Raising Girls
with ADHD

The second edition of the best-selling *Raising Girls with ADHD* features the latest information on research and treatment for girls with ADHD presented in an easily accessible format.

The book is packed with expert information to empower parents to make decisions about identification, treatment options, behavioral strategies, personal/ social adjustment, educational impact, and many other issues from preschool through high school. Featuring practical suggestions and interventions, this book is a comprehensive guide for parents interested in helping their daughters with ADHD reach their full potential. Based on the author's years of personal and professional experience, this book covers topics not often found in other parenting guides, such as the preschool years and early diagnosis, a **Dynamic Action Treatment Plan** parents and their daughters can work on together, as well as guidance for teens on money management, getting their first job and post high school planning. In addition to expert guidance, this new edition also features interviews with girls and their mothers sharing their personal strategies for success in managing ADHD.

Full of tactics, resources, and tools, this book will provide the support you need to build a positive relationship with your daughters while seeking the most appropriate treatments and support.

Mary Anne Richey, M.Ed., is a Licensed School Psychologist who worked for the school district of Palm Beach County for many years and now maintains a private practice in Florida. She also has experience as a middle school teacher, administrator, high school guidance counselor, and adjunct college instructor. She is also the author of *Raising Boys With ADHD: Secrets for Parenting Healthy, Happy Sons*, 2nd edition, and co-author of *The Impulsive, Disorganized Child – Solutions for Parenting Kids with Executive Functioning Difficulties; Stressed Out! Solutions to Help your Child Manage and Overcome Stress*; and *The ADHD Empowerment Guide*.

2nd Edition

Raising Girls
with ADHD

Secrets for
Parenting
Healthy,
Happy
Daughters

Mary Anne Richey

Routledge
Taylor & Francis Group

NEW YORK AND LONDON

Cover image: © Getty Images

Second edition published 2024
by Routledge
605 Third Avenue, New York, NY 10158

and by Routledge
4 Park Square, Milton Park, Abingdon, Oxon, OX14 4RN

Routledge is an imprint of the Taylor & Francis Group, an informa business

© 2024 Mary Anne Richey

First edition published by Prufrock Press 2014

Library of Congress Cataloging-in-Publication Data
Names: Richey, Mary Anne, 1947– author. |
Forgan, James W. Raising girls with ADHD.
Title: Raising girls with ADHD : secrets for parenting healthy,
happy daughters / Mary Anne Richey.
Description: 2nd edition. | New York, NY : Routledge, 2024. |
Revised edition of: Raising girls with ADHD /
James W. Forgan, Ph.D., and Mary Anne Richey. 2014. |
Includes bibliographical references.
Identifiers: LCCN 2023052264 (print) | LCCN 2023052265 (ebook) |
ISBN 9781032428178 (paperback) | ISBN 9781003365402 (ebook)
Subjects: LCSH: Attention-deficit hyperactivity disorder. |
Attention-deficit-disordered children. | Girls–Mental health. |
Child rearing. | Parent and child.
Classification: LCC RJ506.H9 F668 2024 (print) |
LCC RJ506.H9 (ebook) | DDC 649/.154–dc23/eng/20231226
LC record available at https://lccn.loc.gov/2023052264
LC ebook record available at https://lccn.loc.gov/2023052265

ISBN: 978-1-032-42817-8 (pbk)
ISBN: 978-1-003-36540-2 (ebk)

DOI: 10.4324/9781003365402

Typeset in Minion
by Newgen Publishing UK

Access the Support Material: www.routledge.com/9781032428178

Dedication

I dedicate this book to a number of special people in my life. First of all, my first born son, Neal, who died at 2 years of age from neuroblastoma, heightening my understanding of just how incredibly precious each child's life is. That kindled my desire to help and motivate parents who may have children who require extra effort and care, such as girls with ADHD. With proper love and treatment, these girls can develop their strengths and lead their best lives.

I am indebted to my children and their spouses – Kate, Kent, Bryan, and Jessica – and to my grandchildren – Matthew, Maxwell, Molly, Cole, Teddy, and Charlotte – for all the joy and love they have brought. Finally but certainly not least, I thank my husband, Bill, for his tolerance of the writing process and excellent proofreading skills.

Contents

Contents

Figures

Tables

Acknowledgments

Projects like this require the work of many individuals. Many thanks to my editor at Taylor & Francis, Rebecca Collazo, for her prompt response to questions, insightful advice, and effective management of the project from beginning to end, and my copy editor, Barbara Legg, for her knowledge, thoroughness, and patience in proof reading. I also greatly appreciate Dr. Sari Katz, pediatrician, and Dr. Michelle Chaney and Dr. Marshall Teitelbaum, psychiatrists, for sharing their medical expertise by providing valuable, in-depth information about diagnosis and treatment of ADHD in girls. I am grateful for the girls and their mothers who were so willing to be interviewed about their experience with ADHD in hopes of helping others navigate their own journey. Obviously, their names have been changed to protect their identities.

Introduction

From my personal and professional experience, it seems that behind every successful girl with ADHD is a very tired parent. I bet you can relate to that! I often say that it is like a second job to stay on top of the support and services needed, the latest research and changes that occur as she ages. Please know it is well worth your time and effort.

This second edition is designed to:

- ▷ bring you the latest research on ADHD in an easily accessible form,
- ▷ help you gain a strong understanding of the nature of the disorder and its impact,
- ▷ suggest practical, effective research-based strategies so you can help your daughter make the most of her strengths and shore up her weaknesses,
- ▷ provide insightful interviews with girls with ADHD and their mothers, and
- ▷ offer encouragement to keep you focused on the most rewarding prize – helping your daughter be the best version of herself.

DOI: 10.4324/9781003365402-1

You are poised to be one of the most influential people in guiding her toward success in life. It will be a journey influenced by parents, siblings, relatives, caregivers, teachers, and others. I've been down a similar path in my personal life, and I am honored to continue to work with parents and teachers of girls with ADHD in my professional life. I firmly believe that these girls often have so much untapped potential.

In this book, I encourage you to be both optimistic and realistic about your daughter's future by learning what you can do to make the most of her strengths and help her improve in areas that might keep her from using those strengths. There is an explosion of knowledge about ADHD. Much of it points to the vulnerability girls with ADHD have for anxiety, depression, substance abuse, and development of other comorbidities. I want to present some of the most relevant research in parent-friendly terms so that you can be well informed and intentional in your parenting and diligent in helping your daughter discover her passions. Your daughter with Attention-Deficit/ Hyperactivity Disorder may seem like any other girl in many ways but has characteristics that must be looked at through the lens of ADHD, especially its neurological effects.

She has her own set of strengths and unique skills but may not be able to use them to their best advantage because of the complications of ADHD. One thing I have observed to be true for most girls with ADHD is that they are *consistently inconsistent*. Some days your daughter has you glowing with pride, and other days, you are scratching your head in amazement at how it could have all gone so wrong. Please be confident that you can help nurture your daughter's qualities to help her grow into a successful person who will make you proud.

Your daughter with Attention-Deficit/Hyperactivity Disorder (ADD/ADHD) may seem like any other girl in many ways but has characteristics that must be looked at through the lens of ADHD, especially its neurological effects.

Scope of Your Challenge

As the parent of a daughter with ADHD, you face issues that generally aren't on other parents' radar screens such as:

- ▷ impulsivity in acting before considering the consequences,
- ▷ other parents' perceptions that you don't know how to discipline your daughter,
- ▷ embarrassment by the impulsive things she says or does,
- ▷ intensity of her emotional displays,
- ▷ fragile self-esteem,
- ▷ automatic negativity and self-doubt,
- ▷ discouragement (yours and hers),
- ▷ relationship issues and social difficulties,
- ▷ organizational problems,
- ▷ constant procrastination,
- ▷ daydreaming and missing information,
- ▷ underachievement, and
- ▷ severe homework struggles.

Fortunately, there are professionals and resources to help you work through many of the parenting challenges of raising girls with ADHD. *You don't have to conquer everything on your own.* With some effort, you can find support groups with other parents of girls with ADHD, valuable books, and professionals such as counselors, psychologists, or medical doctors. Locating the right people to help you can take some energy, time on the phone, and research, but it *is* worth the effort. Not only will you feel less alone, but you'll also be making an investment in your daughter. As one wise mother of adult children told us, "You pay now or pay later." It is much better to be proactive and provide assistance to ward off problems than to be reactive and face even larger problems. Your daughter may be too young or too immature to realize and verbalize it, but she'll thank you later.

It is much better to be proactive and provide assistance to ward off problems than to be reactive and face even larger problems.

If you cannot afford a professional to guide you, don't worry. Fortunately there are non-profit, reputable groups like CHADD (Children & Adults with Attention-Deficit/Hyperactivity Disorder) and ADDA (Attention Deficit Disorder Association) who disseminate very helpful information and offer parent support groups at no charge. If you are lucky, there might even be a local affiliate of CHADD meeting in your area. Books like this one and many others available in the public library share valuable tips and strategies with you. It is important to make sure the information presented is based on research and currently accepted wisdom and not presented by a group with a vested interest in selling a product.

I understand the struggle of "being in the trenches" but also know how critical it is for your daughter's future for you to be informed and intentional in your parenting. Two key studies, the Berkley Girls with ADHD Longitudinal and the Massachusetts General Hospital studies, documented the increased rate of anxiety, depression, self-harm, eating disorders, and other behavioral problems that can exist in girls with ADHD. It is considered to be a chronic disorder so helping your daughter develop an understanding of her ADHD and how to manage it across her lifetime can be critical. Proper treatment, intervention and informed parenting can make a real difference in the outcome. I am sharing valuable strategies from some of the most respected experts in the field and presenting the latest research on ADHD in an accessible form to fortify you on your parenting journey.

Proper treatment, intervention and informed parenting can make a real difference in the outcome.

ADD versus ADHD: What's the Difference?

Before you read too far in this book, I want to explain the ADHD and ADD terminology, because it can be confusing. Some professionals and parents use the acronyms ADD and ADHD inter-changeably. Others use ADD to describe behaviors of forgetfulness, not paying attention, and distractibility; they apply the term ADHD to describe behaviors of hyperactivity and impulsivity. Within current professional literature, ADHD is considered the umbrella term that is used to describe both students with inattention as well as students with hyperactivity and impulsivity.

There is ADHD predominantly inattentive presentation, which used to be called ADD. There is also ADHD hyperactive-impulsive

Figure 0.1
Types of ADHD

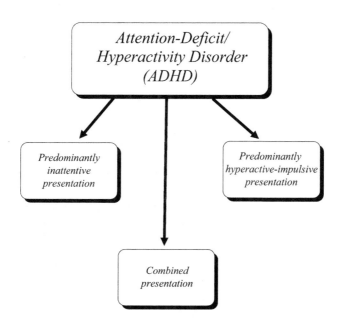

presentation, and that was called ADHD. There is also ADHD combined presentation, where a certain number of symptoms from both ADD and ADHD are met. In this book, I use ADHD as the general term that includes ADHD and ADD. The diagram in Figure 0.1 provides you with a visual of the many variations of ADHD.

How to Use this Book

I value your time and have tried to make the information in this book easily available for the busy parent. You can read the book all the way through, or you can turn to the chapter or part of the chapter that is more relevant to you at the time, such as treatment or need for academic support. The middle chapters are divided into the major developmental periods, including infancy and preschool, elementary, middle and high school. I discuss topics relevant to the age band and include sections on issues you might face in school, at home, and in the community.

At the end of each chapter, you will find points to consider and action steps you can take right away to help your child. Share these with your spouse or a family member so you'll have an ally in choosing the best strategies for supporting your daughter in school and at home.

Knowledge is most useful when you put it to work so there is a **Dynamic Action Treatment Plan** at the end of the book (Chapter 9). It is most helpful if you begin personalizing it as you read through the chapters and hit upon things that might help your daughter. I encourage you to take the time to put your plan in writing because that will help you stay much more focused and purposeful. The beauty of your **Dynamic Action Treatment Plan** is that it will allow you and your daughter to build upon today's successes while following a plan for her promising future. As soon as your daughter is mature enough, include her in helping develop the plan. It is amazing to see the insight some girls have into their own issues and how to work on them. Obviously, as your daughter ages, it will require revisions and updating. You can download the format for the **Dynamic Action Treatment Plan** from www.routledge.com/9781032428178.

Chapter 1

Girls and ADHD

SELF-ASSESSMENT: Where Am I Now?

Each self-assessment helps you reflect on your daughter and your parenting practices and is a preview of the chapter's content.

1 When I think ADHD and my daughter, I …
   a am still deciding if she really has ADHD or not.
   b am overwhelmed with all the supports she needs.
   c know she has ADHD, and I'm ready to take action to help.
   d am hoping this is a phase that she will quickly outgrow.

2 I think my daughter's type of ADHD is …
   a hyperactive-impulsive.
   b inattentive.
   c combined type.
   d I don't know.

DOI: 10.4324/9781003365402-2

3 My daughter's ADHD occurs with …
   a   anxiety.
   b   depression.
   c   low self-esteem.
   d   learning problems.
   e   other.
   f   none of the above.
4 When I think about my daughter's greatest challenge, I believe it is …
   a   friendship.
   b   schoolwork.
   c   organizational skills.
   d   behavioral control.
5 When I think about my daughter and her ADHD, I believe …
   a   she has more strengths than weaknesses.
   b   she has more weaknesses than strengths.
   c   she has an equal number of strengths and weaknesses.
   d   she may have a very tough road ahead.

There is no doubt that raising a girl in our complex world is difficult but raising a girl with Attention-Deficit/Hyperactivity Disorder (ADHD), whether inattentive (what once was called ADD), the hyperactive-impulsive, or the combined presentation, is even tougher. Factor in comorbid disorders, like anxiety, depression, oppositional defiant disorder, or a learning disability, which are often co-occurring with ADHD, and the challenges for you and your daughter just magnified.

While I certainly don't think of ADHD as a gift because of all the complications it can bring, I don't want you to get buried in the negatives. Girls with ADHD can often:
   ▷   think outside the box
   ▷   see creative solutions to problems

▷ hyperfocus on areas of interest, and
▷ exhibit a high energy level which can allow for significant accomplishment.

Helping your daughter make the most of her strengths will be her gateway to success so developing a strong relationship with her and encouraging her along the way will be key.

For so long, girls with ADHD took a back seat to boys in every aspect – diagnostic criteria, research, articles, and books – all with boys as the subject. Thankfully that is changing as more information is coming out about the impact on girls socially, emotionally, and academically. Much of it focuses on the need to have a comprehensive treatment plan as ADHD is now considered a chronic disorder to be managed throughout life.

Helping your daughter make the most of her strengths will be her gateway to success so developing a strong relationship with her and encouraging her along the way will be key.

Girls with ADHD Are Everywhere

It's harder to recognize girls with ADHD than boys, but believe me, girls with ADHD are *everywhere* and are found in every country. ADHD is not a disorder exclusive to the United States. The American Psychiatric Association (2013) stated in the fifth edition of the *Diagnostic and Statistical Manual of Mental Disorders* (DSM 5) that, "Population surveys suggest that ADHD occurs in most cultures in about 5% of children" (p. 61). Furthermore, ADHD is diagnosed more frequently in boys than girls, with a ratio close to 2:1 in children. However, as the DSM 5 states, "Females are more likely than males to present with primarily inattentive features" (p. 63).

The prevalence of ADHD in the United States varies from 5%–12%. As you can imagine, the actual numbers are imprecise and quoted differently in various publications because of so many variables in populations studied – whether it is from the general population or from clinical samples, age ranges, diagnostic criteria, how the data was collected, how the information was reported, and so many other things. The Centers for Disease Control and Prevention (2023) website indicated that parents reported that approximately 10.8% of children 3–17 years of age (6 million) have been diagnosed with ADHD as of 2010. Boys (14.6%) were more likely than girls (6.9%) to have ever been diagnosed with ADHD as children. Ultimately, the ratio becomes more even as more females are diagnosed during adolescence and adulthood.

In case you are interested in data from other countries, data from the United Kingdom indicates 3.62% of boys and 0.85% of girls between the ages of 5 and 15 years had ADHD (Hire et al., 2018). The prevalence estimates of ADHD in Mainland China, Hong Kong, and Taiwan were 6.5%, 6.4%, and 4.2%, respectively, with a pooled estimate of 6.3% (Liu et al., 2018). There was no breakdown provided between boys and girls.

ADHD Affects Girls into Adulthood

Two widely reported comprehensive studies following girls, the Berkeley Girls ADHD Longitudinal Study (BGALS) and the Milwaukee Study, showed that girls with childhood ADHD continue to exhibit impairment into adulthood and may need ongoing treatment (Hinshaw et al., 2012). Biederman et al. (2010) reported on an 11-year follow-up study, "By young adulthood, girls with ADHD were at high risk for antisocial, addictive, mood, anxiety, and eating disorders."

Even though it's harder to identify girls because they are not as hyperactive/impulsive and don't stand out as much as boys with ADHD, it is critical for girls to receive a correct diagnosis to begin the journey of learning how to manage symptoms and receive support. Many girls with undiagnosed ADHD have hidden struggles, but they struggle just the same with maintaining attention, completing homework, staying organized, keeping up with family chores, and relating to peers – especially to other girls. Unfortunately, your daughter may be taking to heart the many negative comments that come her way to indicate she is falling short in her schoolwork, peer relationships, or behavior at home. In an article in *Attitude* magazine, Dr. Kathleen Nadeau (2023), an author and advocate for females with ADHD, expressed concern about what she termed "complex trauma" coming from the "countless daily criticisms, rejections, and blame that add up into a significant and ongoing trauma response – 'trauma by a thousand cuts'" (p. 27). As parents we must help our daughters understand the impacts of ADHD in a non-judgmental way, problem-solve how to identify their needs. establish an evidence-based treatment plan, help them develop their passions and strengths, and build and maintain a strong bond with them. That is a tall order but by reading this book and doing other research, you are on your way!

As parents we must help our daughters understand the impacts of ADHD in a non-judgmental way, problem-solve how to identify their needs. establish an evidence-based treatment plan, help them develop their passions and strengths, and build and maintain a strong bond with them.

Did I Cause It?

Not intentionally, but in many cases a parent's genetics probably contribute to a child having ADHD. When a child is diagnosed with ADHD, parents often comment that their daughter is a lot like they were as a child. It doesn't help one bit to cast blame on yourself or your spouse and wonder who your daughter "got it" from. Instead, try to find some understanding and compassion for what your daughter is facing. If you think you might have ADHD, share your suspicions with her and especially any strategies you have used to your advantage.

It is important for you to remember that your parenting style and the decisions you've made usually are not your girl's main issues. Poor parenting does not *cause* ADHD, but it certainly can aggravate the situation. Being a more skilled parent with a strong understanding of ADHD will not make it go away, but it can have a profound influence on the outcome. Can we, as parents, improve the way we deal with our daughters with ADHD? Absolutely, and a good bit of this book shares ways to help you do just that.

> *Being a more skilled parent with a strong understanding of ADHD will not make it go away, but it can have a profound influence on the outcome.*

Differences between Girls with ADHD and Boys with ADHD

Many people, teachers included, are familiar with how ADHD presents in boys but are less clear about its presentation in girls. In addition to the obvious boy-versus-girl gender differences, there are distinct differences in the presentation and effects of ADHD in boys versus girls. This is an area of emerging research, so always be on the lookout for new information. In my review of the literature about the differences in ADHD in girls and boys, I found that girls with ADHD:

> ▷ are diagnosed with ADHD at an older age;
> ▷ are more frequently diagnosed with inattention and have less hyperactivity;

▷ have more emotional comorbidities during the teenage years;

▷ have a greater likelihood of internalizing and emotional regulation problems, which can lead to self-esteem issues;

▷ have increased feelings of guilt and self-doubt;

▷ have more hormonal issues, specifically with estrogen, which may impact medication;

▷ can have greater risk of early sexual activity;

▷ may experience more friendship difficulties;

▷ have greater turmoil in the mother–child relationship;

▷ struggle more with societal expectations, which traditionally have expected girls to be more nurturing and accommodating;

▷ may be held more accountable for poor organization and sloppy papers in school, which may be excused as typical "boy" behavior in males;

▷ may work harder to compensate for or hide their symptoms to meet parent/teacher expectations;

▷ may be misdiagnosed with other forms of psychopathology – for example, inattention and poor peer interaction may be misdiagnosed as depression;

▷ have differences in brain structure and development;

▷ have lower levels and different manifestations of oppositional defiant disorder and conduct disorder than males – girls may be more likely to have covert behaviors like lying whereas boys may have more overt, aggressive symptoms like physical aggression;

▷ are more disliked than boys with ADHD by ratings of same-sex peers and have higher peer rejection rates;

▷ are more likely to self-harm, cut, and self-mutilate; and

▷ exhibit more excessive talking.

Girls with ADHD Can Be Successful

Parental Commitment – A Critical Component

I often think that behind each successful girl with ADHD is a proud but weary parent. That is because ADHD, especially if there are comorbidities like anxiety, depression, learning disabilities, or oppositional defiant disorder, can complicate your daughter's life significantly and will require more patience, understanding, and intervention. More than likely, there will be days when you need hope, inspiration, and encouragement to keep your eyes focused on the successful young woman with ADHD your daughter can become. This book seeks to arm you with knowledge about the possible challenges you and she may face and how best to support her.

I believe in the expression "knowledge is power," but more importantly, *applied* knowledge is power, and that is why you'll find many self-reflection activities throughout this book. I start with the one below to set the positive tone of this book. Read through the list of positive words that follow in Figure 1.1 and place a check mark next to each word that describes your daughter. I hope you remember these positive attributes and (perhaps when you feel discouraged or are butting heads) look back at this list to reaffirm that she is full of natural talent.

Remember, although much of the research literature on girls with ADHD may appear pessimistic and girls with ADHD do face challenges, they can become highly successful women. Some examples are: Mary Kate and Ashley Olsen (actresses), Karina Smirnoff (dancer on Dancing with the Stars), Lisa Ling (journalist), Michelle Rodriguez (actress), Simone Biles (gymnast), Laurie Dupar (entrepreneur and career coach), and Katherine Ellison (journalist and author). The military, medicine, education, business, and law are full of successful women with ADHD.

Yes, it's challenging to raise a successful girl with ADHD, but here's the good news, it's not impossible. You can raise a successful girl with ADHD by surrounding yourself with the right support people and sources of information, maintaining a positive attitude, accepting her strengths and weaknesses, providing structure for behavior, establishing a strong relationship with her, instilling confidence, and nurturing her natural abilities.

You can raise a successful girl with ADHD by surrounding yourself with the right support people and sources of information, maintaining a positive attitude, accepting her strengths and weaknesses, providing structure for behavior, establishing a strong relationship with her, instilling confidence, and nurturing her natural abilities.

Figure 1.1
Identifying Your Daughter's Strengths

▶ creative	▶ artistic	▶ outdoorsy
▶ intuitive	▶ exuberant	▶ sensitive
▶ emotionally expressive	▶ funny	▶ flexible
▶ kind	▶ considerate	▶ thoughtful
▶ energetic	▶ humorous	▶ imaginative
▶ smart	▶ attractive	▶ curious
▶ athletic	▶ friendly	▶ visual
▶ likes building	▶ likes designing	▶ musical
▶ spontaneous	▶ effective in problem-solving	▶ can be a leader
▶ works quickly	▶ processes information quickly	▶ sees solutions quickly

Despite her ADHD, you can nurture your daughter's qualities to help her grow into a successful woman. Like other people, she has four fundamental needs that must be met: sense of worth, belonging, purpose, and competency. Your daughter can probably accomplish anything she sets her mind to if you nurture these four areas.

What Does Success for Girls with ADHD Look Like?

Everyone has their own definition of success because it is a very personal concept. When I think about success, I don't view it in terms of "things" or "prestige" but making the best of your skills and talents to live a satisfying, happy life. I think most parents feel their daughters are successful as adults if they are happy, live independently, earn a living in a field that brings satisfaction, and contribute to making our world a better place.

I think one important factor in laying the groundwork for your daughter's success is your acceptance of who she is – her strengths, weaknesses, and ADHD and all its complications. Even though it may be hard to wrap your head around it, her path to success may be very different than the one you envisioned but may end up being just as wonderful. Parenting your daughter is not a high-paying or cushy job, but it is *extremely* rewarding and, in my opinion, one of the most important jobs you'll ever do.

Stella grew up in a family with very educated people. She loved academics and was her high school valedictorian. She earned degrees from prestigious universities, including a Ph.D. When her second daughter, Margaret, was born, she was eager to share her love of reading but as a toddler, Margaret would never sit still for more than a minute. Stella persisted in exposing her to books and thought that things would be different when Margaret enrolled in preschool. Much to her dismay, Margaret excelled in everything non-academic – especially playground – and was especially rambunctious during story time.

Ultimately Margaret was diagnosed with ADHD, combined presentation. With all the rigor she had put in on her studies and her career, Stella worked to establish a comprehensive treatment plan for Margaret including executive functioning skills coaching, tutoring to shore up any academic deficits, and ultimately medication. Margaret had ups and downs in school and was never able to say she enjoyed any aspect of it except for sports and extracurricular activities. She developed a keen interest in baking and eventually found an after-school job in a local bakery. She was adamant that she did not want to go to college but wanted to attend a culinary school instead.

Stella's family was often critical of her parenting and felt she should be more demanding of Margaret. Stella tried to help them understand Margaret's challenges with school and remained an advocate for Margaret. She realized that if she did not put her dream of Margaret getting a college degree on the back burner, their relationship would suffer. Stella knew that the world is full of successful, happy women who have not pursued college but secretly hoped that one day, Margaret might choose that path for herself.

Mentally Preparing Yourself for this Parenting Journey

Rather than focusing on the label and its cause, focus on proactive steps you can take to help your daughter. To raise a successful daughter with ADHD, you must start doing things differently as soon as possible after you first learn she has ADHD.

To raise a successful daughter with ADHD, you must start doing things differently as soon as possible after you first learn she has ADHD.

Recognize that ADHD Is a Disorder

ADHD is listed in the *Diagnostic and Statistical Manual of Mental Disorders* (DSM-5). Brain imaging studies document structural brain differences in people with ADHD, so there is no denying it's a true neurobiological disorder. Even though your daughter looks fine on the outside, her mind is wired very differently. Those diagnosed with ADHD:

> … have been shown to differ in the rate of maturation of specific areas of the cortex, in the thickness of cortical tissue, in characteristics of the parietal and cerebellar regions, as well as basal ganglia, and in the white matter tracts that connect and provide critically important communication between various regions of the brain. (Brown, 2013, p. 5)

Taking a "disorder perspective" provides understanding, but it is not who *she* is. Her brain is not broken, it receives and responds to information differently. Another important perspective is that many skills, like self-regulation and organization, may lag behind her age mates in development of up to two to three years. She may be ten years old but functioning like a seven-year-old in some areas. Recognize her as an individual first and then consider how ADHD impacts her. In other words, the ADHD does not define her but rather, she defines how ADHD affects her. Part of your parenting job is helping her

Table 1.1
Myths and Facts about ADHD

Myth	Fact
Poor parenting causes ADHD.	ADHD is neurological and often genetic.
If you have one child with ADHD, all your children will have it.	Not all children in the same family have ADHD.
ADHD is not a real disability.	ADHD is a recognized disability in the Americans with Disabilities Act (ADA) and the Individuals with Disabilities Education Act (IDEA).
Medication is the only treatment for ADHD.	Medication is only one treatment option.
Teachers want inattentive girls on medication.	Teachers want their students to give their best effort.
If a girl is not hyperactive, then she doesn't have ADHD.	Girls who are inattentive but not hyperactive can have ADHD.
A girl who can focus for long periods of time on an interest cannot have ADHD.	Girls with ADHD can focus, even hyperfocus, on topics of interest to them.
A girl with good grades can't have ADHD.	Girls with ADHD can and do have good grades.
Only a psychiatrist can diagnose ADHD.	Pediatricians, psychologists, neurologists, psychiatrists, and other mental health and medical personnel all diagnose ADHD.

Table 1.1, *continued*

Myth	Fact
Psychologists prescribe medication.	Only medical doctors such as pediatricians, neurologists, and psychiatrists, or nurse practitioners prescribe medication.
An equal number of boys and girls are diagnosed with ADHD.	In childhood, more boys than girls are diagnosed with ADHD but by adulthood the ratio narrows.
Most of the behavior of girls with ADHD is willful.	Girls with ADHD are not always able to control behavior. They are often inconsistent in their behavior.
ADHD is a societal fad and will go away.	ADHD has been recognized since the mid-1800s but has been called by different names.
ADHD and ADD are the same thing.	ADHD is an umbrella term used in the DSM-5. What was called ADD is now called ADHD, inattentive presentation.
ADHD is not recognized internationally and is mainly an American diagnosis.	ADHD is recognized globally in developed countries.

Note: From *Raising boys with ADHD*: by Forgan & Richey (2012). Copyright 2012 by Prufrock Press. Reprinted with permission.

understand how she can manage her ADHD, and you are taking a big step by reading this book. Increasing your knowledge about ADHD is key to raising a successful girl. Surprisingly, many myths about ADHD exist (see Table 1.1). Are there any you still believe?

Another important perspective is that many skills, like self-regulation and organization, may lag behind her age mates in development of up to two to three years.

If your child was diagnosed with ADHD using the DSM-5 classification, then current diagnostic criteria require that your daughter presented with symptoms before age 12. She must have several inattentive or hyperactive-impulsive symptoms in two or more settings. There should have also been "… clear evidence that the symptoms interfere with, or reduce the quality of, social, academic, or occupational functioning" (APA, 2013, p. 60). In addition, the clinician may have added a qualifier to the diagnosis, like mild ADHD, moderate ADHD, or severe ADHD. Many professionals believe subtle changes in the DSM-5 ADHD diagnostic guidelines are more lenient and may result in more children diagnosed with ADHD.

Try to Become More Understanding and Patient

Through my experiences, I've learned that changing your daughter's behavior often means changing your behavior as well. If you know she has ADHD, then respond differently to her behavior. As you learn more about ADHD and its neurobiological basis, it will be easier to see your daughter's behavior through that lens rather than as being willful behavior making your life miserable. That doesn't mean you will let your daughter "get away with things," but you will need to learn to respond in a way that doesn't escalate the situation or reinforce negative behavior, but rather, teaches her how to respond more appropriately.

When Becky got upset or frustrated with her daughter, Martine, she tended to point her index finger at her and shake it up and down as she scolded her. Becky became so frustrated at herself that she was determined to stop this automatic response which only infuriated her daughter. One day she decided to write the letters "u" and "p" on the edge of her finger. When she got upset and pointed her finger at Martine, she had an automatic visual reminder

> *to have understanding and patience. Ths simple strategy worked to change her behavior so that she could help Martine figure out a better way to handle a similar situation next time rather than complain about what she did wrong in a threatening and rude way.*

Recognize the Importance of Relationship with Your Daughter

As all parents do, you will have ups and downs with your daughter. It is important for her to know that you are trying hard to be the best parent you can be for her. That means not only understanding the nature of her disorder, but also providing the structure and routines that will help her learn to make the best of her strengths. In his book, *Straight Talk about ADHD in Girls*, Dr. Stephen Hinshaw (2022) calls for what he terms:

> … radical acceptance of her differences from other girls (sometimes subtle, sometimes quite overt) paired with a radical commitment to changing the family climate, altering many of your parenting strategies, and working in conjunction with her teachers, other school personnel, clinicians, and supports in the community. (Hinshaw, 2022, p. 2)

Locate Support Personnel

Begin to locate different support personnel such as educators, coaches, therapists, and doctors who can serve as resources throughout the years. Part of raising a successful girl with ADHD is recognizing that it's very tough to try to do it alone. If she is going to be successful, then at the very minimum you must have her teacher's support. Take extra time to develop a rapport with her teacher and help him or her understand your daughter's strengths and weaknesses.

If you are searching for a professional who specializes in ADHD, one of the most respected sources of information is Children and Adults with Attention-Deficit/Hyperactivity Disorder (CHADD). CHADD maintains a searchable professional database of ADHD experts who may help you with your daughter's ADHD. You may have to interview several professionals to locate the right match for you and your daughter. The important key here is not to give up too soon. I've seen many clients start counseling for anxiety or other mental health issues and then quit because the child does not relate well to the therapist. Then, the parent will say, "We've tried counseling and it didn't work." After probing deeper, I learn that it may not have been the right connection, and in counseling, a strong relationship makes all the difference.

Additionally, if you are lucky, there may be a local CHADD chapter in your area. They are spread throughout the United States, and you can check (www.CHADD.org) to see if there is a chapter in your area. These groups often hold meetings with speakers of interest who might be professionals you would want to connect with and most importantly, you will have the opportunity to learn from other parents of girls with ADHD.

Realize that Your Daughter's Symptoms and Challenges May Change as She Ages

One family I worked with had some frustrating years with their daughter after her diagnosis in first grade. At one point, they said, "Surely we won't be dealing with these types of behaviors in fifth and sixth grade." To their surprise, when seventh and eighth grade came around, they still had to address issues – different ones related to puberty – but they finally acknowledged ADHD was here to stay.

Realize that very likely, you and your daughter are going to have good periods and very rough patches and that meaningful change will gradually occur. Recognize and celebrate those positive changes because more than likely, they required hard work from both of you. Maturation sometimes results in improvement in boys with ADHD because their hyperactivity seems to lessen with age, but girls often have more problems during the teenage years.

At times you may feel like you've taken one step forward and two steps backward, so it helps to reflect and see just how far you've come. That's why completing the **Dynamic Action Treatment Plan**, which is integrated into most chapters and found at the end of the book, is useful. It documents five years of growth and serves as a written plan that shows her progress and needs. You can modify the plan as her needs change.

Questions that May Come to Mind

How Long Does ADHD Last?

Most researchers agree that ADHD lasts a lifetime and should be managed like a chronic condition. A model has been developed called the Life Course Model for Treatment of ADHD. that "prioritizes helping youth with ADHD improve competencies and develop into independent, healthy adults who achieve occupational, personal, and recreational success" (DuPaul et al., 2019; discussed in more detail in Chapter 3 – "Treatment Options for ADHD"). Many longitudinal studies on both males and females have reported that ongoing interventions are necessary to maintain any treatment gains. ADHD is clearly a chronic condition requiring ongoing treatment and monitoring, even into adulthood.

Studies have reported that young adults in their 20s don't always recognize the degree to which their ADHD continues to impact their lives when filling out self-reports. On the contrary, parents' reports of these same young adults show clearly that ADHD is still interfering with their daily living. It's not until many women with ADHD are in their 30s that they begin recognizing how their ADHD is still a major factor. The impact of ADHD on adults is currently the topic of many studies.

ADHD is clearly a chronic condition requiring ongoing treatment and monitoring, even into adulthood.

Why Do Some Say ADHD Is a Gift?

Whether or not your girl's ADHD contributes to success or failure is influenced by many factors including her temperament, attitude, resiliency, home life, and available supports. There will be countless times when your daughter's ADHD seems far more like a burden than a gift.

So, when *can* ADHD become a blessing? When a girl's self-regulation skills have developed and she understands and accepts her strengths and weaknesses, she may be able to use her unique skills and natural talents to their best advantage. For example, some girls with ADHD seem to have intuition that others lack; can see the big picture; have the energy to participate in many extracurricular activities; excel in art, music, or academic subjects that interest them; or interact very effectively with people, especially older or much younger children. Many believe these kinds of characteristics enable them to be very effective when channeled in the right direction and can then be considered gifts. In addition, many successful people with ADHD note they learned the value of hard work very early, which has served them well in life.

You understand your daughter with ADHD best, so think about her natural talents. What are they? Your insight will help identify her strengths. Ask yourself these questions:

    ▷ What comes naturally to her?

    ▷ What does she enjoy spending time doing?

    ▷ What makes her smile and laugh?

    ▷ What type of careers do I picture for her?

Girls with ADHD are often described as social, spirited, loving, sensitive, and/or very observant. These positive qualities should not be overlooked and can become huge assets. However, your nurturing and guidance will likely be required to help develop these qualities.

> *For example, when Sarah's daughter, Matilda, considered a career in veterinary medicine, she and Matilda made frequent visits to the library to check out books on animals. They visited animal shelters and even volunteered as a mother–daughter project at one. While on vacations, they always checked out any zoos in the area. Matilda didn't end up pursuing veterinary medicine, but those positive experiences served her well.*

I believe your child's strengths will carry her through life. School is the only place where we are expected to perform well in *all* subjects, but that's not the case in life. If your child is a C student in math, then perhaps take the viewpoint that it's satisfactory and instead of spending hours working with tutors and trying to mold her into an A-level math student, spend time increasing her reading and writing talents.

Girls with ADHD often have strengths in many areas. Reflecting on the beginning of the chapter, which words described your daughter? Now that you've identified some of your daughter's strengths, build upon them. Consider making a list of her talents and special qualities and posting it where you both can be reminded of them. Turn to the back of the book and enter them on the **Dynamic Action Treatment Plan**. Provide various opportunities for your daughter to develop these strengths as well as discover new hidden talents. Your daughter's gifts can take her far and help her have a happy and satisfying adult life. It's our job as parents, guardians, and families of girls with ADHD to nurture those talents.

What May the Future Hold?

In my experience covering many years, I find the parents who take time to educate themselves about ADHD, build a strong relationship with daughters and provide needed support, and learn new parenting skills along the way, have daughters who grow into independent and satisfied women. Girls who have parent or adult support fare better than those who don't. The time you invest helping your daughter will pay off in future dividends. While raising your daughter, keep these points in mind:

▷ Don't back too far away if she tries to push you away.
▷ Consider money spent on ADHD treatments an investment in your family's future.
▷ Continue to provide just enough support that she knows you are there, but don't allow her to become dependent.
▷ Make sure you are not inadvertently reinforcing negative behaviors by allowing her to get what she wants when engaging in inappropriate behaviors (e.g., pestering, arguing, throwing tantrums).
▷ Try not to give in or take the path of least resistance by doing things for your daughter she can do for herself.
▷ Continue to have one-to-one time that allows you to develop your relationship and talk about her hopes, dreams, and desires.
▷ Know her friends.
▷ Help her set goals for the future such as attending college or trade school. The **Dynamic Action Treatment Plan** can help you with goal setting.

References

American Psychiatric Association. (2013). *Diagnostic and statistical manual of mental disorders* (5th ed.). American Psychiatric Association.

Biederman, J., Petty, C. R., Monuteaux, M. C., Fried, R., Byrne, D., Mirto, T., Spencer, T., Wilens, T. E., & Faraone S. V. (2010, April). Adult psychiatric outcomes of girls with attention deficit hyperactivity disorder: 11-year follow-up in a longitudinal case-control study. *American Journal of Psychiatry*, 167(4), 409–417. doi: 10.1176/appi.ajp.2009.09050736. Epub 2010 Jan 15. PMID: 20080984.

Brown, T. E. (2013). *A new understanding of ADHD in children and adults: Executive function impairments.* Routledge.

Centers for Disease Control and Prevention, National Center on Birth Defects and Developmental Disorders. (2023, January 25). *Attention-deficit/hyperactivity disorder (ADHD) date and statistics.* www.cdc.gov/ncbddd/adhd/data.html

DuPaul, G. J., Evans, S. W., Mautone, J. A., Owens, J. S., & Power, T.J. (2019). Future directions for psychosocial interventions for children and adolescents with ADHD. *Journal of Clinical Child & Adolescent Psychology*, 49(1), 134–145. doi:10.1080/15374416.2019.1689825

Forgan, J. W., & Richey, M. A. (2012). *Raising boys with ADHD: Secrets for parenting healthy, happy sons.* Prufrock Press.

Hinshaw, S., Barkley, R., & Hechtman, L. (2012, November). *Montreal study; Milwaukee study; Berkeley girls ADHD longitudinal study.* Presented at the Research Symposium at the 24th Annual International Conference on ADHD, San Francisco, CA.

Hinshaw, S. P. (2022). *Straight talk about ADHD in girls: How to help your daughter thrive.* Guilford Press.

Hire, A. J., Ashcroft, D. M., Springate, D. A., & Steinke, D. T. (2018, January). ADHD in the United Kingdom: Regional and Socioeconomic Variations in Incidence Rates Amongst Children and Adolescents (2004–2013). *Journal of Attention Disorders*, 22(2):134–142. doi: 10.1177/1087054715613441. Epub 2015 Nov 23. PMID: 26604267.

Liu, A., Xu, Y., Yan, Q., & Tong, L. (2018, August 16). The prevalence of attention deficit/hyperactivity disorder among Chinese children and adolescents. *Scientific Reports*, 8(1), 11169. doi: 10.1038/s41598-018-29488-2. PMID: 30115972; PMCID: PMC6095841.

Nadeau, K. (2023, June). Why ADHD is more challenging for women. *Attention*, 30, 27.

Points to Consider

1 Have you accepted your daughter's ADHD as a disability?
2 How can you support the positive characteristics in your daughter you identified in the checklist of attributes?
3 What do you need to do for yourself to equip you to have patience and understanding?
4 Review your self-assessment responses to decide if there are any areas where you still need to learn more.

Action Steps to Take Now

1 Remember that your daughter probably has a fragile self-image. What are some areas where you can offer genuine encouragement?
2 Begin to establish a support system for yourself by enlisting the help of caring professionals (e.g., therapists, physicians, and teachers), researching support groups, and continuing to read and learn about ADHD.
3 Think about your daughter's strengths and needs and complete Step 1 in the **Dynamic Action Treatment Plan**.

Chapter 2

Diagnosis for ADHD

Each self-assessment helps you reflect on your daughter and your parenting practices and is a preview of the chapter's content.

1 When I consider having my daughter diagnosed for ADHD, I …
   a   have no idea where to start so I keep putting it off.
   b   am researching and considering what our best option is based on services and finances.
   c   know I can count on her pediatrician for good advice.
   d   am so confused by conflicting information.
2   My daughter's primary care doctor is …
   a   aware that she has ADHD and has recommended options.
   b   unaware that she has ADHD.

    c understanding and has referred me to another specialist.

    d questioning whether my daughter has ADHD because she is not hyper.

3 If my daughter is diagnosed with ADHD …

    a I will be relieved to know there is a name for the behaviors we have been experiencing.

    b I will be sad about all the potential difficulties it can have for her.

    c I will want to immediately start researching treatments.

    d Family members, including my spouse, will be doubtful about the diagnosis.

4 When I think about sharing an ADHD diagnosis with my daughter …

    a I know she is mature enough to understand and handle it.

    b I would have no idea how to explain it to her.

    c I don't think she needs to know.

    d I think it is critical so we can work as a team to manage it.

5 As I learn more about an ADHD diagnosis, I …

    a wonder why I didn't have my daughter evaluated sooner.

    b am hoping my daughter receives a thorough evaluation.

    c am starting to question if I might have ADHD too.

    d am going to talk to my primary care physician about how to seek a diagnosis for myself.

From the day your daughter is born, she begins attending, learning, and picking up information from her environment as she interacts with it. If she doesn't attend long enough to take in, process, and store information, then her development will be negatively impacted in many ways across many settings. If she is impulsive and has a problem regulating her behavior, you may have many embarrassing moments as a parent. If she is a daydreamer, you may get frequent notes from her teacher. If her behavior results in persistently negative interactions with those around her, her self-concept will suffer. Many parents I worked with in the school system would hear concerns like these about their daughter but not pursue a diagnosis to determine if ADHD really was the problem. For some parents it was a time factor, for others it was cost, and some just wanted to continue ignoring the issues in hopes they would go away with maturity. There is no doubt that it can be painful as a parent to learn your child has a specific diagnosable condition, but you must put that aside to do what is in her best interest. Believe me, ADHD and its implications are just too impactful to ignore if we want the best outcome for our daughters.

Could It Be ADHD?

How do you determine if she is exhibiting age-appropriate behavior or behavior that is unusual and reflective of ADHD? There is no doubt that attention and behavior can be very developmental, but when do you know an evaluation for ADHD is necessary? You can probably arrive at an answer on your own, but you need to consider these four questions to know if your daughter's behavior is unusual:

> ▷ How is your daughter perceived by peers, especially girls her age?
> ▷ Have your daughter's behaviors, including her inattentiveness, been a continuous problem or a response to a temporary situation?
> ▷ Do the behaviors occur in several settings or only in one place, such as the playground, classroom, or home?
> ▷ How intense is your daughter's behavior during these times and how much does it interfere with her functioning?

The first question invites you to think about your daughter among her peers. The research tells us that girls with ADHD are rejected more often by both girls without ADHD and other girls with ADHD. Don't discount her if your daughter tells you that other girls are mean and don't like her. Early elementary peer rejection is a strong predictor of problems your daughter may face during the teen years, including anxiety, depression, eating disorders, and suicide.

Jolissa always wanted to be the boss since kindergarten. It seemed like her teachers were constantly calling home about her difficulty in playing with others. In kindergarten and first grade, her peers tolerated it, and she was still invited for playdates and birthday parties. In second grade she often came home and complained that no one wanted to play with her. When questioned about it, she said she wanted to run around, and the other girls just wanted to hang out and play pretend. Her mom, Monique, tried to arrange playdates with some other active little girls, but they weren't always successful. By the time she reached fourth grade, her teacher told Monique that Jolissa was having a hard time even talking with the other children in the class because she was constantly interrupting and rarely really listening to her classmates. Other children did not like to work with her on projects because her impulsiveness often led to poor results. When Jolissa started balking about going to school, saying she hated it, Monique decided it was time for a thorough evaluation with her pediatrician. Sure enough, her impulsiveness and high activity level in multiple settings led to an ADHD diagnosis.

The second question was, "Have your daughter's behaviors, including her inattentiveness, been a continuous problem or a response to a temporary situation?" If it's truly ADHD, your daughter should have been dealing with the same problem or problems for a period of 6 months or more. The professional who evaluates your daughter will ask questions to differentiate between ongoing problems and short-term problems causing temporary instability, like divorce, death of a family member, teacher conflict, or peer problems.

Nina, the parent of Juanita, sought help at the end of the school year because her daughter had a terrible third-grade experience. Her mother's intuition had warned her in second grade that something was amiss, and now she finally decided that something must be wrong. Through comprehensive testing, Juanita was diagnosed with ADHD and especially had difficulty with shifting her attention. When something was "sprung" on her, she would likely have a major meltdown. Strategies were developed to help her learn to be more flexible in handling change better. Like many girls with ADHD, Juanita performed better in situations that were highly structured, as compared to more unpredictable ones. As a result of the evaluation, her parents created clear house rules, providing Juanita boundaries for her behavior she couldn't provide for herself.

The third question was, "Do the behaviors occur in several settings or only in one place, such as the playground, classroom, or home?" ADHD permeates all areas of your daughter's life, so she may experience difficulties at home, in school, during Girl Scouts, at sleepovers, and at family gatherings. Your daughter's ADHD may emerge anywhere and at any time. She may hold herself together better in school, but her true colors are displayed at home with demands, bossiness, and frustration when she no longer has the energy to manage her behavior. This difficulty is often what leads parents to set up an evaluation.

Megan had her daughter, Tara, in for an annual check-up with her pediatrician. The doctor said, "I've noticed that she doesn't stop moving or talking. We should consider ADHD." A nurse practitioner specializing in ADHD in the office assisted the pediatrician in gathering rating scales from Tara's teacher and her parents which confirmed her behavior was consistent across settings. She also conducted an in-depth social history which indicated several relatives with an ADHD diagnosis. Megan related Tara's history of sustaining injuries from impulsive behavior and complaints every year from teachers about her distractibility and talkativeness. After reviewing all the data, the pediatrician confirmed her initial suspicion and diagnosed Tara with ADHD, hyperactive-impulsive type.

The fourth question was, "How intense is your daughter's behavior during this time or how much does it interfere with her functioning?" If your daughter's mood or behavior drags on and is so severe that no one wants to (or is able to) get near her for an extended period, that's a severe problem. When you consider the frequency, duration, and intensity of her behavior, it may become clear that a potential problem exists. Like one client told me, "When she has a bad day, it's a spectacularly bad day!"

Lindsey had been asked to leave her day care when she was only three because her tantrums would last for half an hour or more and disrupt the entire class. Parents experienced similar behavior when she was denied her own way. She would throw herself on the floor and scream for what seemed like hours. At four, she had behavior therapy through an early intervention program, which seemed to help but didn't take care of the problems. The administrator in charge encouraged the parents to have her evaluated for ADHD.

Eventually all the parents in these scenarios decided it was time for a thorough evaluation to determine whether their child's behaviors were related to ADHD. They began to learn more about how to get an appropriate evaluation.

Why Seek a Professional Diagnosis?

First, it should provide you with a clearer picture of exactly what is going on with her. Part of the reason for seeking a diagnosis is to make sure it is ADHD and not attributable to other disorders, which can look like ADHD and require very different treatment, or ADHD along with many conditions that are often comorbid with ADHD. These include:

▷ learning disabilities like dyslexia or dysgraphia,
▷ mental health diagnoses like depression or anxiety,
▷ behavioral disorders like conduct disorder or opposi-
itional defiant disorder, or
▷ other neurodevelopmental disorders like autism.

Especially in young children, ADHD can be hard to differentiate from other disorders that may share characteristics. For example, inattentiveness may be coming from discomfort caused by anxiety, behavioral outbursts could be caused by autism or oppositional defiant disorder, or failure to follow conversation could be a language disorder. Or the diagnosis could be ADHD along with a co-occurring disorder. A comprehensive evaluation would put you on the road to being a proactive parent seeking appropriate treatment options. When you know your daughter really does have something fundamentally different about her brain structure and wiring, it gives you a much better understanding of her functioning. The more you learn about exactly what is going on with her, the more helpful you can be in assisting her and those around her in addressing the issues. When your daughter is mature enough to understand any diagnosis, sharing information with her can bring a sense of relief that the condition has a name and interventions that can make her life easier as well as an understanding of ways to handle the difficulties she is experiencing.

Second, the diagnosis may provide you and your daughter with access to school accommodations or services but would first require a professional diagnosis or a psychological evaluation. Accommodations are adjustments such as extra time to complete tests or homework, seating near the front of the class, or frequent breaks, whereas services would be specific interventions provided by staff. Accommodations and services are addressed in preschool, elementary, middle and high school chapters as well as in Chapter 8 – "When School Problems Escalate."

Third, the diagnosis allows you, if you desire, the option of trying medication. Not all parents want to try prescribed medication with their child. If you decide to do so, you must have a proper diagnosis before obtaining a prescription, which can only be written by a medical doctor or nurse practitioner.

What Can I Expect to Happen During an Evaluation for ADHD?

ADHD is a diagnosis based on history, observations, or reports of behaviors in more than one setting over a period of time, as well as ruling out other conditions that could cause a similar presentation. The type of evaluation will depend on the specialist you choose. However, standard components of most evaluations include:

- ▷ family history since ADHD can be genetic,
- ▷ clinical interview with your daughter if she is old enough and with you,
- ▷ rating scales or questionnaires completed by you, your daughter if she is old enough, and teachers who may have knowledge of her functioning since behaviors must be present in two or more settings, and
- ▷ examinations as necessary to rule out other conditions.

Much of the discussion with the clinician will obviously center on the presenting behaviors, many of which are negative. Bear in mind that your child has probably been chastised for those behaviors many times over and may be very sensitive to them. I have found that children are much more comfortable in the waiting room than sitting through the parent interview. That also enables parents to be much more open and honest.

The doctor or clinician would decide what components he or she would include. Obviously, medical doctors would include physical examinations, and psychologists would use various instruments assessing intelligence, academics, processing, and possibly executive functioning, emotions, and behavior if required.

Why is Diagnosing Girls with ADHD Considered to Be More Difficult than Diagnosing Boys?

There are many factors that make diagnosing ADHD in girls much trickier than diagnosing boys:

▷ More girls than boys have the inattentive presentation of ADHD which is not easily observable. These girls often do not stand out and call attention to themselves like hyperactive boys.

▷ For decades most of the research and the diagnostic criteria were based on boys and emphasized high activity levels, whereas girls' hyperactivity may present differently. In their book, *Understanding Girls with ADHD*, Nadeau et al. (2016) pose the question of "whether hyperactivity is the same in boys and girls. For example, clinical observation suggests that hyperactivity in girls may be manifested more through hyper-verbalization and emotional excitability/reactivity" (p.11).

> ▷ Many people, including teachers, are not knowledgeable about signs of ADHD and may overlook symptoms or label them incorrectly, like complaining a girl is just a daydreamer when she is inattentive or that she is a social butterfly if she is always talking and not getting her work done.
> ▷ Comorbid conditions more prevalent in girls than boys, like anxiety and depression, can mask ADHD and result in an incorrect diagnosis.
> ▷ Girls often go to great lengths to hide their difficulties and suffer silently, resulting in exhaustion and damage to their self-esteem.

Racial and Ethnic Disparities in Diagnosis and Treatment

There are some racial/ethnic disparities in the diagnosis of ADHD worth noting. Research has shown that African American and Hispanic children are less likely than White children to be diagnosed. Of those who are diagnosed, racial/ethnic minority children are less likely to be taking medication for ADHD than White children (Morgan et al., 2013). The reasons for these differences could be related to access to healthcare, cultural attitudes about ADHD and medications, fewer concerns brought to the parents' attention by school staff, lack of knowledge about ADHD and the consequences of not treating it, or other undetermined factors. For these children, this means the neurobiological effects of ADHD on their behavior are not being considered, and their treatment needs, including school accommodations, are not met.

Much study has been done on adverse childhood experiences (ACES), which looked at the impact of things like exposure to violence, divorce, death of a parent, abuse, and neglect. Childhood exposure to two or more of these potentially traumatic experiences was more likely to result in negative outcomes in a variety of areas, including academic success and health. Studies have shown that African Americans were more likely to have had exposure to two or more adverse experiences than Hispanics or European Americans. Mattox and Vinson (2018) said:

> Asking directly about traumatic exposures is an absolute necessity in working with black youth and families. While trauma-related diagnoses are by no means mutually exclusive with ADHD, if both are present, it is imperative that the family is educated about the psychological impact of trauma and that treatment interventions target both issues. (Mattox and Vinson 2018, *para 5*)

Otherwise, the treatment outcome could be negatively affected. Access to proper diagnosis and treatment as well as culturally sensitive efforts to communicate effectively with all parent groups are important issues going forward to ensure that all children have access to the treatment and the support they need.

Who Can Diagnose ADHD?

Pediatricians

Many people who seek a diagnosis for their daughter begin with their pediatrician, especially if their daughter has a long-standing relationship with the doctor. Pediatricians have strong knowledge of developmental sequences and see children of various ages daily.

One thing to keep in mind is that your pediatrician is seeing your daughter in an individualized setting for a short period of time where little is required of her – very different from school with lots of children, noise, and demands to complete tasks that may be uninteresting. It is your responsibility to bring issues you or the teacher may have noticed to the doctor's attention, especially for inattentive girls. Many parents are reticent to share negative information about their daughter with the pediatrician, thinking he or she is only interested in their physical well-being. The pediatrician must consider all aspects of your daughter's functioning and not just the way she presents in the office and will usually ask for rating scales from you and teachers to get a complete picture if problems are noted.

The American Academy of Pediatrics (2019) recognizes the significant impact of undiagnosed and untreated ADHD and has developed a document entitled "ADHD: Clinical Practice Guideline for the Diagnosis, Evaluation, and Treatment of Attention-Deficit / Hyperactivity Disorder in Children and Adolescents" (Wolraich et al., 2019). The document advises the primary care clinician to initiate an evaluation for ADHD for any child 4 through 18 who is having academic or behavioral problems and symptoms related to ADHD. In the past, many doctors took a "wait and see" attitude since there is a wide range of normal for when many characteristics, such as fine motor skills, visual spatial skills, and attention, develop. Since more research is coming out about the complexity of ADHD and the need to diagnose it properly, more pediatricians are addressing it earlier, especially if concerns are brought up by parents. If you think your daughter has ADHD, it is important to encourage your pediatrician to conduct an evaluation if he or she does not initiate it.

The pediatrician is only one of several medical professionals who can diagnose ADHD. Most pediatricians are effective in treating mild to moderate presentations of uncomplicated ADHD. If your child's picture is complex or she doesn't respond to conventional treatment, your pediatrician may refer you to other specialists. The Society for Developmental and Behavioral Pediatrics Clinical Practice Guideline for the Assessment and Treatment of Children and Adolescents with Complex Attention-Deficit/Hyperactivity Disorder provides some direction for pediatricians for complex cases. Available at https://sdbp.org/adhd-guideline/cag-guidelines/

Other Medical Specialists

If there are complicating developmental issues like autism, a developmental pediatrician would be a good choice. A neurologist may be recommended if there are concerns about brain functioning, such as seizures or tics. A psychiatrist should be consulted for complicated cases involving anxiety, mood disorders, or oppositional behavior. All the above have gone to medical school and can prescribe medication. A nurse practitioner may work under the direction of the physician and can prescribe medication. In my area, most pediatricians and neurologists are covered by medical insurance but not all psychiatrists accept insurance.

Clinical Psychologists, Neuropsychologists, and School Psychologists

Pediatricians are often interested in knowing the level of your daughter's intellectual and academic functioning, as well as her executive functioning skills, to rule out learning problems as the root cause of her symptoms and may refer you to a psychologist. Or they may also suspect emotional disorders like anxiety and depression, behavioral disorders like oppositional defiant disorder or conduct disorder, or developmental disorders like autism. Hinshaw (2022) notes, that "Some of the risk genes related to autism spectrum disorder are essentially the same as those linked with ADHD" (p. 52). Even PTSD or trauma can mimic ADHD.

Clinical psychologists, neuropsychologists, and school psychologists approach ADHD by looking at the cognitive, functional, educational, neurological, emotional, and behavioral perspective. They focus on the impact the symptoms have on learning and general life adjustment. Their training involves using various assessment measures to provide information on the child's functioning and clinical interviews with the child, parents, and sometimes teachers. There is no one assessment that determines the presence or absence of ADHD, but a psychologist can make a diagnosis based on a comprehensive examination, including instruments, clinical interviews, and behavior rating scales. They provide an overall picture of the child in terms of her intelligence, academic strengths and weaknesses, processing abilities, and emotional adjustment. Psychologists do not prescribe medication but often work closely with medical personnel who can. Some psychologists also provide counseling for both the child and the family as well as behavioral therapy. If cost is a concern, it would be important to check with your insurance company to see if psychologists or neuropsychologists in your area are covered.

A psychologist would be a good place to start if you are unsure about the role your child's intellectual functioning plays in her behavior. For example, it is not unusual for gifted children to get into trouble at home and school because they are curious about how things work, or their boredom causes misbehavior as they seek out stimulation.

Claire was a bright and precocious kindergartner who presented as a challenge for her teacher. She came across as an intelligent, talkative, and bossy young girl who was used to running the show. She called out correct answers, demanded attention, and breezed through her assignments so quickly that she distracted others in the classroom. The teacher recommended IQ testing. After testing, the school psychologist reported that Claire's IQ was in the gifted range and recommended a full-time gifted class. Her mom agreed, and Claire's new placement resulted in a better fit to meet her advanced intellectual ability. She was much more engaged with higher level material and was kept busy to minimize her opportunities to distract others.

A psychologist can evaluate a learning disability or processing problems if that is a concern. For example, a child may appear to be inattentive when she is incapable of doing the schoolwork and feels completely overwhelmed in the curriculum. Or a child who is not processing language and doesn't understand what she has been asked to do may appear inattentive.

Lilly was a 5-year-old who attended a private preschool. Her mother was concerned that Lilly might have ADHD, predominantly inattentive presentation, so she brought her for a comprehensive evaluation. After testing Lilly's language, memory, attention, and auditory and visual processing, the psychologist determined that she had memory weaknesses and auditory discrimination issues that presented like ADHD. The recommendations included individual tutoring using the Lindamood-Bell auditory discrimination program and working memory training plus accommodations in the classroom to ensure Lilly understood directions. As Lilly's skills improved, so did her attention.

Licensed clinical social workers and behavior therapists may provide therapy such as cognitive behavioral therapy, behavior modification, or family therapy. Sometimes behavior therapists work in conjunction with the classroom teacher, providing support in implementing behavior management plans designed to increase a student's motivation to comply with teacher requests and complete assigned tasks. Neither social workers nor therapists prescribe medication. Some are covered by insurance.

Whomever you choose will depend on availability in your area, cost, and your child's profile. The roles of the different specialists are very confusing, so a brief overview is included in Table 2.1.

Table 2.1

Roles of Professionals in Diagnosing and Treating ADHD

Specialty	Training	Function
Pediatrician	M.D. or D.O., general practitioner	Oversees wellness of children, diagnoses medical conditions, and prescribes medication
Developmental Pediatrician	M.D. or D.O., specialist in developmental issues	Is consulted for anomalies in development, like autism, diagnoses medical conditions, and prescribes medication
Neurologist	M.D., specialist in neurology and brain functioning	Is consulted for neurological problems, like seizures or tics, diagnoses medical conditions, and prescribes medication
Psychiatrist	M.D., specialist in mental disorders	Is consulted for behavior/mental health issues, diagnoses conditions based on DSM-5, and prescribes medication
Nurse Practitioner	Advanced Practice Registered Nurse (APRN)	Works under the direction of a doctor and prescribes medication

Table 2.1, *continued*

Specialty	Training	Function
Clinical Psychologist	Ph.D. or Psy.D.	Diagnoses conditions and provides therapy, can't prescribe medication
Neuropsychologist	Ph.D. or Psy.D.	Diagnoses conditions, has specialized training in neuropsychology, often does testing, can't prescribe medication
School Psychologist	Master's, specialist, Ph.D., or Psy.D.	Provides testing and consultation regarding problems that impact education, can't prescribe medication
Licensed Clinical Social Worker	MSW or Ph.D.	Sometimes diagnoses conditions and provides therapy, can't prescribe medication
Behavioral Therapist Coach	Master's or Ph.D. Training varies	Provides behavioral therapy, can't prescribe medication Guides management of daily and future activities, especially executive functioning skills but doesn't diagnose ADHD

Note: From *Raising boys with ADHD* (p. 28) by J. W. Forgan & M. A. Richey (2012), Copyright 2012 by Prufrock Press. Reprinted with permission.

A View from the Pediatrician's Office

Dr. Sari Katz, a pediatrician, answered several questions about the process of diagnosing ADHD in her practice.

Q. Many times parents don't bring up school/ home, community issues with their pediatricians. How do you encourage them to do that?

This is true! In my practice, I try hard to establish a close relationship with my families to let them know that I can be a good resource for any issues related to their children's social and academic lives. From a young age, I start all my visits by talking to the patient and asking him or her about school, social groups, interests, and activities. This lets the child know that my office is the perfect venue to discuss such matters. I also end each visit by telling the child he or she can ask me any questions that come to mind and can call me in the future if they think of anything. I want families to know that we can help with these topics, and we are there to treat the whole child. This is an important part of what pediatricians do.

Q. Do you screen for potential problem areas during a routine examination?

Yes. In addition to asking about school and social life, we conduct routine screening forms in accordance with the recommendations from the American Academy of Pediatrics. An example of one of the screenings we conduct is the Patient Health Questionnaire, or "PHQ." This mainly is a tool used to screen for mental health, but it also has questions about focus and sleep. Sometimes the child answers affirmatively when asked about these topics, and it is a window that opens to discuss a concern.

Q. Can you explain your office's process for diagnosing a girl with ADHD, especially the inattentive presentation?

If a child or parent discusses a concern about attention, focus, impulsivity, or academic performance, we ask the patient to schedule an appointment to do a comprehensive evaluation. This can also be initiated with a phone call or electronic message to our staff.

At the consultation appointment, we will carefully and thoroughly review the child's medical, birth, and family history, and current symptoms. The diagnosis of ADHD cannot be made by a blood test or imaging study; it must be made by a comprehensive patient evaluation. We will also use standard screening forms for ADHD. An example is the Vanderbilt Assessment Scale, which will give a total score and evaluate for a subtype, such as hyperactive type, inattentive type, or combined type. Combined type is when the child meets criteria for hyperactivity and inattentiveness. Often, forms will be given to bring to the teacher as well, unless the school has already filled out and given the forms to the parent prior to the appointment. These forms are not perfect tools but aid us in making the diagnosis. A diagnosis is made when the child meets the standardized criteria for symptoms, family history, and screening test results and other physical and psychological causes for the child's symptoms are excluded or "ruled out" as causes for the symptoms.

The Importance of Ruling Out Co-Occurring Disorders and Other Deficits

If your daughter has ADHD, then she has a higher risk for having co-occurring disorders, which could be academic, emotional, or behavioral in nature, so you want to make sure that she is getting a thorough evaluation which looks at all possible causes for her behavior. Some girls are complex, and it may take several specialists from different disciplines to sort out all the issues and it may take time. This may seem like information overload, but it is very important to make sure you and your medical team have as clear a picture as possible of all complicating factors to provide the best advice and help possible.

If your daughter has ADHD, then she has a higher risk for having co-occurring disorders, which could be academic, emotional, or behavioral in nature, so you want to make sure that she is getting a thorough evaluation which looks at all possible causes for her behavior.

To be specific, the most commonly co-occurring disorders for females with ADHD are learning disabilities, depression, anxiety disorders, conduct disorder, and oppositional defiant disorder. The importance of this information is to alert you to be aware of additional problems that could pop up and require immediate attention and intervention. They may not surface at all or may appear over time. The biggest mistake parents make is ignoring problems and hoping they will go away. The best course of action is to recognize them, get early intervention, and develop an ongoing plan to mitigate their impact. Why act early?

When your daughter's difficulties can be recognized and treated for what they are rather than laziness, or lack of will power and/or intelligence – your daughter can begin to receive proper treatment and hopefully build good habits rather than ineffective coping skills. Many girls with ADHD develop negative self-images and internalize their problems, so the sooner you can help her understand her ADHD and any comorbid conditions and build in the supports she needs, you may avoid some rough patches.

Sample of Research Studies Citing Rates of Comorbid Disorders

In case you are interested in the research, there are numerous studies documenting the rates of comorbid or co-occurring disorders in children with ADHD. Wolraich and Hagan (2019) state, "Fifty to 60% of children with ADHD have at least one coexisting condition. More than 10% of children with ADHD have three or more coexisting conditions" (p. 211). There are some specifically studying girls. An article in *Pediatrics* (Tung et al., 2016) cited the following about the percentage of girls with ADHD diagnosed with a comorbid disorder compared to girls without ADHD after review of numerous studies, which I have compiled as Table 2.2.

The Milwaukee Longitudinal Study indicated that the risk of a girl diagnosed with ADHD requiring special education services was more than 50% (Hinshaw et al., 2012). A longitudinal study conducted on girls by Biederman et al. (2010) indicated "a strong association between ADHD and lifetime risks for antisocial, mood,

Table 2.2
Comparison of Girls with and without ADHD

Comorbid Disorder	% of Girls with ADHD Diagnosed	% of Girls without ADHD Diagnosed
Oppositional Defiant Disorder	42%	5%
Conduct Disorder	12.8%	0.8%
Anxiety Disorder	37.7%	13.9%
Depression	10.3%	2.9%

Compiled by author from information in Tung et al., 2016.

anxiety, developmental, and substance dependence disorders at the 11 years follow up" (p. 416).

The Berkeley Girls ADHD Longitudinal Study (Hinshaw et al., 2012) showed higher rates of suicide attempts and self-injury than the group without ADHD but no higher rates of eating pathology, substance use, or problems with driving. Suicide attempts were highly concentrated in girls with ADHD-combined type. In discussing an overview of his findings in this study, Hinshaw (2022) said girls with ADHD compared to girls without ADHD

> had worse performance in reading and math, poorer executive functioning, higher rates of being disliked by their peers (and friendships marked by considerable conflict), more reactive emotional behavior, lower self-esteem, greater levels of parental stress, and higher rates of both anxiety/depression and oppositional/aggressive behaviors. (Hinshaw, 2022, p. 73)

It Is Not Always ADHD

Since there is no specific and definitive test for ADHD, the diagnosis is often very complicated. What may appear at first to be ADHD may not be on further examination. For example, some children choose to act out in an academic setting when they can't do the work rather than have the teacher and classmates see their real deficits. They could have a learning disability, language disorder, or fine motor deficits.

Ariel was constantly out of her seat in kindergarten, going from table to table or getting up to use the bathroom. Her teacher tried everything to keep Ariel focused on classroom activities, but nothing worked. The teacher encouraged Ariel's mother to have her evaluated for ADHD.

Ariel was starting to lag far behind her peers in identifying her letters and numbers and in all aspects of emerging reading and math skills. Ariel's mother decided to address the academic problems first. She hired a tutor, who also noticed that Ariel could not sit still. The tutor had experience with fidgety children, so she utilized lots of different, hands-on strategies to teach Ariel the letters and sounds. As Ariel began acquiring skills, her activity level decreased significantly. Six months later, she was reading short sentences and her hyperactivity had diminished significantly. Obviously, her academic problems seemed to be the cause of her behavior.

Children with significant anxiety can be so preoccupied with their discomfort that they cannot focus or interact appropriately with peers. Others may have their own agendas where they want to do what they want to do at all costs. Where it might initially appear that their behavior is driven by impulsivity, it may be a conduct disorder or oppositional behavior. A wise and thorough clinician can determine the root of the problem and arrive at an accurate diagnosis.

After the Diagnosis

Just going through the diagnostic process can be trying and emotionally exhausting. If she is diagnosed with ADHD, your emotions may run the gamut from relief to finally know the root of your daughter's problems to sadness that your daughter's life may not go exactly as you dreamed it would. Some parents feel guilty that ADHD was passed down from their family line. Whatever your emotion, give yourself time to process it and then move on to the important work of educating yourself about ADHD, figuring out what her treatment needs will be, and explaining how ADHD impacts her to the important people in her life like teachers, grandparents, and siblings.

Explaining ADHD to Others

Explaining ADHD to Your Daughter

You know your daughter and her circumstances better than anyone, so it is up to you when to tell her about her ADHD. For many children, it is a relief to know there is a name for the difficulties they have been having and that there are things that can help. As she gets older, it is important for her to understand ADHD and her role in advocating for herself. Ideally, you and she will become part of a strong team in figuring out what she needs. You don't want her to feel like something is seriously wrong with her brain or use it as a crutch or an excuse for failing to achieve her potential.

Explaining ADHD to the Elementary-Aged Girl

You can provide an age-appropriate explanation of ADHD to elementary-aged children, customizing the sample conversation to your daughter's profile:

Parent: You know we have been working with Dr. Jones because you were frustrated you were having so much trouble paying attention in school and getting your work done. Would you like to know what she has figured out?

Girl: *Sure.*

Parent: After talking to your teacher, she learned that you are awesome at making connections about things you are studying and have such creative ideas but staying focused on everyday tasks is hard for you. Dr. Jones said your brain works differently and is often very busy with many ideas at once. It can be difficult for you to focus on things your brain doesn't find interesting. Also, you might quickly say or do things without thinking. Dr. Jones said you have ADHD. Have you ever heard of that before?

> **Girl:** *Yes, two kids in my class have it. How is that going to help me get my work done? I am tired of my teacher asking me over and over to hurry and finish. I think other kids don't think I am smart.*
>
> **Parent:** *As far as kids thinking you are not smart; they are totally wrong. Your teacher is quite sure you are very smart because of the way you always see the big picture of any lesson. I can understand you feel annoyed when your teacher keeps telling you to focus but she wants to make sure you get your work done. We can talk to her about ADHD and figure out some ways to make school better for you. It is interesting that you know some other kids with ADHD because it is actually very common. There are many very successful people who have ADHD. We have to work together to figure out what will help you manage it, so it won't interfere with your success.*

You may find it easier to explain by reading a children's book about ADHD to your daughter.

Reading books helps your daughter identify with a book's character and realize that she is not alone with her ADHD. A book also becomes a nonthreatening way for you to have a simple conversation about school and behavior. Listed below are a few books currently available to explain ADHD to a younger child:

- ▷ *Baxter Turns Down His Buzz. A Story for Little Kids About ADHD* (ages 4 to 8) by James M. Foley
- ▷ *Shelley, The Hyperactive Turtle* (ages 5 to 6) by Deborah M. Moss
- ▷ *Mrs. Gorski I Think I Have the Wiggle Fidgets: An ADHD and ADD Book for Kids with Tips and Tricks to Help Them Stay Focused (The Adventures of Everyday Geniuses)* (ages 5 to 7) by Barbara Esham
- ▷ *My Busy, Busy Brain. The ABCDs of ADHD, a Resource and Children's Book about ADHD* (ages 5 to 8) by Nicole Russell

> ▷ *ADHD is Our Superpower! The Amazing Talents and Skills of Children with ADHD* (ages 7 to 11) by Soli Lazarus
> ▷ *Learning to Slow Down and Pay Attention: A Book for Kids About ADHD* (ages 7 to 10) by Kathleen G. Nadeau, Ph.D., and Ellen B. Dixon, Ph.D.
> ▷ *Putting on the Brakes: Understanding and Taking Control of Your ADD or ADHD,* third edition (ages 8 to 13) by Patricia O. Quinn & Judith M. Stern
> ▷ *The Adventures of Phoebe Flower: Stories of a Girl with ADHD* (ages 7 to 11) by Barbara Roberts
> ▷ *Thriving with ADHD Workbook for Kids. 60 Fun Activities to Help Children Self-Regulate, Focus, and Succeed* (ages 8 to 11) by Kelli Miller

Explaining ADHD to the "Tween" or Teen

If your middle school or teenage daughter has recently been diagnosed with ADHD, you'll handle it a bit differently. Ideally, the person who officially diagnosed her will provide an age-appropriate explanation of her ADHD. Below is a brief explanation one psychologist provides to teenage clients:

> *Jasmine, the testing you completed with me showed that you have quite a few strengths, and some of them include (fill in the blank with her strengths). The testing also showed there are some things that are much harder for you, compared with other girls your age. For example, you mentioned that it is difficult for you to (fill in the blank: e.g., keep your mind on important facts when reading, keep your materials organized, easily hold back your anger, etc.). This difficulty is related to Attention-Deficit/Hyperactivity Disorder or ADHD. Have you heard of ADHD?*
>
> *The testing process indicated you have ADHD. It doesn't mean you are not smart, but your brain functions differently causing you to have difficulty*

*paying attention and focusing on what is important
right now. You have difficulty with (fill in the blank)
because of the way your mind is wired. This difficulty
is not going to stop you from being successful in school;
it won't stop you from going to college or technical
school or having a good career. You can be successful,
but you are going to have to work harder than many
people your same age. It also means that you may need
more support, like having a counselor, coach, or person
to help guide you. You and your family may consider
trying different treatments to help you, like medication. The important thing for you to remember is that
you can't use your ADHD as an excuse not to do well
in school. As I already said, you can be successful, but
it takes hard work. What questions do you have?*

If the professional you worked with did not explain ADHD to
your daughter, you can provide the explanation, and use books to fill
in the gaps. Here are resources you can share with your teenager:

▷ *Attention, Girls! A Guide to Learn All About Your AD/HD*
(ages 9 to 12) by Patricia Quinn, M.D.
▷ *The ADHD Workbook for Teens: Activities to Help You Gain
Motivation and Confidence* (teens) by Lara Honos-Webb)
▷ *Thriving with ADHD Workbook for Teens. Improve Focus, Get
Organized, and Succeed* (ages 12 to 17) by Allison Tyler
▷ *Help4ADD@HighSchool* (ages 12 to 17) by Kathleen
G. Nadeau

Once your daughter understands her ADHD, she can begin to
learn to work through and around it. An age-appropriate explanation
provides relief to many girls and affirms that they are not broken or
weird. The explanation and label can help clarify your daughter's
weaknesses so she can move forward with an attitude of hope and
optimism.

Explaining ADHD to Others – How and When?

Siblings

Siblings often suffer in their own way when having a sister with ADHD. They may feel like the target for her impulsive behavior, annoyed by the hyperactivity, or have resentment about the chaos it can cause. Many families find it is best to be out in the open with the diagnosis because it likely has an impact on everyone. By acknowledging it, ADHD just becomes part of family life and hopefully some of the stigma is removed from it. All of us have our unique make-up and ADHD is just one aspect of your daughter's life – it should not define her. A sample conversation could go something like this:

> *Parent*: *You know Josey has a hard time when she gets frustrated or upset. She often reacts before she thinks things through.*
>
> *Sibling*: *Yeah, when we are playing a game, she gets mad and quits if she is not winning.*
>
> *Parent*: *We took her to a doctor who said she has attention-deficit hyperactivity disorder or ADHD. She is very smart but the connections in her brain sometimes work differently. She has trouble sitting still and focusing on things that aren't interesting to her.*
>
> *Sibling*: *What caused it?*
>
> *Parent*: *No one caused it. It is usually genetic. It makes many things harder for her, but we are going to work together as a strong family team to figure out how to help her. You can help by being patient and guiding her to make good choices.*

All of us have our unique make-up and ADHD is just one aspect of your daughter's life – it should not define her.

Other People in Your Community, Teachers, or Relatives

If your daughter has ADHD, should you tell other people outside your immediate family? Do you worry about people judging your parenting skills and your daughter? Are you concerned with her having a label? Will her ADHD prohibit her from getting a job? These are just some of the issues on parents' minds. It is a very personal decision based on many factors.

If your daughter's behavior is intrusive, the sooner you can explain to family, teachers, and key people that impulsiveness and difficulties with self-regulation often come with ADHD, you may cut down on the disapproving looks she and you receive. If your daughter is younger, you will make that decision. If she is older and depending on her maturity level, it might be helpful for her to be part of the decision. As you can guess, many teens are very opposed to telling coaches, but it might make everyone's life easier if the coach has some background.

Figure 2.1 is a letter that one of my clients gave to their daughter's third-grade teacher before the school year started. It highlighted her strengths and potential areas of weakness and offered suggestions for accommodations as well as supports the family was providing outside of school. Often, it's helpful to personally meet with your daughter's teacher either before the first day of school or within the first week of school. Whether in person or via e-mail or phone, it's important to start the school year advocating for your daughter, letting the teacher know how to best work with her, and setting up a way to communicate frequently.

Figure 2.1
Sample Letter to School

Third grade letter

Dear Teacher,

We are pleased that Tara has you for a teacher this year and look forward to a great school year. Each year I give Tara's teacher a letter to explain her strengths and weaknesses and offer my two cents about how to help her in your class.

Tara has a caring heart and loves to help others. She is an only child and loves to help me around the house. If you give her responsibilities that allow her to help you she'll work extra hard for you. Simple things like allowing her to pass out papers, erase the board, or put items up on a bulletin board thrill Tara. Her second-grade teacher allowed Tara to read books to kindergarten students and this boosted her self-confidence. I believe the better bond Tara creates with you, the more she will put effort into learning because she will want to please you.

Tara was diagnosed with ADHD, Predominantly Inattentive Type at age 6 and memory is one of her weaknesses. We've known this since about age 3 because she had difficulty remembering colors, letters, and names. This has hindered learning and has made it especially hard for her to memorize math facts and spelling words. You can help Tara by following her IEP accommodations and allowing her to use a math fact table and by reducing the number of spelling words she must memorize each week. There are many more accommodations listed on her IEP that I attached to this letter. Tara also has a very hard time with writing narratives and teaching her a writing formula or series of steps seems to help her.

I'm fortunate to be a stay-at-home mom and want you to know I am here to help you in any way. I'm available if you need a classroom volunteer or room mom. I hope this a great year for Tara.

Sincerely,

Stephanie G.

References

Biederman, J., Petty, C.R., Monuteaux, M., Freid, R., Byrne, D., Mirto, T., Spencer, T., Wilens, T., & Farone, S. (2010). Adult psychiatric outcomes of girls with attention deficit hyperactivity disorder: 11-year follow-up in a longitudinal case-control study. *American Journal of Psychiatry, 167*, 409–417.

Forgan, J. W., & Richey, M. A. (2012). *Raising boys with ADHD: Secrets for parenting healthy, happy sons*. Prufrock Press.

Hinshaw, S., Barkley, R., & Hechtman, L. (2012, November). Montreal study; Milwaukee study; Berkley girls ADHD longitudinal study. Presented at the Research Symposium at the 24th Annual International Conference on ADHD, San Francisco, CA.

Hinshaw, S. P. (2022). *Straight talk about ADHD in girls: How to help your daughter thrive*. Guilford Press.

Mattox, G., & Vinson, S. (2018). Culturally competent approaches to ADHD: Issues in African-American populations. *Psychiatric Times, 35*(9). www.psychiatrictimes.com/view/culturally competent-approaches-adhd-issues-african-american-populations

Morgan, P. L., Staff, J., Hillemeier, M. M., Farkas, G., & Maczuga, S. (2013). Racial and ethnic disparities in ADHD diagnosis from kindergarten to eighth grade. *Pediatrics, 132*(1), 85–93. https://doi.org/10.1542/peds.2012-2390

Nadeau, K. G., Littman, E. B., & Quinn, P. O. (2016) *Understanding girls with ADHD: How they feel and why they do what they do* (2nd ed.). Advantage Books.

Tung, I., Li, J. J., Meza, J. I., Jezior, K. L., Kianmahd, J. S., Hentschel, P. G., O'Neil, P. M., & Lee, S. S. (2016). Patterns of comorbidity among girls with ADHD: A meta-analysis. *Pediatrics, 138*. https://doi.org/10.1542/peds.2016-0430

Wolraich, M. L. & Hagan, J. F. (Eds.). (2019). *What every parent needs to know ADHD* (3rd ed.). American Academy of Pediatrics.

Wolraich, M. L., Hagan, J. F. Jr, Allan, C., Chan, E., Davison, D., Earls, M., Evans, S. W., Flinn, S. K., Froehlich, T., Frost, J., Holbrook,

J.R., Lehmann, C. U., Lessin, H. R., Okechukwu, K., Pierce, K. L., Winner, J. D., & Zurhellen, W. (2019, October). Subcommittee on children and adolescents with attention-deficit/hyperactive disorder. Clinical practice guideline for the diagnosis, evaluation, and treatment of attention-deficit/hyperactivity disorder in children and adolescents. *Pediatrics*, 144(4), e20192528. doi: 10.1542/peds.2019-2528. Erratum in: *Pediatrics*, 2020 Mar;145(3): PMID: 31570648; PMCID: PMC7067282.

Points to Consider

1 Do you feel your daughter has had an appropriate evaluation and accurate diagnosis of ADHD or do you think she needs further evaluation? What is your next step?
2 What is your plan for telling your daughter about her ADHD?
3 When will you share information from her diagnosis with her school?
4 Do you plan to seek accommodations or services from the school?

Action Steps to Take Now

1 Remember your daughter has probably heard far more negative comments than positive ones. Look for areas where you can offer genuine encouragement.
2 Make sure you have identified your daughter's natural talents. List and post them. Together identify one activity or experience to build on those strengths.
3 Have a discussion or write a letter to one person who needs to have a better understanding of your daughter's ADHD.
4 Begin to establish a support system (physicians, teachers, therapists, etc.) to help you develop a comprehensive treatment plan for your daughter.

Chapter 3

Treatment Options for ADHD

SELF-ASSESSMENT: Where Am I Now?

Each self-assessment helps you reflect on your daughter and your parenting practices and is a preview of the chapter's content.

1 When I consider treatment for my daughter's ADHD …
   a I have no idea where to start.
   b I am researching what our best options are based on services and finances.
   c I know I can count on her pediatrician for good advice.
   d I am so confused by conflicting information.
2 When thinking about resources in my community, I think …
   a there are a wealth of resources and services for children with ADHD.
   b I will see if there is a local CHADD group in my area.
   c there are very few options.
   d I have to do my research.

DOI: 10.4324/9781003365402-4

3 When considering the possibility my daughter has another co-occurring condition in addition to ADHD …
   a I have no idea.
   b I do suspect anxiety because it runs in my family.
   c I am almost too afraid to explore the idea.
   d I am sure ADHD is the root and only cause of all her problems.
4 When I think about giving medication to my daughter …
   a I am dead set against it.
   b I want to try behavioral interventions and parent training first.
   c I hear so many different opinions that I don't know what to think.
   d I know she needs it because she is struggling, so I am all for giving it a try.
5 When considering treatment options, I …
   a know medication can't solve all her problems and will explore psychosocial treatments.
   b am going to check with my insurance company tomorrow about coverage.
   c am going to start with medication.
   d wish I had more time to help her take advantage of several treatment options.

Kim was concerned and went to her pediatrician to have her 8-year-old daughter assessed for ADHD. After the doctor reviewed the behavioral rating forms, she diagnosed Kim's daughter with ADHD. The pediatrician talked about starting a trial of medication, but Kim wasn't prepared to fully consider all the doctor was saying. She was in a state of shock, felt confused, and did not know what to do first. Should she put her daughter on medication? What other options did she have besides medication? Should she tell her daughter's teacher? Should she tell her daughter? Kim was weighed down by her questions. She feared the future but knew that she must put that aside and take positive steps to help her daughter. Learning more about treatment options was the way forward for Kim.

Management of ADHD is a highly charged issue which can be quite confusing. As with most medical conditions, treatment for ADHD is evolving as more research is done and more is learned about the neurobiology of the ADHD brain and the chronic nature of ADHD. Historically, medication has been the most widely used intervention and found to be effective in the large majority of cases because it regulates neurochemicals in the brain, mainly dopamine and norepinephrine, and relieves many symptoms. No doubt medication can be a life saver for many children and families and improves symptoms, but it doesn't address the skill deficits that plague many children with ADHD. From my extensive review of the literature, the need to have a comprehensive plan that addresses ways to improve functioning is becoming important in ADHD treatment. In *Understanding Girls with ADHD*, Nadeau et al. (2016) write:

> We want to help parents and other professionals to move away from a polarizing debate about medication vs. alternatives to medication. Instead, the discussion should focus on developing a treatment plan that focuses on improving cognitive functioning and quality of life that may or may not include medication. (Nadeau et al., 2016, p. 239)

Life Course Model for Treatment of ADHD Recommended

The disparity between the large number of children diagnosed with ADHD who receive medication versus the ones who received other interventions, like behavioral parent training, behavior therapy and /or classroom management training, or a combination of treatments including medication, has been noted. Some thoughts about why large numbers of children may not be receiving other kinds of treatments besides medication could be:

> ▷ professionals dealing with the children aren't well-trained in evidence-based practices,
> ▷ parents may not see the value or have the time,
> ▷ access to services is limited, and
> ▷ the delivery system across the various disciplines is not organized.

Of course, giving medication is much easier for busy families than engaging with other supports but does not address the skill deficits. A **life course model for treatment of ADHD** since it is considered a chronic, life-long disability is recommended (DuPaul et al., 2020). The model's four levels include:

> ▷ Foundational strategies to establish appropriate structure and support in home and school (e.g., parent–teacher communication).
> ▷ Psychosocial interventions to increase competencies and address impairments in academic, behavioral, and social functioning (e.g., organization interventions).
> ▷ Medication treatment.
> ▷ Accommodations to adapt environments to children's limitations (i.e., reductions in expectations). (DuPaul et al., 2020)

The Society for Developmental and Behavioral Pediatrics' Clinical Practice Guidelines for Treating Complex ADHD in Children and Adolescents (Barbaresi et al., 2020) takes a similar approach and advises:

> Treatment should focus on areas of functional impairment, not just symptom reduction, by incorporating developmentally appropriate strategies for self-management, skill building, and prevention of adverse outcomes (e.g., substance use, conduct problems, depression/anxiety, suicidal ideation, educational failure). (Barbaresi et al., 2020)

Furthermore, they recommend monitoring across the lifespan with particular emphasis on transitional periods, like preschool to elementary school, elementary to middle school, middle to high school and high school to postsecondary.

Every case of ADHD is unique. The keys are figuring out what your daughter's major deficits are and how to provide supports for a comprehensive plan. Medication can be an emotionally charged topic but sometimes that is critical for your daughter to be able to take advantage of some of the other treatments. Try to be open-minded as you learn and develop a comprehensive treatment plan that can help your daughter on her journey. It can take time, your own research, and the expertise of others, so hopefully you are motivated to seek answers and can assemble a good team to guide you. ADHD is considered an invisible disorder and can be easily pushed aside, but the consequences of not addressing it with a comprehensive life course plan can be significant.

ADHD is considered an invisible disorder and can be easily pushed aside, but the consequences of not addressing it with a comprehensive life course plan can be significant.

Progress in Understanding and Treating ADHD

As overwhelming as the prospect of developing a life course model for treating ADHD can seem, there are some bright spots on the horizon. As a practitioner who has followed the literature and research for decades, I see progress in the understanding of ADHD, including:

- ▷ characteristics that impede functioning like executive functioning skills deficits and developmental delays;
- ▷ more studies being done on ADHD and its presentation in girls and women;
- ▷ its persistence as a life-long issue requiring ongoing monitoring;
- ▷ the associated risks of not treating it;
- ▷ the emphasis on developing strengths and not fixating on the deficits; and
- ▷ the move to document skills acquisition that transfer to everyday life.

There is sensitivity to the effort required for people with ADHD to function in a linear world and an appreciation of their unique abilities related to their neurodivergence, including their ability to see the big picture, their emotional sensitivity, and ability to hyper-focus on areas of interest. While it is just one more thing to add to your busy life, it is important to stay connected on new developments in ADHD treatment as they unfold.

The treatments which are widely supported by research and practice to date include:

- ▷ parent education and training on understanding the disorder, setting up a consistent environment, and learning how to effectively manage behavior;
- ▷ behavioral treatment, which could include teaching parents and/or teachers to use contingency management (behavior

modification) to improve behaviors and teaching skills to children – continuing until they become routine;

▷ cognitive behavioral therapy or other mental health services for the child if needed;

▷ coaching and organizational training if needed;

▷ parent–teacher communication and educational accommodations when needed; and

▷ medication when necessary, with careful monitoring.

Your child will likely not need all of these, but it is important to know what they are.

What the Research Says About Treatment

As you can imagine, research on the effectiveness of treatments for ADHD is difficult because of so many variables. Those include:

▷ population studied,

▷ type of diagnosis whether inattentive, hyperactive-impulsive, or combined,

▷ how the diagnosis was made and documented including methodology used,

▷ length of time populations were studied,

▷ settings,

▷ how improvements in functioning were measured, and

▷ variables involved in therapy.

Those coupled with unique presentations of ADHD affecting so many areas of functioning don't allow for clear comparisons in studies but in case you are interested, below are some brief summaries of some of the largest studies.

The Multimodal Treatment Study of ADHD (MTA) sponsored by the National Institute of Mental Health is one of the largest and most widely reported studies. It was begun in 1999 with follow-ups in 2002 and 2010 and studied psychosocial treatments (behavior therapy and community care) for ADHD with and without medication in boys and girls. The main findings were that medication alone was more effective than behavior therapy alone but there were some positive results of medication in conjunction with behavior therapy.

The Berkeley Girls ADHD Longitudinal Study (BGALS) led by Dr. Stephen Hinshaw started in 1997, also funded by National Institute of Mental Health, and followed girls from childhood to adulthood. He found that girls with ADHD showed higher rates of later depression than did the girls without ADHD and greater incidences of self-harm, including cuticle-picking and hair pulling on the milder end to cutting, burning, or head-banging – referred to as Non-Suicidal Self-Injury (NSSI). He stated, "A core idea is that when teens experience really difficult and toxic emotions, with no apparent solution, they might engage in NSSI as a means of experiencing physical pain, which temporarily (but only temporarily) alleviates the deeper emotional distress" (Hinshaw, 2022, p. 74). He found that ADHD in girls with both *inattentive symptoms and hyperactive-impulsive symptoms* had a higher risk for self-harm. His recommendations included reducing ADHD symptoms, supporting girls in developing academic and social competence, treatment for serious anxiety and depression if present, and fostering a consistent, supportive home environment.

Treatment Should Address Your Daughter's Need

The key is figuring out what the treatment plan should look like for your individual child and family based on the impact of her symptoms in her daily life, services available, and your financial ability.

The key is figuring out what the treatment plan should look like for your individual child and family based on the impact of her symptoms in her daily life, services available, and your financial ability. Some girls with ADHD do not have impairment severe enough to warrant medication. Non-medical treatments, like behavioral therapy, coaching, and/ or home and classroom supports, may enable them to manage relatively well. Other girls would have an exceedingly hard road without medication. If medication would make the difference between success and failure for your daughter, how could you pass on that option without trying it? Even for girls who take medication, it is important to realize the value of other treatments that build skills and teach strategies as an adjunct.

One thing to keep in mind is that ADHD is a very complex disorder with very diverse presentations. What works for your friend's daughter may not work for yours. As she advances in age and gains skills, her treatment needs might change. It is important for you to be aware of all the supportive options for your daughter so that you can be an educated partner in choosing the right treatment interventions to help her develop her strengths and learn to strengthen or manage her weaknesses.

For example, if your daughter is withdrawn and depressed, she may benefit from cognitive behavioral therapy (CBT) as part of her treatment program to help her reframe her thinking. Parent Behavior Management Training can be a critical component because it educates parents about the complexities of ADHD and how best to manage the behaviors and emotions in the home setting using reinforcement, routines, and firm limits. If your daughter's presenting problems are daydreaming to the point where she is missing much of the classroom instruction despite interventions and has ongoing social problems, she may benefit from her teacher using behavior modification strategies like monitoring and positive feedback to encourage better classroom functioning, social skills training, and/or medication. Other girls with ADHD have varying degrees of difficulties with their executive functioning – those skills required to get tasks done – which may require the intervention of specially trained teachers or ADHD coaches to learn and apply some new skills until they become routine. Many children with ADHD also have learning disabilities and may need specialized tutoring and educational accommodations.

Medication can improve functioning by addressing symptoms, which in turn may help her take better advantage of other services, but it does not teach skills that may need reinforcing or developing, like planning, organization, and social skills deficits. Therefore, a trusted professional who is knowledgeable about ADHD and can see your daughter's complete picture and help you choose the best treatments for her unique needs can be invaluable.

Medication can improve functioning by addressing symptoms, which in turn may help her take better advantage of other services, but it does not teach skills that may need reinforcing or developing, like planning, organization, and social skills deficits.

Try not to be overwhelmed, especially if your child is complex. For her sake and yours, prioritize her needs and don't try to do everything at once. When looking at treatment, take a deep breath and try to make the best decision you can with the information you have acquired from trusted sources. Medication is the most widely used treatment, but other non-medical treatments can be a critical part of your daughter's treatment plan. Since generally much less is known about them compared to medication, I have included them at the beginning of the chapter, so they don't get lost among all the other information.

Non-Medical Treatments Including Evidence-Based as Well as Complementary Interventions to Improve Behavior and Functioning

Non-medical treatments like parent training in understanding ADHD, evidence-based behavioral and academic interventions implemented at home and in school, coaching and or organizational skills training, mental health therapy, educational accommodations and frequent communication with teachers can be highly effective components of your daughter's plan, depending on her needs. When you consider the nature of ADHD with accompanying deficits in many areas of executive functioning and the extra burden on parents, it is very logical that these types of interventions could be advantageous. In my work, I have seen very positive results from a combination of many of them, especially when tailored to the girl's specific needs. Your journey can be complicated enough; you don't need to go it alone without support if you can have access to help. There are costs associated with some of the interventions, some of which may be covered by some insurance, but there are also some supports available for free.

Parent Behavior Training and Behavior Management

If you are like most parents of girls with ADHD, you cannot even begin to count the times you have thrown your hands up in dismay over the years at the daunting task of parenting.

How many times have you wished for just one skill that would make you feel like you had some impact on your daughter's behavior? No doubt about it – parenting a daughter with ADHD adds extra challenges, especially demands on your time and patience. You are already busy providing for your family and yourself, so at the end of the day you may feel like you've given so much that you don't have anything left. That is totally understandable because you are only human. You want the best for your daughter but may be at a loss as to how to make that happen.

Parent behavioral training can ultimately make your life and your daughter's much easier even though it is one more demand on your time. As you know, the ADHD brain isn't intrinsically motivated in the same way as others, has difficulty with organization of actions and thoughts, and is often very impulsive. What works for non-ADHD children may not work with your daughter, so you need new strategies and tools.

Your knowledge about ADHD and how it impacts your daughter's behavior are very important in her treatment plan. After all, you are with her probably more than anyone else. The structure you provide for her when she can't provide it for herself, your knowledge about what behavior she is able to control and where she still needs support, and your ability to help her problem solve will be invaluable. And don't underestimate the value of the relationship you build with her. She needs to know you want the best for her and will never give up on helping her develop her strengths and determining how to manage the challenges ADHD brings to her life.

> *The structure you provide for her when she can't provide it for herself, your knowledge about what behavior she is able to control and where she still needs support, and your ability to help her problem solve will be invaluable.*

Parent behavior training is so important that it is recommended to be the first treatment prescribed for preschoolers diagnosed with ADHD. Especially at that stage, children with ADHD typically lag behind peers in development of emotional control, social skills, and fine motor. It is important for parents (and teachers if the child is in preschool) to learn about developmental stages, how to intervene and change negative behaviors like tantrums, the importance of consistent boundaries, frequent rewards for behavior, and setting up the environment to encourage success.

Unfortunately, parent training may not always be easily available in your community (see resources below for online programs) and components and methodology can vary greatly. Some parent trainings are in groups with other parents of children with ADHD, others are individual, and they may be in person or online. However, most of the recognized programs share common main goals:

> ▷ increasing knowledge about ADHD,
> ▷ strengthening the parent–child bond to encourage cooperation and communication,
> ▷ utilizing practices like positive reinforcement and consequences for managing and changing behavior.

In *Taking Charge of ADHD: The Complete, Authoritative Guide for Parents*, 4th edition, Barkley (2020) urges parents to have a thorough understanding of ADHD and its impact on behavior. He states, "ADHD does not directly *cause* children to refuse or defy your requests" (p. 192) but it can interfere with children's follow-through. We know children with ADHD:

> ▷ crave stimulation and novelty and often avoid boring or tedious tasks,
> ▷ may have a defeatist attitude about even beginning a difficult task because of negative feedback received in the past,
> ▷ have a faulty sense of time and lose track of time before doing a task, and/or
> ▷ may become easily distracted in the middle of tasks.

Even though it may take extra effort, Barkley warns parents about the dangers of not following through with requests. He says, "Parents also train children with ADHD to become defiant when their response to an initial emotional display teaches the children that resistance, defiance, and negativity are effective means of avoiding work" (p. 192). He further recommends using incentives and positive reinforcement before consequences including time-out or having a child lose points on a system you have implemented ahead of time since children with ADHD typically receive so many negatives in their day-to-day life.

Hinshaw (2022) in *Straight Talk about ADHD in Girls* discusses many principles of behavioral family treatments, like "applying a functional analysis – that is, understanding the sequences of antecedent → behavior → consequence that can promote measurable change" (p. 123) and breaking down behaviors you want to change into small steps. If you can understand the circumstances that contribute to the behavior, you can sometimes manipulate the environment to make it more conducive to better behavior or coach your daughter on ways to respond to a challenging situation.

Consequences can mean natural consequences, like no longer having a toy to play with that was smashed in anger, or an imposed consequence, which would be part of your behavior plan. For example, if she was defiant and wouldn't get ready to leave the house with the family, she may lose time from a desired activity. It is very important to look at the dynamics of the behavior and make sure whatever happens following the behavior isn't reinforcing it. Some girls value attention so much that even negative attention following poor behavior is better than no attention and inadvertently reinforces the behavior you want to eradicate.

In *What Every Parent Needs to Know ADHD* by the American Academy of Pediatrics, editors Wolraich and Hagan (2019) suggest praising behavior you want to continue, ignoring behavior that is not problematic, and having consequences to stop behavior that is dangerous or intolerable. For those behaviors that need to be addressed, they suggest giving a simple statement of what you want your daughter to do, such as, "Please stop arguing with your sister." If she doesn't stop, follow with a warning and a specific consequence for not following. They advise,

> Keep in mind that you have given a warning and a terminating command and spelled out the consequence for complying or disobeying, if she does not follow your instructions you have not 'put her in time out' – she *has* 'chosen' the time out for herself as an alternative to following your command. (Wolraich & Hagan, 2019, p. 130)

Parent training to assist in the understanding and management of ADHD is widely available on the internet. Some in-person training may be available in your community, often offered through schools or other organizations supportive of children. Below are a few resources, some of which are free.

Children & Adults with Attention-Deficit Disorder (CHADD) https://chadd.org/ a non-profit organization disseminating information about ADHD, offers a number of parent resources which include:

> ▷ Parent to Parent Family Training through e-learning, webinars or in-person webinars,
> ▷ Ask the Expert series, and
> ▷ Resource Directory of coaches, psychologists, or other services.

***ADDitude* magazine** www.additudemag.com/ disseminates information on ADHD and related conditions and offers:

> ▷ Webinars
> ▷ *ADDitude* magazine with timely articles appealing to all ages
> ▷ ADHD Parenting – articles and videos on behavior, schooling, treatments, and parenting

Triple P Parenting www.triplep-parenting.com/us/triple-p/ is a self-directed, evidence-based program parents can do online. It provides guidance in preventing and treating behavioral problems in children and teens.

Incredible Years Parenting Program www.incredibleyears.com/programs/parent/ is an online program out of Australia designed to treat behavior and emotional problems in children from birth through age 12. It does not specifically address ADHD, but does have a program called Stepping Stones Triple P designed for parents of children with disabilities.

Parent–Child Interaction Therapy www.pcit.org/ is an international evidence-based program designed for children aged 2–7 with behavior problems whereby a therapist coaches parents in interactions with their child through play and behavior therapy.

One parent of an 8-year-old told me, "I feel lost as a parent. I feel like I can't get control of my daughter, Hilda. She's out of control, I'm not in control, and I'm not sure how to rein in her behavior." In this case, Hilda's behavior was much worse at home than at school because she responded to the tightly structured environment provided for her at school and had strong academic skills. Hilda's family was reluctant to engage in family behavioral therapy but realized they had no other choice if they were to help her.

Her parents were not organized people themselves but realized they had to "tighten up" their ship, provide consistency, and hold Hilda accountable for her behavior. It went against their nature to be so scheduled, but they knew it was what Hilda needed. They found that the techniques they had used when she was younger no longer worked, so they had to acquire new tools and strategies. They learned she needed cues and prompts to guide her behavior. Even these didn't always work but were generally helpful.

They had developed a very critical and negative atmosphere in their home which they could see had to change. The therapist asked them to pay more attention to Hilda's behavior when she was doing what she was supposed to do and ignore low level negative behaviors that weren't really that important in the scheme of things. They made a pact to try to give five positives to every negative to Hilda, which seemed to turn her attitude around.

Classroom Interventions, Including Classroom Behavior Management

Since most girls spend a large chunk of their day in the classroom, the American Academy of Pediatrics recommends that the school program be part of an ADHD treatment plan with teacher-administered behavior therapy as a component. Girls with ADHD often face difficulties in the classroom with staying focused, starting and completing their work, not bothering fellow students, and following classroom routine. Teachers with good behavioral classroom management often use the principles of behavior modification, including positive reinforcement of desirable behaviors through a reward system or daily report card. This represents one more task for the teacher, who is probably already overworked and bombarded with paperwork, but can make a huge difference in motivating your daughter to comply with teacher expectations. It will be critical for you to maintain good communication with the teacher and possibly follow through with rewards for good school behavior at home. If your daughter is mature enough, it might be advantageous for her to be involved in setting the goals and rewards.

Classroom accommodations and interventions to help students manage ADHD are an important component and discussed at length in Chapter 5 under the pullout section for your daughter's teachers entitled "Information for Your Teammates – Your Daughter's Teachers" and in Chapter 8 under "School Accommodations and Supports".

Mental Health Therapy If Needed

Many girls with ADHD, especially those with self-esteem issues and self-regulation challenges, find help working with a counselor or mental health therapist. If your daughter has been diagnosed with anxiety and/or depression, mental health therapy will be especially critical. It can take many forms from individual to group counseling and can sometimes even involve the whole family if there are family structure, communication, or sibling issues. Sometimes it is much more appealing to a girl if she thinks of the therapist as a "coach" – especially if she is involved in sports and understands a coach's role in improving performance, as opposed to seeing the therapist as a person who will try to "fix" what is wrong with her. It can be costly but often counseling is short-term, solution-focused, and a game changer for some girls. Some medical insurance covers counseling with specific counselors who are on their plan, so be sure to explore that option. Also, check with any community agencies or your daughter's school for counseling options.

If your child is preschool or early elementary school age, the sessions will be structured around play therapy rather than "talk" therapy and centered on practical issues like sharing, respecting personal space, and curbing aggressive behavior, like hitting. The therapist will likely use toys and games to teach skills. Maturity levels vary significantly for elementary age girls with ADHD. Most younger girls benefit more from a reward-based, behavioral approach than talk therapy, but older girls may benefit from discussing situations faced in their everyday life with an objective listener and receiving help reframing some of them and figuring out effective strategies. Hinshaw reports that many studies support a "CBT approach that emphasizes self-monitoring, self-reward, organizational skills, time management, and anger control" (Hinshaw, 2022, p. 133), especially for teens.

Key to success will be having a counselor with a good knowledge base about ADHD, how it can impact functioning, how to motivate change and develop new habits and routines, and how to help your daughter set treatment goals and work toward them. Finding the right match for your daughter in terms of personality and style will also be of utmost importance. Having a strong, trusting relationship will make or break how well counseling works. Therefore, it is very important to talk to the counselor about this from the start. You should know after three or four sessions if it's the right pairing. Ask your daughter questions such as, "How do you like the counselor? Do you feel like he or she listens and understands you? Are you becoming comfortable talking to him or her?" Likewise, ask the counselor if your daughter is expressive, open, and honest. From this point you can make the decision to stay or find another counselor. Don't stay just for the sake of "doing something" or because the counselor is on your insurance plan because counseling will not work if it's not the right fit. Please don't give up if the first or even second counselor you try isn't the right match if your daughter really needs counseling.

Here are some questions to ask when choosing a counselor for your daughter:

▷ What is your experience in counseling girls with ADHD?
▷ What is your philosophy toward helping make meaningful change?
▷ What type of counseling is used?
▷ How long does the average girl with ADHD remain in counseling in your practice?
▷ What are common causes for leaving?
▷ What is the most frequent age range of girls you counsel?
▷ How are parents and/or family involved?
▷ Do you communicate with teachers or school staff if we give permission?

Identifying the specific issues for the counselor to address will be a collaborative task with input from you and your daughter. Many girls with ADHD benefit from counseling to maintain a positive mindset, appropriately express their frustrations, and/or deal with anger at having to work so much harder than classmates for less than stellar results.

> *Maria was a teenage girl who was overcome with self-defeating thoughts. She had a negative outlook on herself, school, and life that lowered her self-esteem and impacted her academics. She approached each situation from a negative rather than positive perspective. For example, when Maria's mom, Beatrice, suggested she spend the day at a nearby water park for a break, Maria could only think of the long lines she might encounter.*
>
> *Maria finally agreed to see a counselor to appease her mother. To help Maria gain an understanding of how often negative thoughts popped into her head, the counselor gave Maria a click-counter and asked her to hold it for an hour and click it each time she had a negative thought. Maria was shocked to realize she had 19 negative thoughts in one hour. Over time by learning to use positive self-talk to fight back at her negative thoughts, she was able to reduce them significantly, improving her and her family's lives.*

In my experience, parents typically seek counseling when they feel they have done everything they know how to do to support their daughter's emotional functioning, yet there are still problems. When your daughter's challenges reach crisis level, it may prompt you to reach out for a professional's support. As one mom told me, "I just couldn't take one more phone call from the school telling me about her peer problems and self-defeating attitude. I had to do something." It is often more advantageous to seek counseling when problems first begin cropping up rather than waiting until they have reached a flash point and your daughter's self-esteem has been damaged. Habits develop quickly. Remember that it is much easier to change behavior before it becomes an ingrained pattern.

> *Remember that it is much easier to change behavior before it becomes an ingrained pattern.*

To have the most benefit, counseling usually involves you, your daughter, and possibly the immediate family. If some of the issues are school-related, it will be critical to keep the teacher in the loop and anyone else who may be part of your daughter's team, such as her pediatrician or psychiatrist. One benefit of counseling is that families often figure out some of their own solutions when talking about things with a non-judgmental third party.

Types of Counseling

Cognitive behavioral therapy is one of the most common therapeutic approaches used by therapists and counselors. It is based on the premise that a person's thoughts, not external events or people, cause feelings and behaviors. The goal is to change behavior by helping the client shift their mindset about what is happening. Some question the advantages of CBT for girls with ADHD, stating girls most often know what to do but may be hijacked by impulsivity or have trouble following through on doing what they know. However, if your daughter has anxiety or depression, it can be invaluable. Often girls with ADHD are good at catastrophizing, or immediately going to a negative thought when something happens. It may start as a small thought and get to a near-panic level quickly. The therapist will try to help the girl learn to examine her thoughts for irrational thinking and develop a more positive approach.

Cognitive behavioral therapy has a solid research base and is short-term, goal-oriented, and instructive. It can be as short as 12 weeks or as long as a year or more, depending on motivation to change and circumstances that brought your daughter to therapy. During counseling, girls are taught how to identify and express concerns, problem solve, and apply what they learned. The sessions also involve learning to take responsibility and make measurable steps toward achieving the desired outcome.

Another type of counseling is called Dialectical Behavior Therapy (DBT) which includes mindfulness, emotional regulation – including developing tolerance of uncomfortable feelings – and interpersonal effectiveness. Both CBT and DBT are behaviorally focused therapies, but DBT also adds the mindfulness component. Like CBT, DBT can be anywhere from 12 weeks to 1 year. It may also involve some group therapy.

Some schools have mental health counselors, guidance counselors, or school psychologists who offer some counseling, whether individual or group, at no cost. It is often more generic, of shorter duration and more focused on school-related issues than outside counseling. Mental health seems to be becoming more of a priority in schools following the increased incidences of depression and anxiety in the general population, so be sure to inquire about any supports available at your school, especially if your daughter is having difficulty, primarily at school.

To summarize, counseling is a way for your daughter to learn to manage her ADHD and build a skill set for life, especially important if she has internalizing or emotional problems. The goal of counseling is to help girls with ADHD learn to manage their emotions. Goals would be for them to stay calm and in control, have a plan in place to manage their impulsivity, and avoid situations that bring on misbehavior. It is not unusual for girls to seek counseling throughout their lives to help manage obstacles that pop up during different life stages. If you have tried it in the past and it didn't work, perhaps it wasn't the right time for your daughter to take advantage of it or wasn't the right counselor. Don't give up on it altogether if it sounds like something she may still need.

Coaching for Children and Parents

Coaching generally deals with management of practical aspects of ADHD, such as organization, scheduling, goal setting, and time management. Research (Merriman & Codding, 2008) indicates it is an effective and complementary approach for helping people with ADHD develop or improve these executive functioning skills so necessary for success in everyday life. Older elementary students, teenagers, and adults are the most likely candidates to find success with coaching. Coaching is often more action oriented than counseling and is most effective when the girls are motivated to make changes in their daily life and don't have emotional problems that would be better served through mental health therapy. It is often of shorter duration than counseling, depending on the issues involved and your daughter's willingness to implement strategies. The coach will often assist the person with ADHD in breaking down tasks into short-term goals and will check in frequently to see how the person is progressing toward those goals. Ideally, they will oversee practice of skills until they become automatic.

In *The Essential Guide to Raising Complex Kids with ADHD, Anxiety, and More*, Taylor-Klaus (2020) focuses on educating and supporting parents as they develop a "coach approach" in collaborating with their children to create a more peaceful household. The basic tenet of coaching is to motivate people to do things that help them reach their full potential. Taylor-Klaus's four phases of parenting include:

1. Motivate effort and direct work.
2. Motivate ownership and model organization.
3. Transfer ownership and support organization.
4. Empower, champion, and troubleshoot. (Taylor-Klaus, 2020, pp. 65–66)

Coaching as an industry has been evolving over time and becoming more organized and consistent in delivery. It can be in person or accessed virtually. There are now several organizations involved in disseminating research and information about coaching and most importantly, establishing certification and delivering training for coaches. Some of the organizations offering coach training and certification are ADD Coach Academy, JST Coaching & Training, and ADHD Coaches Organization. Some programs confer titles like Professional ADHD Coach, which means he or she would have met the requirements of the International Coaches Federation and have additional hours in ADHD specific training. Jodi-Sleeper Triplett is a nationally recognized authority on ADHD coaching and has authored several books on the subject.

Like counseling, it is important to interview the coach to ensure he or she is trained, understands ADHD and accompanying executive functioning problems, can address your daughter's issues in a way that will resonate with her, and develops a plan so you can monitor progress. Since the coach will likely be helping your daughter set up routines to help problematic tasks become more automatic, it is critical for the coach and your daughter to establish a respectful, working relationship. Making changes in behavior is not easy, so you want the coach to be able to help your daughter become vested in the process. It will be most helpful if those changes can become routine. Make sure to ask questions like:

- ▷ What is your training specific to coaching ADHD?
- ▷ How many girls with ADHD have you worked with? Please provide some examples of successes you have had.
- ▷ Describe your approach and how you monitor progress.
- ▷ Do you offer check-ins between sessions through texts or calls if needed to prompt change?
- ▷ How do you communicate progress with parents and will we be involved in the coaching?

Medication

Advice from the Medical Community

Medical doctors are a source of a wealth of knowledge, but sometimes it is hard to take in all the information in an office visit. I asked Dr. Sari Katz, pediatrician, and Dr. Marshall Teitelbaum and Dr. Michelle Chaney, both psychiatrists, to answer common questions parents have about medication and ADHD.

Dr. Sari Katz, pediatrician

Q: What are the risks if parents decide not to treat their daughter with medication, behavior therapy, coaching, and/or counseling?

Parents are often understandably concerned about the risks of treatment with medication. There is a wealth of incorrect information and misconceptions in the lay public and on the internet about ADHD medicines. As a general strategy, we try to manage symptoms first with counseling and behavioral modifications without the use of medicine. Medicine is usually reserved for cases refractory to non-medicinal treatments or cases that are severe enough to cause significant academic disruption.

This question is a great question, because many parents do not consider the risks of not treating ADHD. These risks are significant, based on the current research. For one, girls with Attention-Deficit/Hyperactive Disorder face poor academic and vocational outcomes. The impulsive nature of these girls can also cause significant social impairment. Girls who try to compensate for suboptimal focus and attention will often spend many hours studying and reviewing material. Due to gender norms, girls are expected to be dutiful and more responsible than their male peers. This can lead to loss of sleep, increased stress, missed social activities, missed extracurricular activities, decreased self-esteem, and subsequent feelings of depression and anxiety. Girls with ADHD have a higher risk of self-harm than their peers. In addition, there is data to show that girls with ADHD have higher chances of encountering situations for which there is risk of personal injury or harm. For example, rates of unplanned pregnancy and personal trauma are higher in girls with ADHD than their peers. Furthermore, girls with ADHD have higher chances of self-medicating their symptoms in the future and higher rates of substance abuse and addiction. So there are definitely known risks to holding back the treatment of ADHD. Giving a child proper treatment for ADHD gives her the best chance for future success and safety.

Q: What happens in your practice if a girl does not respond to the medication or has too many side effects?

After initiating a treatment plan, we always see the child in a few weeks to talk to the child and parent and assess the success of the plan. If there has been a lack of response to a medicine, there are many possible reasons. Sometimes, a higher dose is needed for therapeutic effect. Often, a different medicine should be tried. Luckily, there are many different medicines and pediatricians can often tell by the response and adverse effects, if any, which medicine might be a better fit for the child. Once a child has tried a few medicines without success, reconsideration of the diagnosis is in order. Either the diagnosis is not correct, or a known comorbidity is the major cause of the impairment and needs to be addressed and treated to help the patient achieve symptom relief.

Q. How do you monitor a child's progress?

The child is seen a few weeks after starting medicine. Careful attention is paid to physical and mental effects of the medicine. Once the child is stable on medicine, in-office visits are conducted every three months. We reassess the treatment plan and make sure the child is comfortable taking the medicine and agrees with the benefits. Children as young as six can explain whether they like the medicine and how it benefits them. It is very important to talk to the child, in addition to the parent, because the children often do not voice concerns about the medicine or any adverse effects unless directly asked. Sometimes the child expresses a concern about the medicine but agrees that the side effects are minimal, and the benefit is great. It is important to me that the child agrees with the treatment plan and is an active participant in decisions about medicine and other treatment.

Dr. Marshall Teitelbaum, child and adolescent psychiatrist

Q. Is medication for ADHD essential?

Whether medication is necessary is often perceived as controversial. Usually the decision is clinically straightforward, however. The issue is more one of evaluating what the true diagnoses are first, and if ADHD is either the or among the diagnoses, how the symptoms are interfering in the girl's life. If there are biologically associated diagnoses present, such as obsessive-compulsive disorder, a chronic tic disorder (including Tourette's syndrome), or bipolar disorder, then consideration must be given to the potential risk of using a medication for

ADHD in combination with the related condition. If there are behaviorally associated comorbid conditions present, such as Oppositional Defiant Disorder, conduct disorder traits, and/or low self-esteem/depressive disorders, then the likelihood of a more aggressive measure, such as using medication, becomes practically essential.

The bottom line is that ADHD presents differently, and how it specifically is affecting the given person is what needs to be considered the most when it comes to treatment decisions. If there are significant effects, or a near-term expectation of one or more of these, on behavioral, social, or academic function, the ADHD symptoms need be addressed immediately. The goal is to avoid the future consequences for what happens if these problems are allowed to evolve, such as lower school and/or career achievement, higher risk for substance abuse or legal problems, more relationship challenges, more injuries, ER visits, and moving traffic violations. In other words, we all worry about the potential risks of medications, but we also must worry about the potential risks of not using medications.

There are a number of ADHD medications available. These medications are primarily categorized into two groups, **stimulants** and **nonstimulants**. I will summarize them below along with pertinent information about their use.

The FDA approved **nonstimulants** are Qelbree (viloxazine), Strattera (atomoxetine), Intuniv (long-acting guanfacine), and Kapvay (long-acting clonidine formulation). These options are typically slower to take effect and less potent, although they can be used in combination with stimulants when necessary to augment treatment, as well as to assist with later-day stimulant rebound. Intuniv and Kapvay are based on alpha-2 agonist blood pressure medications that have been used for years off-label to treat ADHD, but longer-acting versions came out on-label and with greater ease of use (as the prior ones often required three to four dosages per day). The alpha-2 agonists can be helpful with ADD-associated insomnia and tic disorders, thus assisting when this genetically linked condition is part of the equation. Given the potential for blood pressure effects, they must be increased slowly, and after having been used for a sufficient length of time, have to be reduced gradually. Qelbree and Strattera work by blocking uptake of the neurotransmitter norepinephrine. Qelbree can be sprinkled into pudding or applesauce for those who have difficulty with pill-swallowing. Strattera needs to be swallowed intact to prevent irritation of the esophagus. Any of the medications can be of value if a stimulant is not considered a safe medical option or if the necessary adequate dosage of stimulant medication is not tolerable, thus sometimes requiring a combination.

The **stimulant** medications are the more well-known FDA approved ADHD treatments. This class is predominantly broken down into two types, those related to methylphenidate (i.e., Ritalin) or amphetamine (i.e., Adderall or Dexedrine). They all tend to cause appetite suppression, but for most children, it can be managed well with appropriate interventions.

Methylphenidate-based medications include shorter-acting (usually no more than 4 hours) and longer-acting (upward of 8 hours) medications. The shorter-acting medicines include methylphenidate (Ritalin) and dexmethylphenidate (Focalin).

The longer-acting methylphenidates include Concerta, Ritalin LA, Metadate CD/ER, Ritalin SR, Aptensio XR, Adhansia XR, Jornay PM, Cotempla XR-ODT, Quillivant, Quillichew and Daytrana, along with the related dexmethylphenidate (the right chemical half of the methylphenidate molecule), Focalin XR and Azstarys (pro-drug of dexmethylphenidate). Daytrana is a patch that goes on the hip, rotating sites daily to lessen the risk of skin irritation. It can allow for better morning symptom management if applied while your daughter is still in bed and can allow more active management of the wear-off time based on when it is removed, regardless of the time it is applied (e.g., if you have a teenager who likes to sleep in on weekends). Jornay PM is provided at night with the goal of delaying its effect until the next morning while still having a full day of efficacy. Concerta, Ritalin LA, Metadate CD, Aptensio XR, Adhansia XR, Cotempla XR-ODT, Quillivant XR, Quillichew XR, Focalin XR and Azstarys (pro-drug of dexmethylphenidate) are medications with differing delivery technologies that increase the likelihood of ongoing benefit throughout the day. Concerta may last longer for some, although Focalin XR may kick in faster. There are various deliveries with fruit flavorings, such as dissolving in the mouth rapidly (Cotempla XR-ODT), liquid (Quillivant XR), and chewable (Quillichew XR). There are others that can be opened and sprinkled, such as Focalin XR, Azstarys, Adhansia XR and Aptensio XR. The goal for many is to make dosing easier if unable to swallow pills, but some can also allow easier finessing of dosages for those who do best on "in between" strengths. The times of day that require better medication coverage need to be kept in mind when using these.

Shorter-acting (up to 4 hours) amphetamine-based medications (admit it, the name is scary) include Adderall (mixed dextroamphetamine at 75% and levoamphetamine at 25% salts), Evekeo (regular and orally disintegrating tablets with mix of 50/50 proportion of dextroamphetamine and levoamphetamine salts, and for some may have a longer duration), Dexedrine (dextroamphetamine), Zenzedi (dextroamphetamine) and ProCentra (liquid dextroamphetamine), with ProCentra being useful at times for kids who cannot swallow pills. Longer-acting versions include Adderall XR, Mydayis (longer-acting version of Adderall XR), Dexedrine spansule, Vyvanse (capsule and chewable versions), Dyanavel XR and Adzenys ER and XR-ODT. The longer-acting medications are more likely to allow better full-day coverage, with Dexedrine spansule typically lasting 6–8 hours, Mydayis lasting 12–16 hours, Vyvanse lasting 10–14 hours, and the others usually being effective for

10–12 hours. Vyvanse is a pro-drug, meaning it is turned into its active product (lisdexamfetamine into dextroamphetamine) only after the body begins to metabolize it. Some can be opened and sprinkled into food, such as Adderall XR and Dexedrine spansule, although typically this should be done in a tablespoon to ensure full medication ingestion. Vyvanse capsules can be opened while pouring the powder into a few ounces of water, yogurt or orange juice to dissolve. For those with difficulty swallowing who don't want to open capsules, Vyvanse also has a chewable version, Dyanavel XR is available in liquid (allowing greater ease for those needing unusual dosages), and Adzenys XR-ODT dissolves rapidly in the mouth.

As I'm prone to reminding parents, non-school hours are often as or more important, as these can be times of higher risk. Driving while distracted can be a major danger, for instance, and the GPA is irrelevant when someone is in the emergency room. There can be more difficulty getting homework completed independently, social disruption, family conflict, defiance, higher-risk behavior experimentation, and self-esteem problems, with all over time leading to much larger challenges, even if only occurring a few hours per day or a few days per week.

There are a variety of other medication classes still being researched, as well as medications that are used for off-label treatment (medications that are thought to be of value at times but that are not formally approved by the FDA for the given medical indication) of ADHD. It is always of the utmost importance that the risks for both treating and not treating ADHD medically are fully explored to help dictate the appropriate treatment course.

Q: How do you know when to stop using ADHD medications with your daughter?

The issue of knowing if or when it might make sense to stop ADHD medication is often quite challenging to decide, especially if the girl is doing well. There are many considerations. First, if your daughter is on a faster-acting medication, such as a psychostimulant, have there been days of missed doses, and if so, what transpired on these days? If the girl had a miserable day with the original symptoms of ADHD seen prior to medication initiation, likely the medication needs to be continued. If she has been doing well for an extended time, it is usually wise to reassess the medication need at least annually, and usually at a time when it would be the least problematic if reduction causes symptom recurrence. For instance, stopping a girl's medication just prior to final exams or some other type of big event would be silly. Often lowering the dosage when there is less going on at school, and possibly with the teacher's awareness, makes it easier to assess the efficacy. Other times it can be less risky to reduce when school is out, although if the main issues of ADHD are on the inattentive (vs. impulsive) spectrum, it can be more challenging to evaluate.

The most important issues have to do with whether the symptoms of ADHD are still there, which is usually the case to at least some degree for many affected individuals, and what ways the residual symptoms are still interfering. A girl who has problems with socialization or behavior when off medication is likely to have a variety of problems if taking an extended break from medication over the summer, for instance. If she is either having no further life interferences without medication or is having minimal enough disturbance that can be addressed in other ways (e.g., organizational coaching, psychotherapy), then it may be reasonable to stop medication.

It is hard being a parent. It is even harder when you have a daughter with ADHD, as often you do not get the support of others like you do with a child with other medical problems. However, it is your responsibility to make the decisions that are in the best interest of your child, regardless of whether they are easy or popular. I often compare the condition to severe allergy or vision problems, as none are thought of as immediately life threatening, but the quality of life and potential risks going forward, if ignored, can be severe. If the medical issue is interfering with your daughter's life, then it is your responsibility as a parent to make decisions, even those that you do not like. Keep in mind that your daughter is not choosing to have ADHD (i.e., be distracted, disorganized, hyperactive). So, take advantage of all the resources that this modern society has to offer!

Dr. Michelle Chaney, child, adolescent, and adult psychiatrist

Q. Can you explain the two classes of medication, stimulants and nonstimulants, for ADHD and how they work? How do you choose which medication is appropriate?

Stimulant medications appear to normalize biochemistry in the parts of the brain involved with ADHD. When a child takes a stimulant, the neurotransmitters dopamine and norepinephrine are released more effectively. Stimulant medications enhance nerve-to-nerve communication by making more neurotransmitters available to boost the signal between neurons. In addition, they block the recycle mechanism or reuptake of the sending nerve cell, leading to an accumulation of the neurotransmitter. Overall, enhancement of dopamine and norepinephrine actions in certain brain regions are thought to improve attention, concentration, and wakefulness, as well as decrease hyperactivity.

The non-stimulant treatments vary in their mechanism of action. Strattera (atomoxetine) and Qelbree (viloxazine) are highly specific presynaptic (sending neuron) noradrenergic reuptake inhibitors. This ultimately makes more norepineph-rine available for nerve-to-nerve communication. The alpha agonist medications (including guanfacine and clonidine) have action on receptors in the prefrontal cortex of the brain, which is thought to be responsible for modulation of working memory, attention, impulse control, and planning.

Choosing which medication will work best for your child typically involves considering how the ADHD symptoms are most impacting their lives. In addition, a family history of responding particularly well with any specific medication is considered (as we know, there is a genetic component to this disorder). Comorbidities that may play a role in the child's overall presentation, such as anxiety or tic disorders as well as appetite challenges, are also considered. First-line treatment is typically stimulant medication unless there are good reasons to consider alternative options. These reasons may include high levels of anxiety, sleep difficulties, appetite challenges, medical issues such as cardiac abnormalities, and a family history suggesting stimulants may not be well tolerated.

Q. What is your advice on "drug holidays," not taking medication on weekends or summer vacations?

All non-stimulant ADHD medications must be given daily to be effective, and "drug holidays" are not permitted. Stimulant ADHD medications do not have this requirement and can sometimes be held if needed or preferred. My guidance for families regarding "drug holidays" is to keep in mind that ADHD symptoms do not disappear just because children are out of school. There are many reasons why continuing to treat on weekends or over the summer vacation are necessary, including being able to sustain attention at camp or other activities generally, needing to complete summer homework or reading, listening and interacting socially with peers and family members with greater success, as well as driving without distraction (if applicable). Despite these benefits, parents may conclude that their child is able to accommodate well without medication when they are outside the school setting and wish to give a "break" in these situations. Sometimes, if their child sleeps in very late on non-school days, taking the medication early enough to avoid side effects may be particularly difficult. If a child experiences side effects from the medication (including lower appetite and sleep difficulties), holding the medication on the weekend and over vacations may even be beneficial. This decision is very individualized; each child's risks and benefits must be carefully considered.

Q. What are the challenges you see in treating girls with ADHD?(hormonal fluctuations, peer pressure, self-esteem, etc.)?

Often, the biggest challenge I see in treating girls with ADHD involves making the appropriate diagnosis in the first place. This diagnosis can be missed in girls because they don't always present with classic hyperactive challenges that catch the attention of teachers and parents immediately. Instead, symptoms may be considered personality characteristics that could be overlooked including appearing withdrawn, daydreaming, being more sensitive, being unmotivated, or not listening well. Girls who do struggle with hyperactive and impulsive symptoms are frequently viewed as overemotional rather than evaluating these symptoms more completely. Girls may place greater blame on themselves for problems they are experiencing which can take a significant toll on their self-esteem and lead to higher levels of anxiety than their peers.

The hormonal fluctuations that occur during the menstrual cycle can potentially worsen symptoms of ADHD for girls. Some studies indicate that girls have more severe ADHD symptoms during the third and fourth weeks of the menstrual cycle (when progesterone levels are higher); these hormonal fluctuations may make the medication less effective and treatment more challenging.

Q. Can you provide information about comorbidities most often seen in girls with ADHD and how they might be treated?

Comorbidities are often seen in girls with ADHD, as approximately 75% of children diagnosed with ADHD have at least one additional mental health or learning disorder during their lifetimes (American Academy of Child and Adolescent Psychiatry & American Psychiatric Association, 2013). Common comorbidities include anxiety disorders, depressive disorders, learning and language disorders, Tourette's syndrome, and oppositional defiant disorder. These comorbidities are diagnosed by having a comprehensive evaluation by a skilled practitioner, often a psychiatrist, a neurologist, a clinical psychologist, or a neuropsychologist, depending on the presenting symptoms. Only psychiatrists and neurologists can prescribe medication but they often work collaboratively with clinical psychologists and neuropsychologists. Typically, this evaluation will include an extensive diagnostic interview and may incorporate rating scales, usually completed by the child's parents and teachers. Because many psychiatric conditions have symptoms that can overlap (e.g., poor concentration may be seen in an individual struggling with depression and anxiety as well as with ADHD), it may be beneficial to treat the condition that appears to be having the greatest adverse effect first and then reassess. Psychological testing can be important to better understand emotional and cognitive functioning and possible learning disorders.

Q. Are there any new advances, either in diagnosis or treatment, on the horizon that you think might be promising?

There is ongoing research using brain scans that I am hopeful will one day be beneficial for diagnosis and treatment in a number of psychiatric conditions including ADHD. However, currently, they do not have much value in clinical practice.

Thanks to Drs. Katz, Teitelbaum, and Chaney for sharing their valuable insights. It's not often that parents are afforded the time during their daughter's doctor's visit to hear this type of in-depth information because many doctors are pressed for time. And even if we had the time to hear this from a doctor, it would be too much to quickly take in, so it is nice to have an explanation in writing to read and reference as needed.

Tina is a working single parent, and her daughter, Carmen, is a ninth grader in high school. Carmen was diagnosed with ADHD in third grade by her pediatrician. Since that time she had been on and off medication. She was not a stellar student but earned mostly grades of B, C, and an occasional D. Carmen was not currently taking medication and her grades were slipping. Tina felt like she had to be on Carmen's case all the time. In addition, Tina was concerned because Carmen was choosing friends who were not known for good grades. Tina decided it was time to have Carmen reassessed, so she scheduled an appointment with a psychiatrist.

Following an additional evaluation, Carmen was iden-tified with serious emotional issues with depression and anxiety. She was surrounding herself with people who had an equally poor self-concept because it helped her feel less inadequate. The psychiatrist felt strongly that Carmen's emotional issues should take priority and required medication as well as weekly therapy with a mental health counselor for cognitive behavior therapy. His plan was to reassess her ADHD after she had become more emotionally stable. Carmen also did not have well-developed study skills, so another part of her plan was to receive assistance at school on how to sort and prioritize the quantity of information her teachers gave her each day and develop a schedule to get her assignments done. While there was still a lot of work ahead, Tina and Carmen could see they now had a plan.

Really, Should I Medicate My Daughter?

Some risk accompanies almost all medications, and most have some side effects, which can usually be managed. Concerns parents sometimes have about medication for ADHD include decreased appetite, impacted sleep, growth retardation, potential for addiction, and heart problems. These concerns are understandable, but having good medical information from research and your doctor can alleviate some of the concerns and allow you to weigh the benefits against the side effects.

Issues with appetite can often be addressed by working with your doctor on timing of medication, dosages, and/or adding calories. If your daughter takes medication in the morning, many doctors recommend providing a protein rich breakfast and a substantial after-school snack since she may have a decreased appetite for lunch. Insomnia may be addressed through helping her establish an appropriate routine conducive to sleep prior to bedtime, such as limiting screen time or exciting activities, and/or consulting your physician.

Much research has been done on the issue of growth retardation. Brown (2017) summed up some of the research on children on ADHD medication and their delays in reaching their full height: "Most of those delays were minor and transient, involving differences of one centimeter or less, relative to predicted height for age, differences that almost always disappear in later childhood or adolescence" (p. 199). Brown recommended having your daughter's height and weight monitored while on medication, and modifications to treatment investigated if your daughter is very small for her age.

Numerous studies have **not** found increased risk of drug abuse by those who were taking their stimulant medication properly as prescribed. According to Chang et al. (2014), "If anything, the data suggested a long-term protective effect on substance abuse." Many believe that proper treatment with medication when needed leads to improved self-esteem and better overall functioning, which can be protective factors against self-medication and use of illicit drugs.

Large-scale studies have reviewed the possibility that medications for ADHD might be related to cardiovascular problems. In discussing his review of research related to this topic, Brown (2017) said:

> Large studies of children and adults with ADHD taking stimulants compared with others of similar age in the general population have shown that the rate of serious adverse cardiovascular events such as severe hypertension, heart attacks or strokes is no greater among those treated with stimulants than in the general public of the same age without such treatment. (Brown, 2017, p.10)

If your child has any cardiac defects or a family history of any, you could ask your doctor about ordering an electrocardiogram (EKG) before starting stimulant medication.

Sometimes parents need more time to process the medication decision and seek second opinions from professionals knowledgeable about ADHD. Some questions a parent may consider include:

1 How is your daughter's self-esteem? If she is feeling bad about herself to the point you worry about depression, then her ADHD may be significantly impacting her daily functioning and a medication trial may be warranted.

2 How is her school performance? Is she failing classes? Does she detest going to school? Do you receive frequent calls about her troubles from school staff? Does she say other kids don't like her? If she is having major school issues and you have ruled out learning disabilities or other causes for her problems, a medication trial may be needed.

3 How is your home life? Does your daughter's moodiness seem to put everyone in a bad mood? Are you constantly being embarrassed by her behavior? Is her ADHD causing relationship stress? If your home life is super stressful, then a medication trial may be warranted.

If you choose medication, be assured that there is much research to back up its benefits and safety when it is prescribed judiciously and carefully monitored by you and your physician. As a concerned parent myself, I am presenting information to you as straightforwardly as I can, but it is your decision. My perception is that some mainstream media can sometimes portray ADHD medication in an unfavorable way when the reality is that medication helps a lot of girls work up to their potential. I know this from my professional and personal experiences.

If you choose medication, be assured that there is much research to back up its benefits and safety when it is prescribed judiciously and carefully monitored by you and your physician.

When or Whether to Stop Medication

Dr. Teitelbaum provided some good advice for you to consider. It is hard for a doctor to predict the long-term need for medication because it is dependent on so many things – maturation, effectiveness of interventions and accommodations provided, degree of development in executive functioning skills, situational demands, and your daughter's motivation. I have seen girls who have learned to use strategies effectively, relied on their strengths to supplement their weaknesses, and found themselves in supportive educational environments where they no longer needed medication in their current situation. When demands increased, such as when they entered high school or started college, some found they needed to restart medication. On the other hand, there are others who need to continue medication into adulthood to be successful. Of course, medication isn't something that you and your daughter should start and stop without medical supervision.

> One colleague and her husband had expended lots of time and effort in getting their fifth-grade daughter, Jennifer, the help she needed for ADHD, combined type. She had a comorbid reading disorder and had had years of specialized reading instruction, which had brought her to grade level. They had identified her weaknesses in getting her assignments done on time and keeping up with her belongings and had been proactive in helping her learn to use organizational strategies to improve in those areas. She had accommodation at school through a 504 plan. They communicated with their doctor about their desire for Jennifer to have a trial of stopping medication to see how it worked and received his approval to have a summer trial without medication. It went fairly smoothly, but they and the doctor felt Jennifer needed to restart the medication at a reduced dosage when school started.

If you feel that your daughter's functioning and self-control have improved to the point you could consider stopping the medication, talk to the prescribing doctor. It is important to consider your daughter's input, but if she is opposed to taking the medication and you and her doctor are convinced she still needs it, it is important to help her understand the rationale to continue taking it. If your daughter is resisting, often the doctor can help work through problems she may be experiencing with the medication. I have also seen ADHD coaches and therapists help a reluctant teen understand the benefits of medication and assist them in developing a plan to get off the medication responsibly with the assistance of their doctor.

Treatments Considered Alternative or Requiring More Research

The media is full of claims for the effectiveness of treatments, such as omega-3 supplements, diets, computer training programs including working memory training, and neurofeedback, on ADHD. Often testimonials and research are included for many of these areas, but current peer-reviewed research does not yet widely support improvement in ADHD symptomology that generalizes to school or home. Some of these are gaining in popularity and may be promising in the future.

Neurofeedback

Neurofeedback (also called EEG biofeedback or biofeedback) is a type of brain exercise or training based on the premise that people can learn to control brain wave patterns and thus impact their inattention, hyperactivity, and impulsivity. The hope would be that children can translate this to their everyday environment to improve behavior and schoolwork.

Simply stated, the goal is to mediate the symptoms of ADHD by decreasing theta (slow) waves often seen during daydreaming and increasing beta (fast) waves present when a person is thinking and interacting with her environment, often through specialized electronic games. Electrodes are attached to your daughter's head or to a cap to monitor wave patterns while she engages in a computer-based activity designed to teach her how to alter brain rhythms. She is notified through beeps or a visual when she has reached a desired level.

But does it work? That answer depends on who you ask and what research studies support their claims. There have been and continue to be many studies in many different countries that show mixed results. Historically, concerns about the studies have focused on inadequate research methodology, such as too few children in the sample sizes, lack of a randomized design, inadequate control group, and/or use of raters who had a vested interest in the outcome (like parents who had put in effort and money for their children to receive neurofeedback or researchers who had a relationship with a company offering the services). Another concern was the lack of an established protocol, which has now been addressed with the general acceptance of three standard protocols for neurofeedback with the Slow Cortical Potential being the most widely used. There is also certification for the person administering the biofeedback from the Biofeedback Certification International Alliance.

Logistics and cost are important considerations. Estimates of the number of treatment sessions range from 20 to 40 sessions lasting between 30 and 50 minutes. Costs are variable but can range from $50 to $125 per session. There are home-based treatment systems which are initially more expensive because you are buying equipment, but you don't have to travel. Negatives on a home-based system are that you don't have the benefit of a clinician to guide you and your daughter and the difficulties that might arise getting her to follow through with a schedule of usage directed by the parent. We all know our kids often perform much better for others than their parents!

Most recently, results have been more promising. Arns et al. (2020) stated,

> Effectiveness in open-label studies was confirmed, no signs of publication bias were found, and no significant neurofeedback-specific side effects have been reported. Standard neurofeedback protocols in the treatment of ADHD can be concluded to be a well-established treatment with medium to large effect sizes and 32%–47% remission rates and sustained effects as assessed after 6–12 months. (Arns et al., 2020)

A current ongoing multisite research study backed by the National Institute of Mental Health conducted by Ohio State University is scheduled to be completed in 2024. The bottom line is that there is not currently widespread agreement among experts that it can be recommended as a fully evidence-based treatment but stay tuned to future research.

Diet and Supplements

There is no question that children with and without ADHD benefit from a well-balanced diet of proteins, fats, and carbohydrates, as well as adequate vitamins and minerals. The natural foods movement has been gaining momentum highlighting concerns about processed foods with many additives. Elimination diets, like the Feingold diet, are not considered effective. Supplementation with nutrients, such as glyconutritional and/or fatty acids, as treatments for ADHD are not considered evidence-based interventions for ADHD but complementary based on information from The National Resource Center on ADHD.

Computer-Based Training/Working Memory Training

The use of computer programs and games to improve working memory and attention has generated interest worldwide. Cogmed Working Memory Training originated in Sweden and has been the focus of many studies, some touting benefits in attention and memory for children with ADHD but most finding little evidence of generalization of working memory to other school-related tasks. This is an internet-based computer software program that the child completes at home with support from her parent as needed along with weekly check-ins and monitoring with a coach. Cogmed is a 5-week, 5-day-a-week program and each session ranges from 35 to 45 minutes. As the child finishes each working memory activity, her performance is recorded within the Cogmed software. While some children enjoy it, it is expensive and doesn't appear to have long-term benefits. The American Psychological Association (2012) stated that "working memory training is unlikely to be an effective treatment for children suffering from disorders such as attention-deficit/ hyperactivity."

A program called LW4K (Learning Works for Kids) was developed by clinical psychologist Dr. Randy Kulman. Children play games like Minecraft and interact with instructors in figuring out how to apply executive functioning skills. The website has many resources for parents but is not considered an evidence-based intervention.

In April 2020 the FDA approved an interactive video game called Endeavor Rx under an emergency release which does have a randomized controlled trial to back it up. Since we live in a technology-oriented society, the use of computers to boost some cognitive skills could be promising, so keep your eyes open for new developments. At the very least, apps and games could be developed that girls and their parents could enjoy doing together.

Aerobic Exercise

The importance of physical exercise for all is constantly in the news and its benefits to ADHD are small but measurable. According to Dr. Stephen Hinshaw (2022):

> A growing set of studies reveals that consistent, at-least-30-minute bouts of aerobic exercise (that is, exercise significantly lifting one's heart rate), several times per week, can help reduce ADHD symptoms and enhance functioning in youth and even adults with ADHD. (Hinshaw, 2022, p. 142)

He noted the effect was small but documented. He felt regular aerobic exercise should be included in a holistic treatment program for ADHD.

The Future of Treatment

Various studies have shown that if an appropriate treatment plan is developed matching the services to the girl's needs, then fewer intensive treatments can be as effective as more intensive ones. The goal of some of the current research is to predict which types of interventions will produce the most effective results for different types of ADHD.

The Bottom Line

The bottom line is that one type of treatment does not work for all girls. Because each girl has unique characteristics, her treatment needs to be comprehensive, customized, and carefully monitored. You should work with a professional who takes the time to understand your daughter within the context of her family and school and then selects treatments that work for her and you.

> *Because each girl has unique characteristics,*
> *her treatment needs to be comprehensive,*
> *customized, and carefully monitored.*

As an informed parent, it will be up to you to consider the big picture – any additional problems in academics, executive functioning, language, and emotional or behavioral functioning that your daughter may have in addition to ADHD, as well as family or school stressors. The **Dynamic Action Treatment Plan** in Chapter 9 will help you develop a written plan to ensure better follow-through. It will include the support you need to obtain for your daughter and action steps you will be taking. Sometimes it helps if you have something concrete to show for your efforts in learning all you can about ADHD and what supports will help your daughter maximize her skills. Lots of planning and intentional parenting can go a long way!

General Management Strategies

Behavior is such a critical issue for parents that it will be mentioned throughout the book. In upcoming chapters, I will discuss techniques targeted to specific age groups, but I am also including general strategies in this chapter because they can be a key part of helping your daughter learn to manage her ADHD. You are probably with her more than anyone else and your interactions can have a profound effect. Strategies applicable across the age span include:

> ▷ establishing structure – girls with ADHD need this but often can't provide it for themselves;
> ▷ creating an environment engineered for success – encouraging proper sleep, nutrition, exercise, and

support when you know your daughter is likely to be overwhelmed;

▷ understanding what your daughter can control and what she needs help managing;

▷ setting realistic expectations for her within her capabilities;

▷ using rewards and incentives meaningful to her as well as positive reinforcement to boost motivation;

▷ assisting in breaking down tasks into smaller, more manageable chunks;

▷ helping her develop resilience and understanding that mistakes present an opportunity to try a different approach next time;

▷ consistently providing immediate feedback and consequences when necessary;

▷ serving as her role model for problem-solving and behavioral control; and

▷ maintaining a relationship with your daughter – spending time having fun with her and having open, honest communications with her.

The following are some additional specific behavioral strategies you may also want to implement that are helpful with girls with ADHD of all ages.

Establishing Clear, Firm Boundaries

One of the secrets of effectively parenting girls with ADHD is to provide clear and firm boundaries for what types of behaviors are and are not acceptable in your home. Remember that most girls with ADHD can't provide these for themselves but need them to help organize and manage their behavior. If you don't establish and continually reinforce acceptable behaviors, she may take advantage of you and her siblings and see how far she can push the limits. Then you will find yourself yelling at your children and feeling like they don't listen or respect you.

Try to complete a plan outlining your non-negotiable house rules with your partner or other adult(s) in the home who will be involved. If your daughter is old enough, it will be helpful to have her participate. The more buy-in you get from her, the greater the likelihood the plan will be successful. Ideally, you want everyone on the same page and responding consistently.

Consider the following process:

1 Identify and write down your five most important house rules.
2 Write down the consequences for not following the rules (e.g., first infraction, second, third).
3 Schedule a family meeting.
4 Discuss the rules and consequences and modify with input from all stake holders.
5 Implement the new plan and revise as needed.

When deciding on your five most important rules, try to keep them short. One parent I worked with, Tom, set up the following rules with 10-year-old Virginia:

> ▷ *no cursing,*
> ▷ *no name calling,*
> ▷ *keep hands and feet to yourself,*
> ▷ *no talking back in a rude, disrespectful manner, and*
> ▷ *complete assigned chores with no more than one reminder.*

Virginia's consequences included a verbal warning for the first offense, time in her room for 5 minutes for the second infraction, loss of privileges for an hour (e.g., video games, iPad, computer) for repeated offenses, and lastly grounding which meant she couldn't play any video games, watch TV, use the computer or iPad, or see or talk with friends for an afternoon. She was allowed to read,

---

draw, or play outside by herself. Tom tried to put supports in place so that grounding wasn't necessary because he knew Virginia's social skills needed continuing development. Time with friends was important, and playing video games for 30 minutes was a way for her to regroup after a tough day at school. When Tom did take away privileges, he talked to Virginia on ways she might prevent that from happening in the future.

As you sit everyone down for the family meeting, structure the conversation by saying something like this:

"You may have noticed that things have not been running so smoothly in our family lately, and there has been a lot of yelling and arguing. It's time to get our family back on the right track and get us working as a team. After all, if we don't take care of our family, who will? It's up to us to make our home run smoother and be pleasant for everyone. We need and want everyone to contribute their fair share, so let's come up with some rules." (Note: Try to get suggestions from your children on new rules. If they are reluctant, question them about certain things, like taking others' things without permission, hitting, etc. Of course, you, as the parent, will have to insist on rules you think are critical, but the more buy-in you can get from your children, the better.) Clearly list the rules along with the consequences for not following them. "Let's go over them together and see if we can all agree to try to follow them so we can have a better time when we're at home. None of us are perfect, so we will slip up from time to time, but it is up to us to help each other get back on track."

By having this type of conversation and agreement with your family, you hopefully will have removed some of the emotion that will occur the next time you discipline your daughter or other children. The clear consequences help you remain neutral because everyone has agreed upon the rules and consequences. For example, if your daughter bellows out a curse word, you can confidently state the warning and inform her that the next consequence is a loss of a privilege. When things have calmed down and you can talk with her, explore more effective ways she could have communicated her dismay. After all, her ability to resolve conflicts will be very important to her future success. These conversations can be difficult to have but can be effective in helping both of you improve your communication. By the way, when you slip up and curse, admit it and talk with your child about strategies you are going to use to avoid it next time.

Expect your daughter to test you on the new rules and consequences for two reasons. First, she is impulsive, and she will know the rule but won't consider it before acting and breaking the rule. Second, she wants to test you to find out if you are serious about enforcing the rules. Many parents I work with notice that their child's behavior temporarily gets worse before it gets better when starting a new plan, so don't give up if you find this with your family. This plan will work, but you must be consistent in using it and following through. Tweak it as necessary. When my children were younger, I used to think to myself, "If I don't follow through, I am going to pay for it next time the situation occurs." It is critical for your daughter to know you mean what you say.

Using Behavior Plans

Behavior charts and plans also work to help shape your daughter's behavior when used consistently. In my experience, parents are challenged to maintain and monitor the plans over time. Most parents start out strong and then fizzle out within a week or two.

Behavior plans can work well for children who do not yet have the natural ability to self-monitor their own behavior and need to be held accountable. Young girls with ADHD are not able to self-reflect very effectively so they benefit from the external control and the reinforcement a behavior plan provides. You don't have to use it for extended periods. After things have gone smoothly for a while, you can fade it out and reintroduce one when or if the need arises.

Carol used behavior plans with her daughter while she was in second grade. Although she did not use them continually throughout the year, she faded them in and out as needed. Carol identified and wrote four important behaviors to be practiced at home and at school on Josey's behavior plan. At the end of each day, Carol reviewed each behavior with Josey based on her observation, her teacher's note, and Josey's input. She found this review became valuable, as Josey gradually opened up about problems she was having because she realized her mom and teacher were trying to help life go better for all. If she followed the individual behavior, then Carol drew a smiley face in the square by the behavior, but if she did not follow the behavior, then Carol wrote, "Try again tomorrow." Each day Josey needed to get three out of four smiley faces to earn a reward, which included things like selecting a dinner menu for the following evening, a special snack, 15 extra minutes of play, special time with a parent, or a sticker for her sticker book. At the end of the week, if she had four out of five days with four or more smiley faces, then she picked a larger reward from a prize box Carol and her husband had created, which contained activities as well as concrete items. This external control and reinforcement helped Josey improve her overall behavior.

You can create a behavior plan or chart on the computer. If you need samples, enter "sample behavior charts" in a search engine, or go to Pinterest to find many examples of behavior plans you can customize for your own use. Your daughter might enjoy the process of helping to create one.

If a behavior plan that encompasses the whole day is not effective, your child may need one broken down into smaller segments of time. She may need more immediate reinforcement for exhibiting good behavior right at the point of performance. Token reinforcement systems provide immediate reinforcement, whether in the form of something tangible like a sticker or checkmark or an intangible like verbal praise, after the desired behavior is displayed.

A key to the effectiveness of behavior plans is having rewards that are really motivating to your daughter. They don't have to be monetary but can be additional time earned toward an activity she enjoys, like tv time, or opportunities to pick family outings or dinners, or activities with friends. Girls with ADHD are easily bored by rewards, so expect to change rewards when they are no longer motivating.

Providing Choices

Which do you prefer, reading a book or watching a movie? Receiving a gift card or being surprised with nice clothes? People like choices, and the same holds true for girls with ADHD. Parents often find their children respond better when presented with two choices, either of which are acceptable to the parent. For example, "You can do your homework now or in 30 minutes," "You may choose to have a birthday party at our house or grandma's house," and "Would you like to clean that one thing up now or clean all of this up before we go to bed?" Giving your daughter choices does not excuse her from the task.

Think about what providing choices does for her. First, it helps her learn to problem solve. For instance, if she is presented the choice of emptying the dishwasher on Saturday before or after her favorite show, then she must think about the benefits. She can watch the show but perhaps dread the ending because she knows the chore is next. If she completes the task before her show, then she can completely relax and does not have to think about her chore. Even though this seems like a simple decision, it requires her to apply problem-solving skills.

Next, providing choices helps your daughter learn to make decisions. As parents we should provide our daughters with age-appropriate decision-making opportunities. If choices are made for her as a child, then your daughter may mature into a young adult who relies upon others to make decisions for her. She may be easily swayed into unhealthy habits or relationships.

Finally, giving your daughter choices can help empower her and make her feel valued. For example, Lisa was given the choice of celebrating her birthday by spending the night at a local dude ranch with her grandparents and cousins or having a party with lots of friends at a local venue. Simple choices like these allow your daughter to feel comfortable making decisions that influence others.

After a workshop I presented for parents, a mom approached me who agreed with giving girls power through choices. She had three children, one of whom was a girl, and she intentionally gave her frequent opportunities to make choices that influenced her brothers. This mom's philosophy was that in the business world it's tough for women to compete with men and that from an early age her daughter needed to become strong at putting up with boys' complaints resulting from her choices.

The main points to remember are that you want your daughter to learn to problem solve and to make her own good choices. To do that, she needs three things from you: opportunity, instruction, and helpful feedback. You can get started today.

Power of Words

You've heard of the self-fulfilling prophecy, which says the words you say, hear, and think determine how you become. Words are so powerful that if your daughter hears you tell her she is lazy and irresponsible, then it is likely she'll grow into that role. On the other hand, if you want your daughter to grow up feeling loved, cherished, important, capable, and special to you, tell her this. As you read this you may be thinking of someone in your daughter's life whom you need to approach about his or her communication with your daughter and its effect on her.

These words also influence your daughter's self-esteem. Our self-esteem reflects how we believe others view us and how we view ourselves. Having healthy self-esteem is important for helping your daughter make it through life, because when she is teased by other girls, she needs to have the strength not to let it permanently affect her. Throughout each chapter, you will find ideas for building up your daughter's self-esteem.

References

American Psychological Association. (2012). *Memory training unlikely to help in treating ADHD, boosting IQ.* www.apa.org/news/press/releases/2012/05/memory-training

Arns, M., Clark, C. R., Trullinger, M., deBeus, R., Mack, M., & Aniftos, M. (2020, June). Neurofeedback and attention-deficit/hyperactivity-disorder (ADHD) in children: Rating the evidence and proposed guidelines. *Applied Psychophysiology Biofeedback*, 45(2), 39–48. doi: 10.1007/s10484-020-09455-2. PMID: 32206963; PMCID: PMC7250955.

Barbaresi, W, Campbell, L., Diekroger, E. A., Froehlich, T., Liu, Y. H., O'Malley, E., Pelham, W. E., Jr., Power, T. J., Zinner, S. H. & Chan, E. (2020, February/March). Society for Developmental and Behavioral Pediatrics Clinical Practice Guideline for the Assessment and Treatment of Children and Adolescents with Complex Attention-Deficit/Hyperactivity Disorder. *Journal of Developmental & Behavioral Pediatrics*, 41, S35–S57. https://doi.10.1097/DPB.0000000000000770

Barkley, R. A. (2020). *Taking charge of ADHD: The complete, authoritative guide for parents* (4th ed.). Guilford Press.

Brown, T. E. (2017). *Outside the box: Rethinking ADD/ADHD in children and adults.* American Psychiatric Association.

Chang, Z., Lichtenstein, P., Halldner, L., D'Onofrio, B., Serlachius, E., Fazel, S., Långström, N., & Larsson, H. (2014). Stimulant ADHD medication and risk for substance abuse. *Journal of Child Psychology and Psychiatry*, 55(8), 878–885. https://doi.org/10.1111/jcpp.12164

DuPaul, G. J., Evans, S. W., Mautone, J. A., Owens, J. S. & Power, T. J. (2020). Future directions for psychosocial interventions for children and adolescents with ADHD. *Journal of Clinical Child & Adolescent Psychology*, 49(1), 134–145. DOI:10.1080/15374416.2019.1689825

Hinshaw, S. P. (2022). *Straight talk about ADHD in girls: How to help your daughter thrive.* Guilford Press.

Merriman, D. E., & Codding, R. S. (2008). The effects of coaching on mathematics homework completion and accuracy of high school students with attention-deficit/hyperactivity disorder. *Journal of Behavioral Education*, 17, 339. https://doi.org/10.1007/s10864-008-9072-3

Nadeau, K. G., Littman, E. B., & Quinn, P. O. (2016). *Understanding girls with ADHD: How they feel and why they do what they do* (2nd ed.). Advantage Books.

Taylor-Klaus, E. (2020). *The essential guide to raising complex kids with ADHD, anxiety, and more.* Fair Winds Press.

Wolraich, M. L., & Hagan, J. F. (Eds.). (2019). *What every parent needs to know ADHD* (3rd ed.). American Academy of Pediatrics.

Points to Consider

1   When deciding on treatment, have you matched her needs to the type of treatment?
2   What choices do you provide your daughter in her day-to-day life?
3   Which supplemental treatments or behavioral strategies do you need to research?
4   Review your self-assessment responses to decide if there are any areas where you still need to learn more.

Action Steps to Take Now

1   In the **Dynamic Action Treatment Plan**, complete Step 2 to create the vision for her future. (**Remember, the Dynamic Action Treatment Plan** can be found in Chapter 9.)
2   Decide which professionals need to be involved in helping your daughter reach her full potential.
3   Determine which topics need to be the subject of further research for you.
4   Decide on one behavioral strategy you can apply or try again.
5   Make it a point today to say three positive statements to your daughter.

Chapter 4

Toddlers and Preschool

Each self-assessment helps you reflect on your daughter and your parenting practices and is a preview of the chapter's content.

1 When I think about my preschool-age daughter, I …
   a am confident her behavioral difficulties are maturational.
   b am concerned she has some characteristics of ADHD.
   c may need to seek a comprehensive evaluation.
   d am still considering my next step.

2 When I think about the support I need to help my daughter, I …
   a haven't really thought about it yet.
   b am researching different supports.

    c   have matched her needs to the right type of support.

    d   am confused by so many options.

3 When considering my daughter's preschool, I …

    a   know it's the right fit for her.

    b   am content but not satisfied it's the best fit.

    c   know I need to locate another school.

    d   need to schedule a meeting to talk to the director about my daughter's needs.

4 When I consider my daughter's preschool teacher(s), I …

    a   know they love my child like their own.

    b   believe they tolerate my child.

    c   am not sure if they understand her uniqueness.

    d   need to encourage the director to provide updated teacher training about ADHD.

5 When engineering success for my daughter at home, I …

    a   need help understanding the symptoms of ADHD.

    b   need to work on structuring her day.

    c   should be more consistent when setting limits.

    d   am barely holding things together and cannot take on another task.

If you are reading this section, you probably suspect that your daughter is different from her peers in how long she can stick with one activity, how emotionally reactive she is, and/or how demanding she is of your time and attention. She may be even more physically active than most. Even though you are captivated by her boundless energy and need for attention, it is emotionally and physically draining for you to meet her needs. You may already know, suspect, or have been told by others that she may have ADHD.

There is no doubt that having a daughter who is more trying than most her age adds another level of stress as you struggle to find answers and interventions for her behavior or locate an appropriate preschool, all while managing your own personal and professional lives. Parenting your daughter can be one of your biggest challenges, but also a time of great satisfaction as you watch her mature and benefit from supports put in place to help her manage her behavior.

Consideration of an ADHD Diagnosis for Preschoolers

One of the most burning questions you may have is whether ADHD can be diagnosed in preschoolers? (I will address that now but encourage you not to overlook the impactful interventions in school and home that come later in the chapter.) So, yes, it is sometimes diagnosed in young children when they show substantial impairment interfering with their daily live. If you passed Chapter 2 – "Diagnosis for ADHD" and Chapter 3 – "Treatment Options for ADHD" on your way to this chapter, you will want to refer back to them later. The diagnosis and especially treatment for preschoolers is a bit different than in older children and is always approached with caution for several reasons:

 ▷ Organization, behavioral control, fine motor skills, language, and attention are all developmental by nature, so behaviors can occur within a range of ages in young children and still be considered within the normal range and not ADHD.

 ▷ Girls' symptoms are not often as clear-cut as rambunctious, hyperactive boys. Remember the diagnostic criteria for ADHD was developed on primarily male samples and favors boys and their hyperactive presentation of the disorder. Girls are much more likely to be inattentive than hyperactive.

 ▷ Most preschoolers, with and without ADHD, need adult support in developing self-regulation skills and have months of testing boundaries and being demanding and obstinate. The term "terrible twos" came to be for a reason!

 ▷ Symptoms can mimic other conditions such as anxiety, depression, behavioral disorders, hearing or vision problems, sensory issues, developmental delays, language processing problems, or lead exposure. A good clinician must look at the root cause of the behaviors and rule out other conditions. Proper diagnoses can lead to effective interventions. Because ruling out other causes is especially difficult in the preschooler population, your pediatrician may refer to specialists like developmental pediatricians, child psychiatrists, or neuropsychologists.

Even if your daughter is diagnosed at an early age, the first line of treatment is behavioral interventions and parent management training unless your child is causing serious behavior problems, at which time medication may be considered. Before delving into the diagnosis and treatment later in the chapter, it is important to be aware of developmental milestones and how your daughter compares to peers.

Developmental Sequences in Typically Developing Children

As noted above, developmental sequences can vary widely and still be considered within the normal range. As we know, girls are generally more advanced than boys in meeting many developmental milestones, especially in language, fine motor skills, and the ability to sit and engage in quiet activities. Many of these skills are interdependent, so delays in one will impact the other. The ability to use language to guide behavior, called self-speech, assists with self-control. When preschoolers have language delays, their behavior will likely be negatively affected too.

Developmental readiness determines what a child can do at any point in time. It cannot be rushed. One parenting secret to successful preschool years is to educate yourself about developmental stages and what you can realistically expect. It will be important to monitor development and provide practice or seek intervention if your daughter lags behind. Don't ignore these delays, hoping she will catch up.

Milestones listed below are estimations generally agreed upon by child development experts as to when behaviors can be expected. The Centers for Disease Control (CDC) has a more thorough listing of behaviors commonly seen in children at specific ages than those listed below on their website (www.cdc.gov/ncbddd/actearly/milesto nes/index.html) and a Milestone Tracker app.

Two years old
- ▷ Begins to notice emotions of others
- ▷ Has temper tantrums and becomes defiant while striving for independence
- ▷ Points to pictures on a page
- ▷ Runs, walks, and kicks a ball
- ▷ Can open simple containers
- ▷ Is learning to use a spoon
- ▷ Begins to play pretend activities
- ▷ Builds a tower from blocks
- ▷ Can sometimes follow a two-step, simple direction like "Go to the door and get your shoes."
- ▷ Often defies directions
- ▷ Can draw straight lines and round shapes

Three years old
- ▷ Can inhibit some behavior
- ▷ May still have tantrums if wants or needs are blocked or routine is changed
- ▷ Wants to play with others
- ▷ Takes turns, sometimes needing prompting or support
- ▷ Turns pages in a book
- ▷ May become upset if routines change
- ▷ Can put on some clothes by herself
- ▷ Can use a fork
- ▷ Crying usually stops after 10 minutes of being left in a new but welcoming place
- ▷ Asks questions, like "Where are we going?"

Four years old
> ▷ Asks to go play and engages in interactive play, not just playing beside others
> ▷ Can attend to non-preferred tasks
> ▷ Avoids danger, like high places or hot stoves
> ▷ Changes behavior based on where she is, like refrains from loud talking in a movie theater
> ▷ Answers simple questions
> ▷ Draws a person with three or more body parts
> ▷ Holds her pencil between her thumb and fingers
> ▷ Catches a ball
> ▷ Speaks in four-word sentences
> ▷ Can play simple board games

Five years old
> ▷ Follows rules in age-appropriate games
> ▷ Can differentiate between real and pretend
> ▷ Can do simple chores like removing the dishes from the table
> ▷ Answers questions about a book read to her
> ▷ Can engage in conversation with three or more exchanges
> ▷ Pays attention to a learning activity, like a story, for 5–10 minutes
> ▷ Recognizes and can write some letters
> ▷ Can manage buttons

Characteristics Common in Children Diagnosed with ADHD

The following is a list of characteristics with corresponding age levels seen in children later diagnosed with ADHD:

Infancy (0–12 months)
> ▷ Is highly demanding of attention

▷ Is rambunctious or excessively active
▷ Is easily frustrated and difficult to soothe
▷ Shows strong responses to stimuli, like noise, light, temperature, or textures

Toddler (1–3 years)
▷ Cannot seem to screen out extraneous stimuli, like noise or movement
▷ Darts from one activity to another every few minutes except for strongly preferred interests
▷ Has little or no interest in sedentary activities
▷ Does not consistently respond to her name and may have poor eye contact
▷ Seems to be in her "own world" many times
▷ Has difficulty regulating behavior, especially regaining control when angry or frustrated
▷ Is highly impulsive and risk taking
▷ Is accident prone
▷ Has sleep disturbances, either falling asleep and/or waking early

Preschool (3–5 years)
▷ Is constantly moving or fidgeting
▷ Has little interest in quiet activities, such as looking at books or listening to stories
▷ Has limited task persistence, changing tasks every few minutes
▷ Shows inconsistent attention skills, especially between preferred and non-preferred activities
▷ Has weak social skills
▷ Has behavioral problems, disobedience, and engages in unsafe behaviors
▷ Talks constantly
▷ Is clumsy or has poor coordination
▷ Has difficulty waiting a turn

> ▷ Shows aggression, such as hitting other children or grabbing items from them
> ▷ Is highly emotional
> ▷ Daydreams and often needs repetition of instructions
> ▷ Has substantial impairment in daily functioning

Questions to Consider about Your Daughter's Development

Now that you have had a chance to compare typically developing behaviors to those which may signal ADHD, think about the following questions:

> ▷ Does her behavior negatively impact her success with peers and/or adults on a consistent basis? Think about how frequently she interrupts, is aggressive, doesn't listen, or insists on having her own way. Do you find that other children don't want to play with her because of her aggressiveness?
> ▷ How does her behavior compare to other girls of the same age and similar temperament? (Remember that even a period of months can mean big developmental leaps, so comparing your daughter to girls very close in age is important.)
> ▷ Does her behavior occur in more than one setting – at home, preschool, or in play groups?
> ▷ Are there other life events that could be contributing to the behavior, such as the birth of a new sibling, divorce or separation, death of a pet or loved one, or a move?
> ▷ Have her behaviors been problematic for at least six months?
> ▷ Could the behavior be caused by other conditions, such as a language delay, allergies, memory weakness, deficits in fine motor skills, or another developmental delay?

Genetic, Prenatal, and Birth Issues

Research reported in *The Lancet*, a British medical journal (Williams et al., 2010), showed that children with ADHD have a larger number of DNA segments that are either duplicated or missing, known as copy number variants. Genetically based neurological characteristics, including less activity in the frontal regions of the brain (especially those areas that inhibit behavior, resist distractions, and control activity level) and differences in the effectiveness of neurotransmitters, have been noted. Because it is genetic, it is possible that you or your partner have ADHD.

Extensive research has been done on the causes of ADHD. In addition to the genetic link, some risk factors can be increased by:
- ▷ prematurity and significantly low birth weight,
- ▷ prenatal exposure to alcohol, tobacco, and illegal drugs,
- ▷ complications of the fetus that interfere with brain development,
- ▷ excessively high lead levels or other toxic agents, and
- ▷ postnatal injury to the prefrontal regions of the brain.

According to the Perinatal Collaborative Project (discussed in Barkley, 2020), some additional specific features in the birth or early development of children have also been identified as having a greater risk of development of ADHD, even though the risks are reported to be low. These risk factors include:
- ▷ delays in motor development,
- ▷ smaller head size at birth and at 12 months of age,
- ▷ amniotic fluid stained by meconium (material from intestine of the fetus),
- ▷ signs of nerve damage after birth,
- ▷ breathing problems after birth, and
- ▷ low birth weight (2020, p. 102).

When Is a Comprehensive Evaluation Warranted?

Now that you have armed yourself with information about typical developmental milestones, behaviors that might be associated with

ADHD, and genetic and prenatal factors, it is time to decide if you should pursue an evaluation. Without a doubt, a preschooler who puts herself in danger by being overactive, distracted, or impulsive and who has difficulty with daily activities such as eating, communicating, playing with friends, attending preschool, and interacting in the community merits a comprehensive evaluation right away. The chances of a child like this growing out of this level of behavior without intervention are slim. Even for other preschoolers who show more moderate signs of ADHD, an early diagnosis can be helpful in minimizing future problems.

But I Have Never Heard of a Preschooler Being Diagnosed with ADHD

Data from the National Survey of Children's Health from 2011–2013 showed that "2.7% of children ages 4–5 were diagnosed with ADHD" according to Patricia Pastor et al. (2015). Although girls are usually older than preschool age when diagnosed, it is not something you should put off if your daughter is engaging in dangerous behavior, is significantly difficult to manage in the home, or is being asked to leave preschools.

The more knowledgeable you are about the disorder, the more you can help your daughter. It is being recognized at earlier and earlier ages for several reasons:

▷ more is known about the condition by the public and medical profession and about the value of early behavioral interventions, and

▷ more preschoolers are attending preschool, where attention and behavioral control may become more of a problem as more is demanded of her than at home.

The American Academy of Pediatrics has come out in support of early recognition and recommends an evaluation for any child from four to eighteen who is having "academic or behavior problems and symptoms of inattention, hyperactivity, or impulsivity" (2019). They also recommend additional training for doctors during pediatric residency in prevention, early detection, assessment, diagnosis, and treatment of ADHD.

See Chapter 3, "Treatment Options for ADHD," for information on the various professionals who diagnose ADHD. In my experience, pediatricians or neuropsychologists are most often the ones to make a diagnosis in young children.

The comprehensive examination for a preschooler would be like that of an older child and is discussed in detail in Chapter 2, "Diagnosis for ADHD." The physician could take a complete history, do a physical examination, interview the parents and child, and get rating scales from the parent and teacher if the child is in school. Wigal et al. (2020) state "Several behavioral rating scales have been validated in children younger than 6 years of age for assessing ADHD." The Clinical Practice Guidelines for the American Academy of Pediatrics state:

> The primary care clinician should include a process to at least screen for comorbid conditions, including emotional or behavior conditions (e.g., anxiety, depression, oppositional defiant disorder, conduct disorders, substance use), developmental conditions (e.g., learning and language disorders, autism spectrum disorders), and physical conditions (e.g., tics, sleep apnea). (Wolraich et al., 2019)

Emily threw a tantrum every morning when she had to separate from her mother. She would not make eye contact with her teachers, did not interact with other children, often looked at objects out of the corner of her eye, became upset if routines were changed, and often appeared to be daydreaming or in her "own world." Her preschool teachers encouraged the parents to have her evaluated for ADHD. However, after a thorough investigation, Emily was

> *determined to have an autism spectrum disorder. Testing showed that her social language skills were very delayed and sensory sensitivities made her very uncomfortable in a large classroom setting. She had difficulty establishing joint attention, reading social cues, and communicating with age-appropriate social language skills. She needed a structured classroom with social skills and language development infused throughout the day and qualified for a special education preschool program offered through her school district.*

Benefits of an Early Diagnosis

Parents often ask about the benefits of seeking an early diagnosis if medication is usually not the first line of treatment in preschoolers. The most important thing is that early detection enables you and those around you who interact with your child to have a better understanding of her behavior and how to support her. Secondly, your daughter may qualify for additional support through state-sponsored programs. (More on sources of information and discussion of these eligibilities at the end of the preschool section.) The preschool years are an important window of time in development. Your daughter will benefit from a strong bond with you so you can establish boundaries for her and help her adapt to more structured settings. Along the way, you will learn to be her advocate and safety net.

> *Lin is a beautiful little girl who has just started preschool for the first time. She darts from one activity to another, like she cannot fully take in one thing before her racing mind pulls her to the next. In fact, children find it hard to follow her in play because she is always jumping up*

and running off to something else without inviting them to join. If not carefully supervised, she never puts away toys before yanking out something else. She is engaging and friendly with adults. In fact, she demands almost constant adult attention and interaction except when she is coloring, her favorite activity. Her parents are beginning to see that she is losing favor with her peers because of her erratic play skills. She is invited less and less often to homes to play. Her teachers are noticing her difficulty in becoming independent and following the routine of the classroom. They often question whether Lin is actually listening to them. Her teachers suggested a simple behavior plan targeting following the classroom routine. Her parents have added more structure to her life at home and also decided to have her see a play therapist who can address her social skills and provide some practice in playing with others since she is an only child and has never been in social situations before. If Lin doesn't respond to these interventions, her parents are prepared to seek a comprehensive evaluation and have already started the discussion with her pediatrician.

Non-Medical Treatments for Preschoolers

There are many fewer studies on the effects of various treatment approaches for ADHD in young children compared to older children. As noted previously, behavior therapy and parent training are the recommended first treatment approaches for preschoolers diagnosed with ADHD. Parent Behavior Training teaches parents how to better manage problem behaviors and how to strengthen the bond with their child. Many preschool teachers are trained in these behavioral techniques and use them in the classroom. Behavior therapy for preschoolers involves using behavior modification strategies as well as play activities, like games and toys, to help children improve behavior. These are research-based interventions which have shown some efficacy. (See the resources for parent training in Chapter 3.)

Although it is not a research-based treatment, some clinicians advocate diets higher in protein and lower in carbohydrates and sugars to provide a more stable sugar level and prevent meltdowns based on metabolic problems, which might exacerbate ADHD.

Medical Intervention with Young Girls Diagnosed with ADHD

The use of medication in young children with ADHD requires careful consideration of the severity of the behavior balanced with the side effects from medication, like increased irritability, impact on weight and height, and sleep disturbances. If parent training and behavioral interventions are not effective or if the child is engaging in dangerous behavior, then medication is often prescribed and monitored carefully. The September 2007 issue of the *Harvard Mental Health Letter* (Harvard Mental Health Letter, 2007) suggested that in addition to parent training, "specialized day care should be considered before resorting to stimulant medication" (p. 1). These early intervention programs are often provided by school districts or through state funded programs – more about those early intervention programs later in this chapter.

"The Preschool ADHD treatment study (PATS) has provided the most extensive efficacy and safety data on methylphenidate (MPH) for ADHD in preschoolers to date, with significant improvement in ADHD symptoms observed with MPH compared with placebo"

(Wigal et al., 2020). Also read a pediatrician's and two psychiatrists' views of medication for girls included in Chapter 3.

Coming to Terms

As noted in an earlier chapter, it is important to put aside any parental guilt if your daughter has or appears to have ADHD. Hinshaw (2022), a prominent researcher in ADHD in girls, states:

> Noteworthy problems in school and in self-control are not typical for girls to display, so, when they appear because of ADHD, they place a great deal of stress on the family (and, I believe, actively promote tendencies for self-blame in parents). Such parenting stress – which involves feeling overwhelmed and inadequate as a parent and questioning the closeness of the interactions with one's daughter – is a predictor of the daughter's key impairments in later life. (Hinshaw, 2022, p. 114)

So do your best to let go of any guilt and focus on developing a strong relationship with your daughter and learning how to help her manage her behaviors.

Since it is considered an invisible disability, people who meet your daughter often don't understand that neurobiological differences in her makeup may make many developmental tasks harder for her and be responsible for a 2- to 3-year delay in the development of many skills. Numerous studies have pinpointed differences in the brain structure, cells, connections, and chemicals of those with ADHD which shed light on the day to day functioning. One of the most recent is a study done on postmortem brains of subjects with and without ADHD by the National Human Genome Research Institute, part of the National Institute of Health, which found that individuals diagnosed with

ADHD had differences in genes that code for known chemicals that brain cells use to communicate. The results of the findings, published in *Molecular Psychiatry*, show how genomic differences might contribute to symptoms (National Institutes of Health news release, Nov. 2022). This research is consistent with current models of the involvement of neurotransmitters in ADHD and other mental disorders.

So your daughter may look like a normal four-year-old girl but have the skills of a two-year-old in some areas based on the fact that her brain functions differently. In addition to the patience required to deal with her inconsistent and often frustrating behaviors, you may be exposed to insensitive, negative comments about her behavior and your parenting skills. Rest assured that much research has documented the genetic, neurobiological nature of ADHD. Although home environment plays a role in improving or worsening a child's temperament, it does not cause ADHD.

Since it is considered an invisible disability, people who meet your daughter often don't understand that neurobiological differences in her makeup may make many developmental tasks harder for her and be responsible for a 2- to 3-year delay in the development of many skills.

In addition to developmental differences and symptom overlap with other conditions, life experiences and parenting styles can also cloud the picture. This doesn't mean that parenting causes ADHD. Rather, chaotic conditions, especially trauma, can seriously impact a child, causing her to have more disorganized behavior, mimicking ADHD. In addition to lack of a secure, structured environment, studies have shown that how parents respond to a difficult child can impact the course of behavior problems. In terms of parenting style, a negative and critical style of management has been shown to predict the continuation of behavior problems into later years. Even parents who take a more positive approach can inadvertently reinforce inappropriate behaviors by giving in and allowing the child to get what she wants following a tantrum or outburst or by providing too much attention to the negative behavior.

Preschool Issues

Preschools are very different settings from home and from most daycares. They have much more structure and more demands. Placing your daughter with ADHD or symptoms that would suggest ADHD in a preschool setting could bring additional stress to both you and your child. It is commonplace for boys with ADHD who are oppositional or aggressive to be kicked out of daycares and preschools, but it's not so likely to happen with girls because their behavior is usually less disruptive.

> *Sienna had fine motor delays resulting in difficulty cutting and coloring in a preschool setting. She quickly lost interest in activities that she could not complete successfully. Teachers were perceptive to her limitations and adjusted tasks to her skill level. Her willingness to engage increased right away. Her lack of interest was related more to a mismatch between her skills and the task requirements than an attention problem.*

When selecting a preschool for your daughter the main secret to success is to find a school that is the right fit. As you talk to preschools, be honest if you have concerns about your daughter's behavior and attention to determine if they have had success in teaching children like her. For example, if she is a daydreamer, do they make efforts to keep her engaged or do they just allow her to play by herself and entertain herself with her imagination? You don't want to set up negative expectations for her, but you also don't want to start her off in a setting that would not help her maximize her development.

Time spent researching the right fit between a preschool and your daughter could pay big dividends and enhance her self-esteem. You want to avoid early experiences of failure because of the stress that brings to you and your child. She is building her sense of self-esteem as a capable learner and participant in the educational setting from these early ages. Because our world is constantly changing, you want your daughter to value learning and see herself as a lifelong learner. Your choices may be limited according to your geographical location, but it will be important to find the best fit that you can.

Helpful Questions in Your Preschool Search

Philosophy

What is the school's mission statement and philosophy? Your goal is to find a preschool that seeks to understand a child's strengths and build on those rather than focusing on the negative. Preschool is only the beginning of a long educational experience, so having it begin in a positive way is desirable. Some questions to consider might be:

> ▷ What are the teacher's expectations for what your daughter should be doing at her age? How do those expectations match her skill set?
> ▷ How adaptable is the program in accommodating individual needs? For example, if a child becomes too stimulated, is there a quiet space where she can go and regroup but still be supervised?
> ▷ What rate of success has the school achieved in successfully engaging girls who are inattentive?
> ▷ How parent friendly is the school? How is communication handled with parents?

Physical Set-Up

▷ Is the environment inviting, warm, and comfortable?

▷ Is it well equipped with colorful materials to develop language, fine motor, early literacy, and math skills?

▷ What is the ratio of preschoolers to staff? Girls with inattentiveness and ADHD-like symptoms function much better in small-group or individualized settings than in large-group activities.

> **Your goal is to find a preschool that seeks to understand a child's strengths and build on those rather than focusing on the negative.**

Structure and Daily Routine

Girls with ADHD benefit from a structured setting with firm boundaries because they are generally unable to provide structure for themselves. They usually have deficits in executive functioning skills, so benefit from routines that help in their development like starting a task, sticking with it, and cleaning up when finished.

▷ Does the teacher explain and model each desired behavior and practice until students know exactly what is expected from them, including how to walk from place to place in line, sit in circle time, and raise a quiet hand to get the teacher's attention? (Some of these may be year-long goals.)

▷ Is movement throughout the day a key feature?

▷ How long are children expected to sit still?

Curriculum

▷ Do they use theme-based units of study that focus on concepts (such as community helpers) as well as social skills? For example, the social skill of being a good friend could be taught through literature, songs, games, and role playing.

▷ What kinds of continuing education do the teachers receive to enable them to keep up with trends and "what works" with children?

▷ Does the curriculum involve learning through experiences and hands-on activities?

Behavior Management

▷ What are some techniques the teacher will use to gain and keep attention? Examples might be frequent visual and verbal cues, like a cue that would bring your daughter back to attention without nagging when she has zoned out, or a visual could be a red stop sign to remind your daughter to stop and think before acting.

▷ Is the teacher proactive in trying to figure out what might be effective for individual children? For example, if your daughter can't sit still in circle time, being given a job to do, such as assisting the teacher in turning pages in a book being read to the group, can redirect her attention in a positive way.

▷ What disciplinary techniques, like simple behavior modification techniques such as star charts with positive reinforcement, are used? Do consequences and rewards follow the behavior as soon as possible so your daughter can easily make the connection with the behavior?

▷ How is time-out used and how often? If time-out does not prove effective for your daughter, what alternatives will be considered? Remember, if your daughter is placed in time-out often, she will miss learning opportunities.

Safety

▷ How closely are children monitored for safety?

▷ If the children go on field trips, what is the procedure for making sure no child is left behind on a bus or at an event?

▷ Are the play areas enclosed?

▷ Is the overall facility secure?

Teacher Characteristics

A preschool teacher who is firm, but loving is important for your daughter. Energy and creativity are important, as well as a love of children and knowledge of their developmental differences. A teacher who is highly organized, is intuitive about behavior, and has situational awareness will assist a girl with ADHD in acclimating to her new situation. The teacher should be effective in communicating concerns and positive accomplishments with you so you can work together as a team.

If possible, it's best to try to observe the teacher in action, even if it means scheduling a time to return another day. You probably don't want a teacher whose demeanor is totally soft spoken and flat because she might not be able to engage your daughter. On the other hand, you don't want a teacher who is gruff and intolerant.

Bottomline

Depending on your circumstances and where you live, it is very possible you may not have many choices. It will be important to make the best choice you can based on your research and feedback from other parents and then try to share with the teacher what seems to work effectively with your child. Children can thrive in many different programs if they feel valued, safe and successful.

> *Corrie's and Toby's daughter, Rebecca, started out attending a Montessori preschool because they had read about the positive impact of this approach. Things seemed to go smoothly at first. Then the teachers reported difficulty with Rebecca "wandering about." She would go from area to area but not really complete any of the lessons, thus interfering with the other children's work. Corrie and Toby decided that the Montessori program was not the*

right fit for Rebecca, so they moved her to a preschool with a traditional schedule. This was the right fit and helped because the class's daily schedule was more structured with a series of short activities.

Corrie and Toby structured the home routine to help Rebecca, using a behavior and reward chart they found on Pinterest that had a place to write the expected behaviors and a spot to place either a happy, sad, or neutral face depending on her behavior. They explained the chart to her and reviewed it daily. For example, one rule was, "No screaming at Mom or Dad." Each day Rebecca could earn a reward if she had a certain number of happy faces. This was a concrete way to teach Rebecca responsibility and help her learn about the importance of self-control.

What about Repeating a Year of Preschool?

Occasionally preschool staff may recommend having a girl repeat a year of preschool or parents may advocate for it with the school. In my experience, it happens more frequently with boys than girls.

Before that decision is made, there are many factors to consider. These include birth date, physical size, social maturity, fine motor skills, and progress in her current setting. Research does not support the benefit of holding a child back a year. I have known parents who held children with August or September birthdates back a year and felt it allowed time to mature and be more ready for the academics presented in kindergarten. Remember that fine motor skills and attention are two of the many skills that are developmental, meaning they don't come online for children at the same time.

You should gather as much information as you can from her teacher and the school. If you are thinking about retention, important questions are:

▷ Would an additional year to mature make a significant difference in her performance and overall adjustment to school?

▷ What would a repeated year in preschool look like for her in terms of curriculum? Would she be bored if material was the same or similar?

▷ How would repeating one year impact future years? After the year was repeated, is it likely she would still have trouble keeping up with the curriculum?

Some parents who choose to hold their daughter back have her repeat in a different preschool, possibly one with a more academic curriculum or at least new activities so she won't be bored. Try to project ahead and think about how this retention would impact her as an elementary school student, a teenager, and a college student. Wouldn't it be nice to have a crystal ball?!

If you are still not sure, take your daughter to a local school or clinical psychologist and have some educational testing done. For an investment of several hundred dollars, a good psychologist can help you determine your daughter's readiness for kindergarten. When your daughter enters elementary school, it becomes harder to retain a student.

When More Preschool Support Is Needed

Despite your best effort to find a good fit in a preschool for your daughter, the teacher may let you know your daughter is having trouble meeting expectations in some or all areas. As a parent, it is easy to take a wait-and-see approach, deny the existence of problems, or postpone action. Early intervention services can be very valuable to your child, so you will want to keep your eyes open to her needs. The neuroplasticity of her brain during these early years makes early intervention services especially critical. You don't want her to go for years with untreated symptoms that may cause difficulty with learning and social relationships and result in low self-esteem.

> *The neuroplasticity of her brain during these early years makes early intervention services especially critical.*

Anna had language delays and difficulty in processing auditory information. Her preschool teachers complained that she did not follow directions but roamed around from place to place in her classroom rather than working on the assigned task. A thorough language evaluation revealed that Anna did not process or understand many of the directions from her preschool teachers, who gave primarily auditory directions. When auditory directions were paired with visuals, such as cue cards to remind her of expected behavior, and a visual schedule to structure her day was developed, her rate of on-task behavior increased significantly. She qualified for language therapy provided by a speech-language pathologist and funded by her state.

How to Access Services for Developmental Delays

It is widely recognized that early intervention of lagging developmental skills can make a huge difference in a child's life. Federal law requires that school districts provide early identification and intervention services for children with disabilities severe enough to impact their functioning. The first step is to register for an evaluation. Even infants and toddlers can qualify for services. Preschoolers (ages 3–5) may qualify for services through the Individuals with Disabilities

Education Improvement Act (IDEA). (For more information on IDEA, see Chapter 8, "When School Problems Escalate.") Your child could be evaluated by a school psychologist, developmental pediatrician, speech-language pathologist, occupation therapist, physical therapist, and/or a behaviorist – depending on areas of concern. Following the evaluations, the team would provide recommendations on services and where you would go to get them.

There is a wide variation from state to state as to how easy it is to obtain these services for delayed skills. As an example, early intervention in language, intellectual abilities, fine motor and gross motor skills, and behavioral regulation are widely available in some school districts and states. Some offer services in the home at no cost to parents. Other areas only offer services at a center or through a preschool program. When a significant level of support is needed, a therapeutic preschool may be required. Some states have scholarships for toddlers with developmental delays for various therapies or private preschools. If you have any concerns about your child's development, it is worth your time to register for an evaluation through your state or school district, which is usually free, and find out about services offered.

Bear in mind that these evaluations are geared toward the child's needs in an educational environment and may not be as comprehensive as those conducted by a clinical psychologist, neuropsychologist, or child psychiatrist. If your child is having significant problems and you have doubts about the thoroughness of the evaluation in any area, you might want to consider an additional private evaluation on your own if you are able to provide that. See Table 4.1 below for developmental concerns and suggestions on which professionals might be able to provide the most helpful information.

My experience has been that a preschooler with a speech or language delay often meets the requirement for speech/language services, and children with cognitive delays qualify easily for services offered at no cost by states for preschoolers. Behavior may be harder to qualify for but children do qualify for services in that area as well. It is always better to have obtained services and not needed them in the long run than to hope for the best and later realize your child really needed early intervention. See Chapter 8 – "When School Problems Escalate" for more discussion of legislation governing disabilities, including preschoolers.

Maria's parents were at their wit's end because she was not successful in her day care. Her preschool teachers complained that she was often grabbing toys from other children, intruding in other children's play without asking, running from place to place, and throwing tantrums if her needs were blocked. Her parents had tried reasoning, rewarding, and punishing – all to no avail. After a thorough evaluation, including a cognitive assessment by a school psychologist, an in-depth speech-language evaluation by a speech-language pathologist, an occupational therapy assessment evaluating fine motor skills and/or sensory issues, and a developmental history, Maria was determined to be eligible for a special needs preschool program that focused on behavioral goals along with emerging academic skills. The classroom had a low pupil-to-teacher ratio, additional assistance from a classroom aide, and a highly structured behavioral management program where behaviors were taught and reinforced. In addition, she had occupational therapy to help improve her deficient fine motor skills, which were impacting her ability to hold a pencil, cut, and color. Maria had her ups and downs but eventually improved in her ability to follow directions, stay in her assigned area, and keep her hands and objects to herself. Without that early intervention, Maria would have encountered much more difficulty in elementary school.

Table 4.1
Guide for Seeking Assessments of Developmental Issues

Concern	Symptoms	Consult	Type of Assessment	Cost
Fine motor delays Sensory issues	Difficulty holding crayon or pencil and drawing. Excessive reaction to sound, light, tags, personal space issues	Occupational therapist	Fine motor skills and/or sensory sensitivities	Covered by some medical insurance
Gross motor skills	Walking, jumping, balance, and using large muscles like throwing a ball	Physical therapist	Large muscle movements	Covered by some medical insurance
Articulation of speech sounds or receptive or expressive language development	Speech errors that are not developmental, difficulty putting words together in sentences, problems understanding language or vocabulary development	Speech-language pathologist	Articulation Vocabulary Sentence usage Understanding language Social language	Covered by some medical insurance

Table 4.1, *continued*

Concern	Symptoms	Consult	Type of Assessment	Cost
Global delays in many areas, including cognitive, social, attention, and/or behavioral	Delays in understanding concepts, learning new things, emotional self-regulation, and/or behavior	Clinical psychologist for milder concerns but a neuropsychologist has more extensive training and generally provides a more in-depth look at neurological issues	Intellectual, processing, evaluation of behavior and emotional status, as well as ruling out other diagnoses like autism spectrum disorder or mental health issues, like anxiety	Out of pocket in most areas, but some may be covered by insurance. Neuropsychological is more expensive but more comprehensive
High activity level or significant distractibility	Engaging in dangerous, impulsive activity, difficulty managing at home or school because of behavior or inattentiveness	Pediatrician	Family history, evaluation of child, and rating scales by family and school. Will rule out other physical issues such as sleep disturbances or hypothyroidism	Usually covered by insurance
Significant difficulty with behavior or emotions	Concerning behavior at home or school	Child psychiatrist Neuropsychologist Clinical psychologist.	Family history, evaluation of child, rating scales by family and school	May or may not be covered by insurance

The value of an assessment cannot be underestimated because it can provide solid information about your daughter's strengths and weaknesses and provide direction on intervention. For example, if your child has delays in fine motor skills, occupational therapy could be recommended, or if there are gross motor delays, physical therapy could be very helpful. At these young ages, there is much neurological growth going on and opportunity to influence development in a positive way.

Parent Interview

Sadie is an 11-year-old girl who was diagnosed at 7 years old with ADHD, inattentive presentation. Her mother is a behavior analyst who is very skilled with behavioral interventions. She was in a small private school until this year when she transitioned to a public middle school.

Q. What are your biggest parenting headaches related to your daughter's ADHD?

Being in a group of people and my child needing my undivided attention. This has gotten better as she has gotten older. When she was little, I could barely have conversations with other people because she was talking a million miles an hour.

Q. What are some positives you notice in your daughter that may be attributed to her ADHD?

She is very in tune with her surroundings. She hears and notices things I may not. When given tasks she enjoys, she can complete them with great proficiency.

Q. What behavioral interventions in the home and in the school have been the most helpful for her?

A predictable routine has always worked great for us at home. When she was younger, we used a visual schedule for morning and night routines. If I had several chores that I wanted her to accomplish, I wrote them on sticky notes. I also give her "choices" for chores – laundry or dishes. She doesn't like either but is more likely to have a better attitude if I give her the choice.

Every year at school I provide all her teachers with an accommodations list for her. I also advocate for her when her teachers complain she is chatty or distracted. I usually ask her teachers if she's chatty and bored. To be bored is okay, but encourage her to finish her task, take a movement break, read a book, etc. At an older age, the ability to check her own grades and keep track of her assignments was critical for her to feel in charge of her own learning.

Q. How was ADHD explained to your daughter and by whom?

She does not know she has ADHD. Only that she is gifted and a bit hyper LOL.

Q. How have you helped your daughter find her passions and strengths?

We have truly listened to her wants and needs. She has tried several sports and not felt connected, so we stopped those. We have exposed her to more of the things she enjoys that are in the same category. She loves art so we do a lot of private art classes, pottery classes, and investing in art supplies she picks out. She also loves music and is great at playing piano.

Q. How has ADHD impacted sibling relationships?

She has a younger brother with more intense ADHD symptoms than she has so that has been challenging. They both want to monologue, without giving each other turns to talk. They both crave space to tinker with their things, but they will also play together for hours at a time if it is an activity they are both in control of, like video games. A board game or really anything that is not simultaneously gratifying is hard to navigate for both of them. On the flip side, they have an understanding of each other's intensities that can be challenging for other children to understand. I am truly grateful they have one another.

Home/Community Issues: Being a Proactive Parent

Whether your daughter has been diagnosed or is suspected of having ADHD, there are a number of things you can do to help manage her behaviors in the home and community. Keep in mind that often young children have not yet acquired the skills they need to manage their behavior and benefit from:

▷ realistic expectations based on their developmental levels,
▷ simple directions, followed by praise for following or correction for not following,
▷ affirming, strong parental bonds,
▷ consistency and structure including firm limits,
▷ supports to help them, like visual or verbal cues, for tasks they can't do independently,
▷ opportunities to try again, and
▷ adults modeling appropriate behavior.

You know your child better than anyone else. If she has ADHD or is suspected of having it, continue to educate yourself to have a thorough understanding of it and how your child's daily interactions are affected. Observe your child's presentation of any of the following characteristics of ADHD at home and determine ways you can assist her with:

▷ excessive daydreaming,
▷ consistently failing to notice when her name is called,
▷ poor attention to tasks,
▷ impaired impulse control and inability to delay gratification,
▷ deficits in memory or storing information to use in guiding future behavior,
▷ difficulties with regulating emotions and motivation,
▷ diminished problem-solving ability,
▷ delayed development of internal language,
▷ greater variability in quality of work, and
▷ hyperactivity.

Be a detective in determining ways your daughter's characteristics affect her daily life and try to provide supports when you can to help her grow in her deficit areas. But don't overwhelm yourself by trying to work on too many things at once. Perhaps pick one or two things to concentrate on at a time.

Be a detective in determining ways your daughter's characteristics affect her daily life and try to provide supports when you can to help her grow in her deficit areas.

At all times, remember that some behaviors may **not** be completely within your daughter's control. You don't want to hold her responsible for things she cannot yet do. For example, if she cannot manage her frustration on her own when she can't do something, work with her to assist her in developing those skills. Often helping her identify and name the feeling is a helpful first step but may not be possible until she has calmed down. For example, it is often helpful if she can recognize and communicate that she is frustrated, sad, or angry. She can use her language to communicate her difficulty and seek help in managing it. For many girls, this is a long, drawn-out process, taking years.

Children are very individual in what helps them manage frustration, so work with her to figure out how to solve this problem. If you can catch the problem when it first begins, some children I have worked with have found the following helpful:

- ▷ learning to take a break and come back to it later,
- ▷ holding or squeezing a sensory toy,
- ▷ taking deep breaths,
- ▷ coloring,
- ▷ using visualization to take a quick mental break and think about something that brings them joy, like a pet or special place, and
- ▷ help in putting the situation in perspective (what they are upset about in the moment may not matter even an hour from now).

As you well know, once the child has completely lost control, the capacity for logical thought has gone. Some children want to be alone when they are upset, others benefit from a hug or presence of an adult. Even though these times can be incredibly upsetting for you, it is important to remain calm yourself. When she has calmed down, work with her to help her figure out how she can learn to calm herself so she can get back to her regular activities. This is a challenge for sure but celebrate even small steps moving in the right direction.

Remember that behavior is often the tip of the iceberg or what is visible. Much more lies beneath the surface, like feelings about previous experiences and relationships. Taylor-Klaus (2020) encouraged parents to suspend judgment about behavior. She recommended "fully understanding and accepting the challenges for what they are" (p. 69).

She suggested parents should approach teaching self-management with patience, helping children learn it "slowly but surely, in developmentally appropriate ways" (p. 69). It can seem like a long haul but just keep your eyes on the prize of having a daughter who ultimately learns to control her behavior.

From my work with children with ADHD, it appears that their behavior breaks down when the demands placed on them exceed their ability to complete the requested task. Your daughter may impulsively tell you she hates you, shut down and withdraw, or purposefully try to push buttons when she is overwhelmed. When your daughter can't perform, she'll let you know it! Your child is fortunate to have a parent like you who is concerned enough to research and learn about techniques that can be helpful.

> *From my work with children with ADHD, it appears that their behavior breaks down when the demands placed on them exceed their ability to complete the requested task.*

Engineering Her Success

Applied knowledge can be a very powerful ally in creating success. A few things I recommend you do to learn more about ADHD include:

▷ *Seek out parent training in effective management and discipline.* If your daughter was diagnosed with ADHD as a preschooler, this is the first line treatment. Your pediatrician may already have given you a referral. If not, contact community agencies or your local school district for information specific to your area. You can access information online through groups like CHADD (https://chadd.org), *ADDitude* (www.additudemag.com), or other sources for parent training listed in Chapter 3 – "Treatment Options for ADHD."

▷ *Learn what management tools are effective with your child.* Distraction is often effective if you see your daughter starting to get upset. Some benefit from reminders (either visual or verbal) to use coping strategies. Teaching calm-down strategies, such as stopping and thinking before acting, deep breathing, mindfulness, or putting the situation into perspective (like reminding her that tomorrow she may not even remember the event that has upset her), can be helpful. Other children become completely overwhelmed by too much stimulation and benefit from a quiet area to regroup. Behavior modification techniques, including immediate reinforcement or consequences (star charts or checklists can be helpful), ignoring negative behavior that is not dangerous, and teaching replacement behaviors (like what she can do when frustrated instead of biting), can be very effective.

▷ *Be positive and focus on strength areas.* If your daughter is creative and innovative, provide activities to encourage those talents. If she enjoys helping others, try to engineer those opportunities. Try to praise your daughter several times a day for things she is doing correctly.

▷ *Create an environment that promotes success.* If your daughter is accident prone, put away items that can be easily broken. If she has trouble cleaning up toys, provide an organizational structure like placing pictures on shelves or drawers where each toy goes and helping her figure out which toy to put away first, second, etc. Remember that many children with ADHD cannot often break down tasks into manageable steps, like being asked to clean up a room without help. For example, ask her to pick up all the dolls first. Next ask her to pick up any dirty clothes and put them in a hamper. If she has trouble transitioning from one activity to another, use a kitchen timer to count down the time before she must switch activities, or give verbal warnings. Time Timer (www.timeti mer.com) is a visual timer that allows the child to see time remaining in an activity.

Structuring Her Day

▷ *Provide a structured environment with adequate opportunities for activity and rest.* Mealtimes, naptime, and bedtime should be consistent. Some children benefit from having a visual schedule that shows their daily routine or a visual cue card to prompt certain behaviors, like remembering to clear their plate from the table. If you enter "visual schedules for preschoolers" in a search engine, you will find many examples.

▷ *Prepare your daughter in advance when a change in schedule is unavoidable.*

▷ *Provide plenty of time for physical release throughout the day, including playing outside or engaging in some energy-releasing activity.* This can be especially important when she will be required to be seated for a while.

▷ *Keep your daughter busy in productive, engaging activities.* Idle time may create problems.

▷ *Make sure media and technology don't replace activities needed for growth and development, such as social interaction, physical activity, creative play, and tasks developing fine motor skills like cutting and coloring..* The American Academy of Child & Adolescent Psychiatry (2020) screen time recommendations are:

  ▷ 18 months or younger should not be exposed to screen time except for video chatting,

  ▷ 18- to 24-month-old should watch educational programming with a caregiver, and

  ▷ 2 to 5 years old should be limited to one hour per day of non-educational programming and three hours on weekends.

▷ Given the rapid development of children's neurological structures during the first 2 years of life, children learn more effectively from interaction with humans than screens. The American Academy of Pediatricians has developed an excellent planning tool for families to create a media plan (available at www.healthychildren.org/English/media/Pages/default.aspx#planiew).

▷ *Plan diversions for times when long periods of sitting will be required*, such as when traveling in a car. Bring snacks, games, books, electronics, and videos to keep her occupied.

▷ *Be prepared to remove your daughter from highly stimulating activities if she becomes easily overwhelmed.* Children frequently cannot calm themselves down and need some quiet time.

Managing Behaviors

▷ *Think ahead about that behavior you expect of your daughter in different situations.* Discussing expected behavior beforehand is often helpful.

▷ *Practice how you would like to respond when she misbehaves in situations to avoid overreacting.* Remember, you are only human, so this won't always work.

▷ *Promote good habits by noticing and reinforcing her positive behaviors.*

▷ *Be as consistent as possible.* It is always important to muster the energy to follow through on directions and consequences. If not, you will likely pay for it later. Consistency enables your daughter to know exactly what you expect and to be clear about the rules. Consistency by parents, caregivers, and teachers in using the same behavior cues can be critical. For example, if your daughter gets too loud, get her attention, and give her a visual cue like motioning with your hand to lower her volume.

▷ *Monitor your daughter's activities closely for safety if she is impulsive.* Cover electrical outlets and lock up cleaning products and other dangerous items. If your daughter is a climber who enjoys getting into kitchen cabinets, provide a cabinet at floor level just for her that contains items of interest.

▷ *Some behavioral problems can be avoided by providing distractions if you see that your child is getting upset.* Suggest stepping outside for a few minutes, listening to a story, or singing a song.

▷ *Help your daughter learn to label the feelings behind the behavior as soon as she is able.* For example, if she is frustrated, help her figure out what that feels like and how to communicate it. The next step will be to help her figure out how to cope with those feelings. Language can be very powerful in helping her manage her behavior. You have probably heard the expression, "Name it to tame it."

▷ *Use time-out judiciously and as an opportunity to regroup.* Some experts estimate that time-out should include 1 minute for each year up to 5 years of age. Time-out can often begin at 2 years of age with assistance. It seems to be most productive if it is framed as a calm-down spot where the child can regain control to continue enjoying her day rather than a punishment.

Teaching and Learning

▷ *Keep eye contact with your daughter, especially when giving directions.* If necessary, gently hold her chin so she is looking right at you to ensure she is listening. (Caveat: Be alert to situations in which holding her chin could set up a power struggle. Sometimes it is better to avoid eye contact in dicey situations so as not to challenge or antagonize.)

▷ *Keep directions clear and simple.* Children with ADHD are especially unreceptive to long directions or conversations. Keep directions to only one step until you are sure your child can handle two-step directions.

▷ *Provide repeated practice for new skills,* especially social skills like sharing a toy. Children with ADHD seem to learn through experience and practice rather than by observing social cues.

▷ *Don't assume that your daughter understands cause and effect.* Specific training in identifying cause and effect relationships in stories, movies, and real-life situations can be helpful.

▷ *Ensure that the environment is free from distracting stimuli when engaging in a teaching activity.* Children with ADHD are often unable to screen out competing stimuli.

▷ *Allow fidgets or items that may help the child sit and focus* – for instance, when a book is read. Effective fidget items are things that keep the child's hands busy or provide sensory input for her body, like sitting on a ball chair or bumpy cushion, or wearing a weighted vest. They serve to calm her but do not become a distraction. Handheld fidgets can be favorite toys, such as a stuffed animal or a squishy, sensory toy, if they do not become distractions. Search online for "sensory fidgets" to see a variety of options. Websites such as www.addiss.co.uk or www.therapro.com are good sources of fidget toys.

▷ *Use as many senses as possible when teaching a new skill.* For example, when teaching the names of fruits, allow your daughter to draw them, touch them, smell them, and taste them. Interactive learning will be the most productive.

▷ *Give her a head start on learning to focus and develop some internal limits on behavior.* As noted above, a kitchen timer or Time Timer (www.timetimer.com) can be used to help your daughter extend the time she can focus on one activity.

Parental Self-Care

There is no question that parents of children with ADHD are under much more stress than parents of children without ADHD. What parent of a girl with ADHD hasn't been impacted by the eye rolls or judgement about parenting? It is no wonder parents of girls with ADHD have self-doubt about their parenting skills and often lower self-esteem. If you have more than one child with ADHD or if you have ADHD yourself, then of course your stress level will be even more elevated. Or what about when a global crisis like COVID interrupts your daughter's daily schedule? Your challenges will be magnified significantly.

Even under the best circumstances, your daughter's behavior may be baffling and often disruptive to the entire family. You may feel you are constantly on guard and never have time to yourself. Even finding a babysitter who can handle your daughter effectively and not barrage her with negative comments may be difficult.

Realize that time away from your daughter is important to allow you to regroup and keep a positive attitude. The search for a competent babysitter who understands your daughter will be well worth it. Find someone who is willing to be educated about her condition. Oftentimes, your daughter will respond more positively to someone who is willing to engage in high-energy or creative activities while keeping in mind the importance of safety. If money limits your ability to have a babysitter, try to exchange babysitting duties with another parent who understands ADHD and its management techniques. You want to avoid putting your daughter in situations that could be damaging to her self-esteem but want to provide some self-care for yourself.

Remember that you are human and will lose your patience from time to time. Build in little breaks that will make this less likely to happen. Finding a support group of parents of children with ADHD may be helpful if that group is positive and focused on sharing what works, new techniques, local resources, and services. They could be a great source of local resources and services. To find support groups, check online, local school systems, pediatricians, or other health professionals.

As noted previously, CHADD, an organization for children and adults with ADHD (www.chadd.org), has support groups in some areas. Parent training specific to children with ADHD is available through a number of organizations, including CHADD, *ADDitude* (www.additudemag.com) and Impact Parents (https://impactparents.com). More intense and specialized training, such as Parent–Child Interaction Training (www.pcit.org), may be available in your community or virtually. See Chapter 3 "Treatment Options for ADHD" for a more complete list. Keeping up with the latest research can be helpful. Search online for "childhood ADHD" or ADHD in preschool" to find the latest research findings Try to use only trusted sources, as there is plenty of inaccurate information out there.

Don't hesitate to use the help of a psychologist, counselor, or coach to learn problem-solving approaches specific to your own family if your finances permit. (Always check with your medical insurance to see what may be covered.) Often family therapy can be helpful in establishing a cohesive family bond. Remember that the same parenting approach that works for one child does not necessarily work for another.

> *Cindy and her partner took two parenting classes that were offered at a local preschool. One class was called Conscious Discipline (https://consciousdiscipline. com), and the other was Redirecting Children's Behavior (www.positiveparenting.com). Even though they knew the classes weren't designed for neurodiverse children, they still thought it would be worthwhile. In one class, they learned a strategy to curb their tendency to overreact to her daughter's behavior – **S**TAR or taking time to **S**top, **T**ake a deep breath, **A**nd **R**elax. To remember to use the strategy, Cindy placed paper stars at strategic places around the house.*

Assistance with Siblings

In addition to the challenges in preschool and in the community, your daughter with ADHD will, of course, bring her difficulties into the home. Her difficulty with listening, impulsivity, and organizing her own behavior will inevitably create conflict with siblings. Brothers and sisters are often jealous of the additional time parents must spend with a child with ADHD. They may view the child with ADHD as lucky and envy her. You want to help other family members have some understanding of ADHD while still treating their sibling as a full and integral member of the family. I often think girls with ADHD are highly perceptive about what others think and pick up quickly on those disapproving looks.

It is important for all children to understand that even in families, everyone has different strengths, interests, and needs. As children mature, short family meetings can help air concerns, establish goals, and assess progress in creating a strong family unit. Some families find it helpful to engage a professional psychologist or counselor to learn problem-solving approaches to sibling conflicts.

I often recommend books to help parents explain ADHD to siblings. Books written specifically for children often allow for an open discussion within a supportive context and enable children to identify with the issue or character. Some good books include: *My Brother's a World-Class Pain: A Sibling's Guide to ADHD/Hyperactivity*; *Learning to Slow Down and Pay Attention: A Book for Kids About ADHD*; and *Cory Stories: A Kid's Book About Living With ADHD*.

Some More Tools for Your Toolbox

Remember that it is often very difficult for a girl with ADHD to hold her behavior together in school and community settings. Her behavior may disintegrate in the home setting, where she feels safe. Providing a quiet place where she can regroup without trampling on the rights of other family members will be important. One technique I encourage parents to do is physically get on their daughter's level when they are talking to her. When standing, parents tower above the child. When talking to, disciplining, or teaching her, parents should kneel, sit, or bend down to look her in the eye. This simple technique has an amazing effect in getting active or inattentive girls to actually listen and understand.

A second technique I have found helpful is to lower one's voice as the girl's voice gets louder. Energetic preschool girls often are loud and have lots of drama with their play and voices. An effective strategy is to talk softer and get down to a whisper as your daughter gets louder. Inevitably, your daughter will take your cue and start to whisper too.

A third strategy that often works well for preschool-age girls is teaching parents and siblings to make a game of things. Preschoolers usually enjoy games, and their competitive nature fits well with playing racing games. For example, when cleaning up toys, race your daughter to see who can pick up the most toys the fastest. Another family I have worked with had an older daughter who often played the game of follow the leader to get her younger sister to go where she wanted her to go or do what she wanted her to do.

Lastly, try to apply a problem-solving approach to each problem. If one potential solution or technique has failed, go to plan B. Ultimately you will likely find an answer that works for your family. Being creative and having a sense of humor can help immensely.

These techniques won't always work, but having more strategies in your toolbox can sometimes make your life much easier. The challenge is remembering them in the heat of the moment when you need them the most. Staying in control yourself when a child's fury is unleashed can be one of the most difficult but helpful things you can do. You are human, so you can't also manage to be calm and in control but hold that as a lofty goal and pat yourself on the back each time you have managed it!

Staying in control yourself when a child's fury is unleashed can be one of the most difficult but helpful things you can do.

Physical and Emotional Health

Self-Esteem

Your daughter's self-esteem is a collection of beliefs she has about herself. It begins developing in toddlerhood and continues throughout life. It fluctuates because it is often based on interactions with others and opportunities for success. It can be defined as pride in oneself or self-respect.

Self-esteem in preschoolers is in its early, developmental stages. The preschool girl with ADHD has likely heard hundreds of redirections from her parents, teachers, caregivers, and classmates. She is likely bombarded with many more negative than positive comments. All these redirections and negative comments can take a toll on her self-esteem.

Preschool-age girls with low self-esteem may say things like "I'm a bad girl" or "Stop it, me. Be quiet." They may hear this from their classmates and even some teachers and parents. You may even overhear your young daughter say these things when she is angry or frustrated at herself. If your daughter makes negative comments about herself, give her a hug and reassure her that you love her just the way she is. You can admit that her behavior sometimes frustrates you but that you still love her very much. Each night when you tuck her into bed, make it a nightly ritual to tell her how much you love her.

General Strategies for Building Self-Esteem

Help your daughter develop a "can-do" attitude based on opportunities to accomplish realistic tasks. Even small successes can help build a strong foundation for good self-esteem. Don't expect more from her than she can do. Her frustration tolerance may be limited, so patience will be required.

Try to help her be as independent as possible. Doing things for herself builds confidence in her abilities. It can be much more time-consuming to allow for independence in things like dressing but is important whenever you have the time.

Focus on building social skills early. Even play dates for little ones where sharing, turn-taking, and recognizing emotions in the playmate, like sadness, anger, and happiness are important.

Give honest, accurate feedback as she develops her view of herself. Focus on what she has done right, perhaps the effort she has put into something, and identify what you are continuing to work on with her to make her life easier.

Do not compare her to other children, especially siblings. More than likely, she will be making her own comparisons.

Provide a safe, secure environment for her, both at home and at school, enabling her to take risks as she strives to accomplish tasks. Give her chances to make some of her own decisions and help her learn to solve problems.

Reading Books Aloud

Most preschool-age girls with ADHD love it when adults read out loud to them. Books are a great resource to help build the self-esteem of preschool girls. A few books I recommend to clients with preschool-age girls include *I'm Gonna Like Me: Letting Off a Little Self-Esteem*; *No, David!*; *Alexander and the Terrible, Horrible, No Good, Very Bad Day*; *Have I Ever Told You?*; and *Love You Forever*. Reading books like these with your daughter helps her identify with the character, learn how the character solves a problem or develops a new behavior, and then apply that to her life. Books provide a nonthreatening and peaceful way to teach your child and build self-esteem.

Begin by asking your daughter to sit on your lap or right next to you so you can both see the pictures. As you read the book aloud, use an animated voice. Help your daughter identify with the character by pointing out similarities between her and the character. Look for positive things that are related to the character and your daughter in addition to troublesome behaviors.

For example, in *No, David!* by David Shannon, the character likes chicken but forgets to chew with his mouth closed at the dinner table.

If this happens to your daughter, mention that the boy in the book forgets to chew with his mouth closed too and talk about what his mom says. You and your daughter can practice chewing with your mouths closed together. At the end of the book, reinforce how much David's mom loves him and how much you love your daughter, too. Most children enjoy having the same book read to them multiple times, so each time you reread the book, you should emphasize different points.

Journaling by Scribbling, Drawing, or Writing

There are additional activities you and your preschool daughter can do to help build self-esteem. One way is to provide your young daughter with an age-appropriate journal. Dr. Janet Mentore Lee wrote a kid's journal, *The Daily Doodle: A Journal for Children Ages 4–7*. Dr. Lee describes her journal as a way to help kids feel reassured, validated, and supported. Each page of the activity book is a writing, scribbling, or doodling prompt that will help your child express her inner thoughts, feelings, and coping skills. Depending on your daughter's developmental level, you can help her draw pictures, or write words or letters. *The Daily Doodle* provides prompts and is a great way to collaborate, create, and connect with your child, critical components to a parent–child relationship and building self-esteem. Caveat – some girls like this type of activity and others don't.

Creating a Self-Portrait

Another activity you can do with your preschool daughter is to help her create a self-portrait. A large piece of butcher paper or many copy-sized sheets of paper taped together work well. Place the paper on the floor and ask your daughter to lie on top of it. Use a pencil or marker and then trace the outline of her body. Tell her you'd like to work with her to make a self-portrait. Use her and your favorite art supplies, which could include crayons, paint, ink, chalk, and so forth. Place a small mirror within reach and encourage her to look at it frequently. Help her by drawing in her ears, eyes, and mouth, and allow her to color her features. Comment about her beautifully colored eyes, nice hair, wide smile, or strong arms. When the project is completed, hang it up in her room. You could even take her picture next to it and tell her you are going to e-mail it to relatives, share it with friends, and brag about how cool she and her portrait look. An alternative to the life-size portrait is just to draw the shape of your daughter's head on paper and then allow her to color in her facial features.

Forging a Strong Parent–Child Relationship

Regardless of the activity you complete with your daughter, reinforce how much you love her and enjoy being with her. Don't stress too much if she is wiggly while you read or squirms as you trace her outline. Try to have fun with her and reinforce her positive qualities. One wise parent of a preschooler with ADHD that I have worked with always strived for a ratio of five positive comments to one negative comment, but he rarely achieved it. To encourage himself he even bought a small counter to keep in his hand and click as he said positive comments. This helped for a while as he tried to change his mindset toward saying more positive comments.

When it is all said and done, having a positive and close relationship with your daughter will be invaluable as you and she tackle any obstacles ADHD might bring. Many successful people with ADHD point to their mother or father who was always there for them and never stopped believing in them. You can be that person for your daughter.

References

American Academy of Child and Adolescent Psychiatry & American Psychiatric Association. (2013). *ADHD parents medication guide.* www.aacap.org/App_Themes/AACAP/Docs/resource_centers/adhd/adhd_parents_medication_guide_201305.pdf

American Academy of Children & Adolescent Psychiatry. (2020). *Screen time and children.* www.aacap.org/AACAP/Families_and_Youth/Facts_for_Families/FFF_Guide/Children-and-Watching-TV-054. aspx

Barkley, R. A. (2020). *Taking charge of ADHD: The complete, authoritative guide for parents* (4th ed.). Guilford Press.

Harvard Mental Health Letter. (2007). *Preschool ADHD.* www/health.Harvard.edu/press releases/preschoolADHD

Hinshaw, S. P. (2022). *Straight talk about ADHD in girls: How to help your daughter thrive.* Guilford Press.

National Institutes of Health. (2022) *Researchers unlock pattern of gene activity for ADHD.* https://nihrecord.nih.gov/2022/12/09/researchers-unlock-pattern-gene-activity-adhd#

Pastor, P., Reuben, C., Duran, C., & Hawkins, L. (2015, May). Association between diagnosed ADHD and selected characteristics among children aged 4–17 years: United States, 2011–2013. *NCHS Data Brief*, 201, 201. PMID: 25974000.

Taylor-Klaus, E. (2020). *The essential guide to raising complex kids with ADHD, anxiety, and more.* Fair Winds Press.

Wigal, S., Chappell, P., Palumbo, D., Lubaczewski, S., Ramaker, S., & Abbas, R. (2020). Diagnosis and treatment options for preschoolers with attention-deficit/hyperactivity disorder. *Journal of Child and Adolescent Psychopharmacology*, 30(2), 104–118. doi: 10.1089/cap.2019.0116. Epub 2020 Jan 20. PMID: 31967914; PMCID: PMC704725.

Williams, N. M., Zaharieva, I., Martin, A., Langley, K., Mantripragada, K., Fossdal, R., Stefansson, H., Stefansson, K., Magnusson, P., Gudmundsson, O. O., Gustafsson, O., Holmans, P., Owen, M. J., O'Donovan, M., & Thapar, A. (2010, October 23). Rare chromosomal deletions and duplications in attention-deficit hyperactivity disorder: a genome-wide analysis. *Lancet*, 376(9750), 1401–1408. doi: 10.1016/S0140-6736(10)61109-9. Epub 2010 Sep 29. PMID: 20888040; PMCID: PMC2965350.

Wolraich, M. L., Hagan, J. F. Jr, Allan, C., Chan, E., Davison, D., Earls, M., Evans, S. W., Flinn, S. K., Froehlich, T., Frost, J., Holbrook, J.

R., Lehmann, C. U., Lessin, H. R., Okechukwu, K., Pierce, K. L., Winner, J. D., & Zurhellen, W. (2019, October). Subcommittee on children and adolescents with attention-deficit/hyperactive disorder. Clinical practice guideline for the diagnosis, evaluation, and treatment of attention-deficit/hyperactivity disorder in children and adolescents. *Pediatrics*, 144(4), e20192528. doi: 10.1542/peds.2019-2528. Erratum in: *Pediatrics*, 2020 Mar;145(3): PMID: 31570648; PMCID: PMC7067282.

Points to Consider

1 Remember that organization, thinking before acting, and being able to sustain attention are all developmental by nature, meaning that behaviors can occur within a range of ages and still be considered within the normal range.

2 Time spent in researching the right fit between a preschool and your daughter could pay big dividends and enhance her self-esteem.

3 As a parent, it is easy to be in denial about problems and postpone action. Be proactive.

4 You will walk a fine line in helping other family members have some understanding of ADHD behavior while treating the sibling as a full and integral member of the family.

5 Review your self-assessment responses to decide if there are any areas where you still need to learn more.

Action Steps to Take Now

1 Develop a stronger relationship with your daughter's preschool and ensure that her needs are being addressed. Use the questions in this chapter if you interview prospective preschools for your daughter.

2 Become a detective in determining ways your daughter's characteristics affect her daily functioning and try to provide supports to help her work around and grow in her deficit areas.

3 Recognize your child's temperament or pattern of personality characteristics. Structure her environment to enhance chances of good behavior.

4 Seek out parent training in effective management and discipline. Add that to Step 3 Action in the **Dynamic Action Treatment Plan** listed at Chapter 9.

5 Try some of the tools suggested in this chapter such as using books, turning tasks into games, or getting down to her level when you talk.

6 Be positive, notice, and compliment the positive things your daughter does.

Chapter 5

The Elementary Years

SELF-ASSESSMENT: Where Am I Now?

Each self-assessment helps you reflect on your daughter and your parenting practices and is a preview of the chapter's content.

1 When I think about my elementary-age daughter, I …

  a feel she is doing the best she can considering her ability and the effects of her ADHD.

  b question whether she is becoming increasingly overwhelmed in her classroom.

  c am concerned she is missing instruction because she is daydreaming too much.

  d am more concerned with her emotional/social standing than her academics.

DOI: 10.4324/9781003365402-6

2 When I think about the support I need to help my daughter, I ...
   a have not had time to really think about it.
   b am confused about all the options.
   c have identified a cadre of people who can help me maximize her strengths and remediate her weaknesses.
   d am in the process of identifying the best people who can help her be successful.
3 When I think about her elementary school, I ...
   a am sure her educational needs are not being met.
   b question whether the right foundation for skills in reading and math are being developed.
   c feel that the school is doing a great job of helping her.
   d think I need to communicate more effectively with her teacher and the school staff to fine tune supports that might help her.
4 When I think about her teacher(s), I ...
   a am sure they do not even know she has ADHD.
   b question whether they have knowledge about ADHD and effective interventions.
   c need to improve the level of communication with the teacher about homework, my daughter's progress, and upcoming longer assignments.
   d am very satisfied with her teacher(s).
5 When I think about my daughter's social skills in the school, community, and home, I ...
   a realize she is delayed in many skills.
   b see that she is increasingly becoming isolated and prefers to be alone.
   c have noticed that she is not invited to birthday parties or sleepovers.
   d see she is well-liked by adults and children.

Here's what's happening: Your daughter's emotions are still developing, but she's probably way behind the curve compared to other kids her age. She may look like a little lady, but she's likely a bundle of raw emotions and feelings strung together in an almost primal way. Although her needs may vary, it is likely she will require lots of your time and patience in teaching her how to compensate for her deficits, especially her tendency to get lost in her own thoughts. You may need to spend extra time teaching her how to stop and think, rather than just react, because it probably will not come naturally to her. Or she may be so scattered, you will need to start at ground level in helping her develop some organizational skills. Perhaps her social skills require specific teaching and structured opportunities to practice what she has learned. Regardless, you'll need a ton of patience, because those times you'll need to do the teaching will be the times you'll be most challenged by her behavior.

Your daughter is in school full-time now, and she'll likely be expected to master the same curriculum as the students around her. Both of you will need plenty of tools to meet this goal without lowering the bar for her academic success. I'll spend a lot of time in this chapter sharing strategies that will help your daughter succeed in the classroom. Your daughter's teachers will be a critical part of her success, and I'll help you identify some of the characteristics of school settings where a girl with ADHD can flourish.

These are the years when your daughter is learning basic skills and work habits she'll use for the rest of her life and developing self-esteem that she will take into adolescence. I'm not going to sugarcoat it – these years can be tough. But there is tremendous satisfaction in knowing that the hard work, patience, and consistency you invest now will establish a firm foundation for your daughter. I've been in the trenches and know that sometimes it seems like the struggles are never going to end. But take my word for it. One day, you're going to look back and say, "Wow, those years went by fast."

Looking Ahead

The chapter is organized according to the following main headings:

> ▷ Section 1: School (the challenges, the changes, and the ways you can help your daughter succeed).
> ▷ Section 2: Community Issues (her relationships with family and friends and activities in the community.)
> ▷ Section 3: Your Daughter's Physical and Emotional Health.

Going to School

Your daughter's elementary school career will likely be full of ups and downs. Each year, she will face new challenges and expectations. As a girl moves from preschool to elementary school, she will be called upon to be more independent, organized, and goal-directed – areas that are weaknesses for most girls with ADHD. Her behavior and adjustment to school will be related to how well she can handle the increased demands on her organizational skills and coping mechanisms. For most students, ADHD impacts not only their focus but also their ability to inhibit behavior and their executive functioning skills (e.g., planning, remembering, and organizing). Her impulsivity prevents her from thinking about the consequences of her actions and may impact her relationships in the classroom. What she needs is not criticism for bad decisions and lack of focus, but support to meet the new demands placed on her.

As a girl moves from preschool to elementary school, she will be called upon to be more independent, organized, and goal-directed – areas that are weaknesses for most girls with ADHD.

Julissa was a mess in third grade. Her teacher said Julissa always had papers everywhere. None of the children wanted to sit at her table because she was always bothering them to ask what she should do next. Furthermore, the class received rewards based on their table's performance, and the children knew Julissa would lose points for her table. Her difficulty in being accepted by her classmates didn't stop there. At recess, none of the children wanted to play with Julissa because she was so unpredictable and usually insisted on everything her way.

Academically, Julissa was falling behind in all subjects, especially reading comprehension and math problem-solving – two of the areas that required the most concentration and memory. Her parents didn't know how to help her when she got home because they could not read the scribbles in her agenda planner, and Julissa never knew what she was supposed to do. They dreaded picking her up from school, because she often had meltdowns in the car based on how her school day had gone. She would cry because none of her classmates picked her for their team and no one wanted to be her best friend. Julissa often said the very words that tear at a parent's heart: "Everybody hates me!" The saddest part was that they knew why she felt that way because she was rarely invited to any birthday parties or to play at anyone's house. They had always known she wasn't the perfect, well-behaved child, but she had managed to fit in much better in kindergarten, first grade, and second grade than she had in third grade. It seemed that the other girls were maturing and leaving Julissa in the dust.

They immediately set up a meeting with Julissa's teacher, who fortunately had a real heart for children with

ADHD. She had a good perspective on Julissa's areas of greatest difficulty. She identified Julissa was below grade level in reading and referred her for additional reading instruction at school where her progress would be monitored. In addition she provided materials which could be used at home to support what would be studied in class. To address her social problems, the teacher recommended parents have playdates structured around a specific activity, like bowling, and prepare Julissa beforehand about how to treat her classmate so they might enjoy being together. The teacher moved Julissa's group closer to her table, so she could more easily keep an eye on her and support her when she appeared lost. She used more visuals so Julissa could see what the finished product should look like and always checked on her after she had started the assignment to answer any questions. She stopped letting children pick their own teams and assigned them instead. She often joined Julissa's team to encourage her participation as well as her inclusion by other team members. As Julissa's confidence grew and her despair lessened, she began to feel like she fit in with her class. Her teacher began to think what had seemed like poor attention and performance was linked to her anxiety and being overwhelmed by the demands. Everyone agreed to continue monitoring her attention as the year progressed. Her parents had already begun the discussion about her school problems with their pediatrician and were open to an evaluation for ADHD.

Problem-Solving Perspective Required

If you are like most parents of girls with ADHD, you will find that your daughter's elementary years will be filled with learning and new challenges for you as well. There will be little room for complacency. Just when you think you've figured out how to handle your daughter's difficulties and are experiencing a period of smooth sailing, a new problem will pop up. If a girl with ADHD is anything during these years, she is consistently inconsistent. Some days, she will amaze you and other days, you will wonder why all the synapses in her brain are not firing together. In talking about kids with ADHD, Goldstein (2004) said, "They know what to do, but do not consistently, predictably, or for that matter, independently do what they know" (p. 1).

I recommend that you adopt this stance: Look at every situation that arises as simply another puzzle with a solution. You and your daughter will fare much better if you keep that problem-solving perspective, because you never know when you will need it. Even when challenges come at you fast and furiously – and I know they will – I encourage you not to feel defeated by problems as they arise. Don't let your daughter feel beaten either. Instead, make sure she knows that together you're going to look at her capabilities along with resources to help her, and then work to make things better. You are not going to ignore problems, because by now you probably know they won't go away unless addressed. As her world has gotten bigger, your team can also grow. You can turn to her teacher, her principal, her school guidance counselor or psychologist, her doctor, and trusted friends for help and support. (Don't be reluctant to approach the principal when you need assistance, especially if he or she is very student-centered and involved with students.) Part of the problem-solving mentality is remembering that you don't have to have all the answers yourself.

Elementary schools are not the same as when you were a student. Your daughter is faced with high-stakes testing, mandatory retention in some schools, reduced opportunities for recess, and a complex social milieu that is often complicated by social media in the later elementary years. Don't despair. Some positive changes in education that have happened in recent years may make your daughter's life easier. Schools and teachers are generally much more knowledgeable about ADHD and how to effectively serve those who are impacted. Research on girls with ADHD is making people, especially teachers, more aware of their struggles. Increased use of technology in the classroom can also be a plus for children with ADHD. There is still much more to do, but girls with ADHD are not being ignored in the same way they have been in the past.

When you factor in her ADHD and the likelihood that your daughter may also have academic deficits, she is going to need your involvement and support if she is to develop and maintain a positive attitude toward learning. That doesn't mean you have to sit with her for the duration of her homework time or that you are going to be doing any of her homework for her. It means you might have to help her get started on her homework, ensure she understands what she is supposed to be doing, help her break the assignment down into manageable chunks, be available for questions, or help her figure out how to make study aides like flash cards. It is well documented that girls diagnosed with ADHD often have learning disabilities and lower performance on standardized testing. There will be increased demands on her organizational skills and persistence, often exceeding her capability. These are critical years for her when she is cementing her view of herself as a learner. Your goal will be to help her be as independent as possible while providing enough support to enable her to view herself as a capable learner. As her study skills develop, remember that it is much easier to establish good habits from the very beginning than to break bad habits. Educate yourself so you can make the best possible choices for her. Check out the **Dynamic Action Treatment Plan** in Chapter 9 and fill in some of your daughter's academic strengths and needs.

Your goal will be to help her be as independent as possible while providing enough support to enable her to view herself as a capable learner.

Melissa was a 10-year-old girl in fifth grade who had been diagnosed with ADHD and was taking medication. Rather than developing more self-control, her parents felt she was displaying less. She would blow up at home at the slightest provocation and seemed constantly stressed. A visit to the doctor prescribing her medication ruled out the medication as the cause of her unpredictability.

Her parents were spending more and more time helping her with her homework but felt like they were presenting material for the first time rather than reinforcing what had been taught in the classroom that day. A conference with her teacher showed she was falling farther and farther behind in the classroom. Her teacher reported that she often looked confused and didn't know where to start on assignments.

Unbeknownst to her parents, Melissa had recently been dropped from her group of friends at school, children she had been friends with since third grade. Her teacher reported overhearing insensitive comments Melissa had made to the other girls prior to the dissolution of their friendship and noted Melissa often wanted to "call the shots" during play. Now at recess, she would wander around aimlessly, as if she did not know what to do with herself. A conference with Melissa, her teacher, and her parents revealed that Melissa was miserable at school, constantly thinking about how sad she was rather than focusing on her schoolwork.

From talking to Melissa about her peers, her parents realized she was not yet able to take the perspective of others and needed assistance in refining her social skills. Fortunately, the school's guidance counselor had a small group focusing on social skills, which Melissa joined. All involved felt Melissa perked up and seemed to benefit from specific teaching about social skills. Her parents helped her identify other students in the classroom who might be good friends and made plans to establish play dates. When watching movies or reading books, they also tried to guide her in anticipating what other children might be thinking. As her social life became less rocky, her attention improved in the classroom and she was better able to control her emotions. The challenges ADHD brought were still there, but at least she wasn't preoccupied with her social problems.

School Choices

Your choice of schools (and whether you have a choice at all) will depend upon where you live, your financial situation, and whether your local school district allows freedom to move from one school to another. In some cases, your local public elementary school may be your one and only option. If that's your family's situation, I encourage you to keep reading because what you learn here may help you advocate for your daughter's school to become a more welcoming place for all children with ADHD.

Many communities offer a variety of choices – public, charter, virtual, private, and home schools. Pod or micro-schools, made up of a small collection of students whose parents hire a tutor or teacher for all or part of the day have popped up in the last decade.

If you have options, select the type of environment that will provide the best learning opportunities for your daughter while not overloading your family with stress. Time spent researching your options will likely pay off and will certainly give you peace of mind that you did the best that you could.

Consider the overall philosophy of the school. Children with ADHD generally do well in schools with structure, good communication with parents, a solid curriculum that matches instruction to the child's abilities, energetic teachers who utilize experiential learning and a variety of instructional techniques, and reasonable class sizes. It is important that the staff understands ADHD as a neurobiological condition with deficits in impulse control and executive functioning, so they don't immediately attribute a child's problems to laziness and lack of motivation. When you're evaluating a school, you might ask some of the following questions:

- ▷ If it is not a public school, ask if the curriculum matches state guidelines. In most states, you can go to your state department of education's website and access the curriculum for various grades.
- ▷ What is the average class size? Smaller is often better; 20 students or fewer is optimal.
- ▷ Does it appear to be an organized and structured environment?
- ▷ Do the students sit in desks or at tables? A highly distractible child usually does better at a desk.
- ▷ Does the school provide opportunities, such as tutoring, for extra help if a child lags behind academically?
- ▷ What kind of success rate has the school had for girls with ADHD?
- ▷ Is close supervision always provided, especially during transitions?
- ▷ What is the school's communication policy with parents?

▷ Is the school willing to accommodate your child's needs with strategies such as preferential seating, frequent cueing to task, or allowing movement if it does not disturb others?

▷ What is the behavior management plan? Is it proactive and designed to eliminate opportunities for misbehavior? In the classroom, children with ADHD benefit from close supervision, clearly defined rules, positive reinforcement, contingency management that uses motivational incentives, and being held accountable for their behavior.

▷ Does the staff assist students in developing organization skills?

▷ Do they make it a priority to help every child feel connected to others in the classroom and try to foster friendships for children who are struggling in this area?

In the classroom, children with ADHD benefit from close supervision, clearly defined rules, positive reinforcement, contingency management that uses motivational incentives, and being held accountable for their behavior.

Teacher/Classroom Match Is Important

If your daughter needs support in the classroom, a good plan of action may be to have a conversation with the principal prior to the beginning of the school year and provide some information about your daughter to help the school make a good teacher match for her. Some teachers are much more effective than others in dealing with girls with ADHD. The ultimate decision will be up to the principal, who must consider many factors. Teachers who are patient, have high energy, and are structured and loving but firm are usually most effective with children with ADHD. One confounding factor about these children is that their focus is often governed by their motivation, so it is key to have a teacher who tries to make learning interesting. Some families have the good fortune to find a teacher who is flexible enough to work with their daughter's built-in restlessness and distractibility while boosting her independence and self-confidence. Having a teacher who can appreciate your daughter for her strengths and does not become too annoyed with her impulsivity, distractibility, or activity level will be invaluable.

Zola was cruising along in kindergarten and first grade. She seemed to be able to hold it together during sedentary classroom time until recess, when her teacher commented she became incredibly active, running about the entire time. At the end of first grade, her best friend (who also happened to be one of the most popular kids in the class) deserted her. Zola's willingness to take the perspective of others had not yet developed.

In second grade Zola found herself without a best friend and in a class with a teacher who was very rigid, cold, and boring. She was advanced academically. When she completed her work before everyone else, her teacher made her sit silently and would not allow her to work on anything else. One day, while her mother was presenting a program to Zola's class, she realized just how sad her daughter had become at school. She had stopped participating in class and lost her spark.

Zola began to balk at going to school. Sometimes she had to be carried to the car, kicking and screaming, because her mother knew that her reluctance to go to school would only grow if she was allowed to miss school after a tantrum. After many conferences and much insistence from her parents, the school transferred her to another second grade classroom, where the teacher immediately recognized Zola's need for permissible movement, stimulating activities when she finished her work, assistance in developing her social skills and boosting her self-esteem. The teacher lovingly said, "She needs fluffing up." Even though the change was positive it took time for Zola to make the adjustment. Her parents had to continue trying to provide opportunities to make social connections and to help her regain her interest in school.

In third grade, Zola seemed completely overwhelmed by the demands of the curriculum even though her parents knew she had grade level skills. A conference with the teacher revealed she was often off task and slow to start on her work. Her parents consulted their pediatrician who had the teacher complete a rating scale, which was very elevated for inattention. She was subsequently diagnosed with ADHD, combined type. She received a 504 plan at school which allowed for more careful teacher monitoring and support in getting stated on her work. Her parents, teacher, and pediatrician were continuing to monitor her progress.

The quality of your daughter's education can have a direct relationship to her adult life, so these years are very important. In my practice, I have observed excellent teachers who know exactly what strategies work for girls with ADHD. As your daughter's most powerful advocate, you should have a solid understanding of instructional techniques that might help her and share them with her teachers in a respectful way. More than likely many of her teachers will already be implementing many of these strategies. You can print and personalize the list below with any additional interventions that might help and share them with new teachers when appropriate. Your goal is always to establish a collaborative relationship, not to tell the teacher how to run her classroom. You might even want to incorporate some of these strategies at home.

Information for Your Teammates –
Your Daughter's Teachers

Classroom Organization/Management

In an ideal world, your daughter's educational environment will include:

▷ A positive classroom environment, especially one in which the teacher understands ADHD and is familiar with strategies to prompt your daughter to become an active participant in the learning process.

▷ Specific classroom procedures established and practiced consistently. In kindergarten, children may need to understand how to stand in line, take turns, raise their hands, and wait to be called on before speaking.

▷ Organizational skills taught and modeled throughout the school day, with assistance where necessary. Use of color-coded folders for each subject and a separate folder for homework can be very helpful.

▷ Seating available for your daughter in a distraction-free area, close to the point of instruction but as far away as possible from air conditioners, high-traffic areas, bathroom access, and other active students.

▷ A study carrel or separate area of the classroom provided where a child can choose to go and work when distractions become too great. In some cases, students have referred to these areas as their offices rather than a punishment.

▷ Work areas kept neat and free of distractions.

▷ Placement near positive role models.

▷ When possible, core classes scheduled early in the day. An optimal schedule for a girl with ADHD is to have lunch and physical education or recess at intervals to break up the day.

▷ Achievement motivators that stress effort and persistence. In other words, the child is rewarded for doing her very best, not for producing an "A" result.

▷ The concept of time out should be used as a chance to regain control and get back into a "learning frame of mind" rather than as a punishment.

▷ Supervision provided, especially during transition times and lunch. Lack of structure allows for more social interaction where potential problems may flourish.

▷ Permissible movement if other students aren't disturbed. For example, the girl with ADHD may be allowed to get out of her desk to retrieve something, walk around the classroom, go to the restroom, or get a drink of water if she doesn't take advantage of the situation. Sometimes the chance to move about can help children refocus if they are willing to get back to work afterwards.

▷ Acceptable substitutes for motor overflow provided, such as allowing the student to squeeze stress balls, sit on a ball chair or bumpy cushion, or chew gum if permitted by the school, if these items do not become a distraction.

Behavior: Rewards and Consequences

Children with ADHD usually require more relevant rewards and consistent consequences for behavior than other children. An individualized behavior plan using tangible rewards is sometimes necessary and can be developed by the teacher, a school psychologist, or a behavior specialist. Stickers, happy faces, or check marks can be redeemed for opportunities for extra computer time, to mentor another student, to be a teacher's helper, or to have lunch with a special teacher or administrator. Sometimes a response/cost plan, whereby a student can lose previously earned points because of poor behavior, works for some students and may be necessary for serious behavior. For example, if a student hits someone or causes a big disruption in the classroom, she might lose some or all her points for the day or lose one of the privileges she had already earned. (A caveat is that some students react very badly to losing things with no opportunity to earn anything back, which makes their behavior more difficult to manage the rest of the day.) Since girls with ADHD often tend to live in the "now," rewards or consequences delivered as closely to the behavior as possible will have the most value. Some other behavioral tips are:

▷ Sincere verbal praise for specific behaviors is invaluable as a tool for reinforcing the desired behavior. Make sure to "catch her being good."

▷ Students can often benefit from monitoring their own behavior with counters or check sheets.

▷ Frequent visual cues between student and teacher help maintain optimal attention and behavioral control. A cue could be a special sign known only by your daughter and the teacher. This is a great proactive way to help a child.

Lesson Presentation

Teaching girls with ADHD sometimes requires a little bit more ingenuity (and a lot more patience). Respectfully ask your daughter's teacher to think of this list as extra tools for his or her toolbox:

▷ Give directions in short sentences, accompanied with visuals when possible. In the upper elementary grades, it is often helpful for a child to see what the finished product should look like before she begins working.

▷ Offer help in breaking down longer assignments into manageable chunks. Some children are overwhelmed by the amount of information on a page and benefit from covering part of the page with a blank sheet of paper. When a child is overwhelmed, she often shuts down rather than attempting to start on a project.

- ▷ Establish eye contact with a child with ADHD before delivering key points of instruction. Watch for signs that indicate lack of comprehension and daydreaming.
- ▷ Provide frequent review and repetition of previously learned material.
- ▷ Understand the child's capability and provide lessons that are challenging without being frustrating.
- ▷ Hands-on, experiential learning is a favorite for children with ADHD. Their attention to task increases significantly when it is of high interest.
- ▷ Ignore minor inappropriate behavior.
- ▷ Provide warnings before transitions (e.g., "Five more minutes before science").
- ▷ Demonstrate proper behavior through modeling. Sharing and turn-taking can be especially difficult for young children with ADHD. Teachers can model behavior, reinforce appropriate behavior, and help the child initiate interactions.
- ▷ Use of computerized instruction as part of the curriculum is a positive way for most girls with ADHD to learn because it is stimulating and interactive.
- ▷ Target her learning style. Because children with ADHD can be incredibly focused on topics or activities of their choice, an effective motivator can be to allow them extra credit on selected topics with the project to be matched to their learning style. If a girl is talented verbally, then she might research something and present it to the class. If she's creative and good with her hands, she might build a project instead.

Your Daughter's Peers

Outside of your family, your daughter's school offers the most important opportunities for her socialization. Elementary school is when your daughter should be making great strides in learning how to appropriately interact with others. During this time, it is common for girls with ADHD to have one of two problems:

> ▷ they may lack social skills appropriate for their age, and
> ▷ they may have the skills but may not stop and think before they act.

If your daughter is having problems with her peer group at school, you need to understand the root of the problem. Is she insistent on being the boss? Does she have trouble following the verbal interactions of girls? Is she unable to read body language and pick up visual clues from others? Is her thinking so unorganized that she can't stay on topic? Does she withdraw from groups because she does not feel accepted? More than likely, her teacher can share information about her functioning in the classroom, and you can make observations on your own at birthday parties or other social outings. Often, she has not yet developed the necessary social skills and may need more assistance.

Difficulties girls with ADHD often have with peers at school include:

> ▷ personal space issues – invading others' personal space or being too sensitive if crowded,
> ▷ turn-taking in conversation and games,
> ▷ issues in sportsmanship, especially losing,
> ▷ listening and following a conversation,
> ▷ wanting to control activities,
> ▷ solving disagreements,
> ▷ being easily bored and losing focus, and
> ▷ accepting criticism.

If you have pinpointed some problem areas for your daughter in the above list, then you can go about helping her acquire those skills:

▷ Communicate with her teacher and solicit his or her help. Sometimes children need to be explicitly taught social skills; they don't acquire them by osmosis. Some schools have social groups run by a guidance counselor or school psychologist where children are taught skills and practice them using role playing. Some classroom teachers are excellent at weaving social expectations into their daily curriculum and setting up opportunities where children can interact successfully.

▷ Some books you can read and discuss with your daughter about friendship issues include:
  Rulers of the Playground by Joseph Kuefler (ages 4–8)
  Circle of Three – Enough Friendship to Go Around by Elizabeth Brokamp (ages 8–12)
  The Friendship Book by Wendy L. Moss (ages 8–12)

▷ There are interactive apps, such as *My School Day* by Social Skill Builder, Inc. (appadvice.com) and digital resources, such as *You Are a Social Detective: Explaining Social Thinking to Kids*, 2nd edition (Socialthinking – Storybook).

▷ Arrange play dates and provide opportunities for your daughter to establish relationships with other girls. Put time and effort into selecting the children and the activities to maximize opportunities for success. Girls who struggle with social skills usually do better initially when activities are highly structured, such as making a craft, bowling, or swimming, and involve only one other child.

Some teachers are very good at setting up social opportunities for awkward students and go the "extra mile" to help students connect. I have observed a teacher grabbing a basketball and encouraging a child who usually hangs on the sidelines to join in a game. Within minutes, other children were joining in. If situations can be set up where children can interact comfortably, little by little, their skills begin to grow.

Bullying

Unfortunately, bullying occurs in all schools, despite careful oversight and strict rules against it. Bullying almost always involves an imbalance of power and is defined as intentional, often aggressive or mean behavior directed toward another. It can take many forms, including physical and verbal attacks, exclusion, and sending threatening messages via e-mail, text, or phone (cyberbullying – discussed in more detail in the next chapter).

Except for cyberbullying, bullying and intimidation have been around for ages and were previously viewed as part of the childhood experience. Research and current culture have pointed out the dangerous effects of bullying. It can make life miserable for the one being targeted, especially for those who are socially naïve and timid. When the victims internalize the bullying, their hurt can lead to anger, loneliness, withdrawal, lowered self-esteem, and depression. In the worst cases, it can lead to self-harm. It is important to talk to your daughter about bullying and make sure she can recognize it and has some tools to handle it.

It is important to talk to your daughter about bullying and make sure she can recognize it and has some tools to handle it.

An official website of the United States government, www.stop bullying.gov, has helpful information about bullying for children and parents. Some suggestions from my experience with managing bullying include:

> ▷ Keep communication open with your daughter. Know the names of children she likes and doesn't like at school and why; find out if she feels left out at school, and encourage her

to tell you if anyone makes fun of her and figure out how to help her respond.

▷ Explain that it is important to tell teachers or principals if she observes or is the target of bullying. This information is usually confidential and is not considered "tattling."

▷ Try to practice or role play some strategies to use if she is bullied.

▷ Model good behavior for your daughter. Handle disagreements with your spouse, friends, or the school without resorting to aggressive, threatening behavior. Bullying is a learned behavior. In my school experience, children who are disrespectful and bully others have often observed similar ways of handling conflict within their home.

▷ Encourage her to be an "upstander" – one who stands up for others who are being bullied.

▷ If you suspect she is being bullied, don't ignore it – get to the bottom of it and see that it is resolved.

Other important pointers for your daughter if she is being bullied include:

▷ Try not to show fear or anger, as this is often the reaction a bully is seeking.

▷ Maintain emotional control so the bully doesn't think he or she is making an impact.

▷ Don't fight back by resorting to bullying.

▷ Calmly tell the bully to stop or simply walk away.

▷ Try to stay with a group of friends, as bullying is more likely to occur when alone.

▷ Don't bring expensive things to school that other children are not likely to have.

▷ If riding a bus, sit near the front of the bus, not in the back.

A Quick Look at Causes, Presentations, and Possible Solutions for Behaviors

As I have stressed throughout the book, no two girls with ADHD will be alike. Your daughter's ADHD may manifest itself in very different ways than another girl's. Scan the chart in Table 5.1 to see if you recognize any familiar behaviors. If you do, it will not only help you understand the likely causes but also suggest ways you might work with your daughter to overcome some of her challenges.

Table 5.1
Causes, Presentations, and Solutions for ADHD

Cause	Presentation	Possible Solutions
Faulty sense of time	► Always late and behind schedule ► Doesn't get started on tasks ► Misses deadlines ► Doesn't start tasks promptly ► Poor planning	► Use agenda or planner ► Create a behavior plan ► Break assignments down ► Use prompts and reminders ► Maintain a schedule
Impulsivity	► Acts before thinking ► Doesn't consider consequences ► Jumps from one task to another ► Doesn't listen to others ► Blurts out in class ► Limited self-control	► Provide structure ► Teach verbal rehearsal – using self-talk ► Share stop/think strategies ► Conduct role playing

Table 5.1, *continued*

Cause	Presentation	Possible Solutions
Inflexibility	▶ Trouble with transitions ▶ Easily agitated ▶ Uncooperative	▶ Give prior notice for transitions ▶ Teach coping skills
Inattention	▶ Disorganized ▶ Loses items ▶ Unable to listen ▶ Forgets task of moment ▶ Doesn't store material in memory ▶ Thinks of many things at once	▶ Teach self-monitoring ▶ Create a designated place for items ▶ Insist on eye contact ▶ Use organization tools ▶ Use memory strategies
Overarousal	▶ Fidgeting ▶ Excessive talking ▶ Constant movement ▶ Easily stimulated	▶ Give student permissible movements ▶ Use of fidget item ▶ Provide calm areas ▶ Ignore low-level behaviors

Note: From *Raising boys with ADHD* (p. 112) by J. W. Forgan and M. A. Richey (2012). Copyright 2012 by Prufrock Press. Reprinted with permission.

Callie breezed through kindergarten and first and second grades. However, in third grade, her academic performance started falling behind her peers. Her school was departmentalized, so she had to travel to different teachers for math, reading, science, and written language. She could never seem to pack up her materials correctly and usually ended up stuffing papers in her backpack. She missed turning in assignments because she couldn't find the papers. She was frustrated that all assignments *seemed longer and more complicated, requiring more concentration and focus. Callie's teacher observed more daydreaming.*

Callie had trouble with reading comprehension, because by the time she finished reading the long passages, she had forgotten what she had read. When reading aloud, she often skipped over words which also impacted her comprehension. Writing seemed overwhelming. Callie rushed through writing assignments and wasn't disciplined enough to effectively use planning strategies or go back and proofread. In math, she was resistant to showing her work on multistep problems.

Callie began to dread going to school. Her parents consulted with their pediatrician who had a long history with the family. After a thorough examination consisting of a social and developmental history, behavior rating scales by her parents and teacher, physical exam, and consultation, Callie was diagnosed with ADHD, inattentive presentation and started on a low dose of medicine. The parents knew more than medication was needed to help Callie get back on her feet at school and acquire some new skills.

Fortunately, Callie was already in a structured, predictable classroom setting with an enthusiastic teacher who was determined to figure out strategies to help her be successful. Some of the strategies that proved effective included:

- ▷ *Her teacher initiated weekly communication with her parents about her progress in class.*
- ▷ *Her parents agreed to have Callie empty her backpack every night and get all the papers in their proper places.*

> ▷ *Her parents helped her establish a designated place by the door where she could put her school items for the next day.*
> ▷ *Callie earned time on an educational video game played at home based on the minutes of independent reading she did.*
> ▷ *Her teacher developed a monitoring checklist (see Table 5.2) broken down by subject. She was placed on a reward system and was able to select her reward from a menu of reinforcers that she could earn dependent on her total number of points, which included additional time on the computer, opportunities to assist her teacher, and homework passes. She was required to self-monitor with teacher oversight.*

In my work as a school psychologist in the public school system, individualized behavior and/or self-monitoring plans are often developed for students. Callie's plan had its ups and downs, but her teacher was able to establish that she did not have academic skill deficits, but rather performance deficits. Everyone was motivated by Callie's progress – her teacher, her parents, and most importantly, Callie herself. Her situation shows that interventions in the classroom and at home are often multifaceted and require commitment from all involved parties, especially the child, to be successful. Of course, it is one more thing for a busy parent to monitor but can pay big dividends. It is critical for interventions to be implemented when your daughter first starts having difficulty – not waiting until her self-esteem has been battered, and she has dug herself into a hole where escape will be difficult. If you think your daughter needs a behavior or self-monitoring plan, list it in the **Dynamic Action Treatment Plan** in Chapter 9 with steps you plan to make it happen.

Table 5.2
Self-Monitoring Chart

All Subjects	Good (2)	Fair (1)	Needs Work (0)
Did I have all materials ready and available?			
Did I catch myself daydreaming and bring myself back to my work?			
Reading			
Did I use comprehension strategies when reading?			
Did I reread if the sentence did not make sense?			
Writing			
Did I complete a brief diagram to organize my writing?			
Did I proofread all my writing for complete sentences, punctuation, and capitalization?			
Math			
Did I follow a plan my teacher gave me to solve math word problems?			
Bonus points for kind deeds, extra work, or exceptional behavior:			

Note: From *Raising boys with ADHD* (p. 115) by J. W. Forgan and M. A. Richey (2012). Copyright 2012 by Prufrock Press. Reprinted with permission.

Consistent Expectations between Home and School

Home plays a far more important role than just a place to do home-work (which I'll cover in the next section). In fact, the expectations you set for your daughter at home are as important to her success as anything that happens in the classroom. I recommend that parents extend the concepts of structure, activity, and discipline existing in school into their home. It's important that your daughter understands that school is not the only place she needs to maintain self-control, nor is it the only place where she can depend on a certain amount of structure and sameness. Some things to try include the following:

▷ Provide a structured home setting with a predictable schedule and try to stick to it.

▷ Try to avoid sending your daughter to school tired. She will have to expend so much energy to battle her ADHD during the day and will need reserves.

▷ Help her establish some order in her room, especially for important things. Choose your battles carefully.

▷ Identify a specific place in the house, preferably near the door, for her backpack, lunch box, or anything traveling with her daily to school.

▷ Until she is disciplined enough to keep her backpack, have her empty it every night and put papers in their proper places.

▷ Make a quiet, uncluttered homework space available. Eliciting her help in selecting and creating the space might result in more compliant use. Many girls enjoy adding their own dec-orative touch to the space.

▷ Offer a healthy, balanced diet that is not loaded with processed food.

Whether your daughter likes it or not, daily physical activity and some opportunities to relax and blow off steam and release some excess energy are important. At home, you might try the following:

▷ Make sure that she has ample opportunity for activity. If she tends to be sedentary, don't give up until you find an active outlet that she enjoys. Some parents find that children benefit from running or riding their bike *before* going to school in the mornings.

▷ Make sure your daughter is not overscheduled, so she has ample opportunity for breaks, activity, and sleep. You want to strive for a balance – enough activities for exposure but not an overload.

▷ Try to avoid placing her in situations where the problems associated with her ADHD will be aggravated. Think ahead.

Never presume that because your daughter is in school, it's now her teacher's responsibility to see that she behaves properly. That job is yours as well. It is often critical to establish a system for communicating with her teacher (whether it is via e-mail, notes in the agenda planner, or on a daily behavior log), so you can work as a team to steadily improve your daughter's focus and self-discipline. At home, try to put these practices in place:

▷ Work to understand the difference between willful acts of disobedience and behaviors that are the result of her ADHD and may not be under her control. Deal with them accordingly because open defiance should have definite consequences. Impulsive actions or behaviors caused by her distractibility may provide teachable moments where you can help your daughter develop strategies for dealing with her ADHD.

▷ Try to make sure you are not inadvertently reinforcing her ADHD behaviors. For example, if a girl receives big payoffs for impulsive outbursts by getting what she wants or receives lots of attention for it, the behaviors will be reinforced. Most behaviorists believe you get more of what you pay attention to because most children crave attention, whether it is positive or negative.

▷ Give directions in short, concise sentences, using prompts or visual reminders if memory seems to be an issue.

▷ Provide plenty of positive reinforcement and limit the negatives to the important things. It is important to pick your battles. Remember, your daughter probably gets plenty of negative feedback outside the home. There is a difference between being firm and being overly critical.

▷ Provide consequences within short order of the offending act. Providing them consistently is also key.

Homework

Be honest. Many of you would rather walk over hot coals than try to get your daughter to do her homework, wouldn't you? It's daunting for so many reasons. If your daughter has had a frustrating day at school, she will not look forward to sitting down at a desk again. Frequently, children with ADHD have great difficulty with executive functioning skills like initiating activity, planning, and organizing. They honestly may not even remember what the teacher wants them to do. Children with ADHD often resist settling down to do homework and usually wait until the last minute. Procrastination can reach a new level on large projects, especially long papers and science projects.

> *For Jabari's daughter, homework was a nightly battle. He recognized this as classic ADHD behavior. Homework requires sustained mental effort – a difficulty for children with ADHD. Over time Jabari and his wife found that applying Grandma's Rule worked – Grandma's Rule means you eat your veggies before dessert. In other words, work comes before play. Jabari's daughter had to complete her homework before she could engage in preferred activities.*

> *Her IEP (Individualized Education Plan) also included a reduction in homework as well as receiving her homework early, so she could get started over the weekend. These accommodations helped reduce frustrations.*

Homework can be very stressful. The following guidelines have worked for many families:

▷ Establish ground rules and stick to them. For example, turn off the television and loud music, and don't permit your child to receive telephone calls or text messages during study time.

▷ Figure out the optimal time for homework in your household. Some children need a break after school, and others cannot be corralled after playing outside.

▷ Determine how long your daughter can work without becoming frustrated. Provide frequent activity breaks and/or snacks. Your daughter needs to be willing to return to work after the break is over.

▷ Remember that she may have difficulty figuring out where to start and how to approach different tasks. Help her learn to prioritize tasks so the most difficult and important ones are done first. Guide her in planning and taking one task at a time. You may need to cut assignments into parts, so she doesn't feel overwhelmed.

▷ Provide help when needed, but do not become so involved that your daughter is not independent – a very tricky balance. She is not developing her skills if you are doing the work for her.

▷ Allow her to use the computer or iPad (with teacher permission) for producing written work.

▷ If homework time produces too much unresolved conflict between you and your daughter, consider the services of a tutor (if you can afford it or can find a college or high school student willing to volunteer his or her time).

High-Stakes Testing

In many states, standardized testing plays a role in a school's evaluation and sometimes in whether a student is promoted. These tests are usually 45–90 minutes long, often have a great deal of information on a page, and can be very tedious and boring – clearly not optimal for girls with ADHD. Accountability is critical in school systems, so it is important to help your daughter make the best of the situation. Many school districts have practice tests on the computer, an effective way for a girl with ADHD to learn. Take advantage of practice opportunities if available.

Work to learn more about what is covered on the test and try to incorporate some of those skills into your daily interactions with your daughter. For example, if fractions are on the test, involve her in measuring when cooking or when building a project. If she might be asked to make a prediction about what she thinks may happen in a story, then ask her to make a prediction when watching a television program together.

Many girls with ADHD have heightened anxiety because of what they perceive to be performance deficits or just generalized anxiety. Try to be sensitive to that possibility and help her figure out coping strategies to use when she is anxious, such as breathing deeply or visualizing herself in a peaceful place. You and her teacher will walk a fine line between motivating her to do her best and putting too much pressure on her. If your daughter needs extended time or other accommodations related to her ADHD, a 504 plan or IEP can be considered (see Chapter 8 – "When School Problems Escalate").

Retention

Most studies have not shown benefits to retention. However, it is a decision that must be made based on individual circumstances, the educational environment, and advice from educators and others involved with your daughter. Some questions to ask are:

▷ Does your daughter's birthday make her one of the youngest or oldest children in the class?

▷ Would the retention be likely to produce long-term benefits? Surely the retention year would be easier for her, but what about subsequent years?

▷ Is she delayed in areas other than academics? What are her social skills like? What about her physical size and development?

▷ If she has siblings, how would that impact retention? If she would end up in the same grade as a sibling, sometimes that can cause conflict.

▷ What is the school's recommendation?

▷ If retention seems to be the best option, can you frame it in a positive way to your daughter?

My experience has been that retention is easier on children than their parents. It is a complex decision that must not be taken lightly. Consideration should be given to repercussions for the retention year as well as its impact on the remainder of your daughter's school career.

Janie had been diagnosed with ADHD in second grade and had been responding positively to medication. However, she began struggling in third grade with all academic subjects. This was the first year the results of standardized testing could result in retention. Janie was so frustrated with the lengthy tests because she called them "boring" and was rarely able to finish them in the allotted amount of time. She was in danger of retention, and she knew it. That seemed to fuel her anger. Her parents were upset that recess was being withheld from Janie because she had not completed her work. They felt, and rightly so, that she needed an outlet for her energy.

Her family consulted with Janie's psychiatrist, who advised against any change in medication but recommended an evaluation through the school district to determine if Janie also had a learning disability. The results of the evaluation indicated that she had difficulty with sequential auditory and visual memory as well as deficits in processing speed. All her academic skills were significantly below grade level, and her class work was at her frustration level. The school implemented intensive, research-based interventions targeted to her academic deficits. She made progress but did not reach her academic goals. Janie subsequently qualified for services with a learning disability and received some of her academic instruction in a smaller classroom setting at her instructional level. She received extended time and breaks as needed on standardized testing. Without significant interventions, Janie might have been retained and her interest in school and her academic skills might also have continued their decline without specialized instruction geared toward her learning disability.

What to Do When There's No Progress

Even after diligent research, excellent communication, and support at home and school, your daughter may be struggling too much in her current setting. If you feel she is not learning and/or is miserable, it is important to be proactive. Schedule a conference with the teacher and ask for his or her honest assessment of the situation. Together, brainstorm additional strategies or accommodations that could work. The pullout section in this chapter entitled "Information for Your Teammates: Your Daughter's Teachers" provides good strategies to share if the teacher is open to it. Other fact sheets are available on websites such as www.CHADD.org or other parent support websites.

Inquire if the school has any additional resources that can be tapped. If she currently has a 504 plan, could more supports be added? Or does she need an IEP, where she would receive direct service from an Exceptional Student Education teacher for part of the day or in certain subjects? See Chapter 8 – "When School Problems Escalate" for a thorough discussion of 504 and IEP eligibilities as well as accommodations.

Is there a guidance counselor or school psychologist who could observe your daughter and provide feedback? Sometimes fresh eyes may look at a problem from a different perspective and come up with solutions. Consult with the principal since he or she is the instructional leader of the school.

Occasionally the match between the teacher and your child is just not a good one. Principals are usually reluctant to change children's classrooms in the middle of the year, but some will with good cause. Emphasize your daughter's strengths, needs, and the teaching style that works best for her. Although most principals cannot honor every parent request, many will listen carefully to what you have to say, especially about a child with a disability. It is often helpful to have another person with you when meeting with the principal or school staff. Bring along your spouse, a friend, or even an advocate. Make sure you keep notes of the exchange and follow up with a letter thanking the principal for his or her time and document decisions or commitments made.

If your daughter is on medication, consult with the prescribing doctor to see if adjustments are in order. If a change is made in medication, sign a release for the teacher to communicate directly with the doctor to provide firsthand information about the effects of the medication during the school day.

If no workable solutions are forthcoming, you could explore the advisability of changing schools. This should not be entered into lightly, because stability is important. However, sometimes the school/student match just doesn't produce the desired results and could end up damaging a student's attitude toward learning as well as her mental health. It is important to be cautious about just how much information you share with your daughter in these situations. My experience has been that girls can quickly pick up on their parents' attitudes about teachers and schools, which can color their own thoughts.

Time to Change Schools?

How do you know when it's time to move your daughter to a different school? I know girls with ADHD have their ups and downs but when the bad times far outnumber the good ones, it could be time to change schools.

If your daughter is attending a private elementary school, the choice may not be yours if she is not asked back for another school year. That can throw you into a tailspin! You may feel panicked, disappointed in your daughter or yourself, or discouraged that you must search for another school. If this happens to you, don't blame her. It won't help the situation and will certainly hurt her feelings, reinforce that she failed again, and decrease her self-esteem. Yes, you want to have a straightforward conversation about her work habits, effort, and behavior, but rarely is it 100% your daughter's fault. Emphasize to your daughter that when a school placement does not work out, there are always a combination of factors. For example, some private schools do not have the resources to make as many accommodations as public schools can.

If you've failed in numerous attempts to work with your daughter's teacher and engaged the principal, school psychologist, or guidance counselor to explore all options, and you still sense a growing despair in your daughter, then you may find it in her best interest to learn what other school choices might be open to her.

Ask yourself these questions:

▷ Am I receiving daily (or almost daily) phone calls about my daughter's school behavior or lack of academic progress?

▷ Is most of the feedback I receive from my daughter's teacher or school negative?

▷ Have I been asked to come pick my daughter up early from school on multiple occasions because of behavior or has she been suspended?

▷ Does my daughter say she hates school or feels sick each morning when it's time for school?

▷ Does my daughter's self-esteem seem low? Does she make statements such as, "I'm dumb," "I'm going to drop out of school," "My teacher doesn't like me and neither does anybody else."

▷ Does my gut feeling or intuition tell me it's time for a change?

If you answered yes to most of these questions, it could be time for a change. If so, the next question is, "Where?" There are positives and negatives to any educational setting. Can you afford to send her to a private school? Does she need a special type of school, like one specializing in dyslexia or ADHD? Should you homeschool or consider a virtual school? Often the answer is not obvious or easy. Check out Chapter 8 – "When School Problems Escalate" for more information on different kinds of educational settings.

Barbara's daughter, Judy, attended public school from kindergarten through second grade, and it was generally a good experience. At the end of Judy's kindergarten year, the school wrote a 504 plan, which allowed reasonable accommodations for her ADHD. This plan was helpful because it allowed Judy to stand up and complete her work, be sent on an errand if she appeared to need movement, and not have her recess taken away if she failed to complete her classwork. Judy's second-grade teacher understood that girls with ADHD had difficulty with

---

attention and often required movement. She allowed Judy to have a two-seat option. She was able to work either at her desk or at a table in the back of the room. She enjoyed this option because it provided choice, and at times one seat felt better than the other one.

At the end of second grade, Barbara and her husband, Brent, decided to move Judy to a private school. Although the public school's third grade had a good reputation, they were very concerned about the mandatory third-grade retention if Judy didn't pass the high-stakes state test. At this age, Judy rushed through her work and gave up quickly if the work became too challenging. Barbara believed Judy would rush through the state test, possibly facing mandatory retention if she did poorly.

When considering the move from public to private school, Barbara and Brent weighed the pros and cons. Some aspects in favor of a private school they were considering included:

▷ no mandatory third-grade retention,
▷ smaller class size,
▷ a more accepting environment with less stress,
▷ daily recess,
▷ lots of parent involvement, and
▷ manageable amounts of homework.

For their family, the only drawbacks were paying tuition and providing transportation.

The first private school they visited wasn't a good fit. After Judy took the admissions test, the principal told Barbara and Brent that the school couldn't meet Judy's needs. Although they were disappointed, they kept a positive perspective that they would find the right place for Judy. As it turned out, they located a private school that *offered small classes, structure, and a supportive learning environment. The principal openly accepted Judy and her ADHD and willingly honored the 504 plan that was already in place, allowing a smooth transition between schools. Judy successfully attended this elementary school from third through fifth grades.*

Parent and Student Interview

Background

Cindy is an 11-year-old who is currently in the sixth grade in the same private school she has attended since early elementary school. She generally did well in school, but her teacher noticed she was very inconsistent in her work and often seemed very spacey. Her parents took her to a neuropsychologist who diagnosed her with ADHD and recommended medication for her inattention. Her parents then took her to a psychiatrist who prescribed medication, which is now working well after several changes.

Parent Interview

Q. Can you describe your initial reaction? Did you feel you received helpful information from the diagnostic process?

Cindy was 10 when diagnosed. We were all relieved to find out exactly how her brain processed information. She had high scores on the logic portions of the evaluation and extremely low scores on the "hit a button when you see a certain symbol pop up on the screen" test. It became clear that she was understanding concepts but not able to focus on boring, menial tasks. The doctor who did the evaluation had a long sit down with us and with Cindy to go over the results and explained why she would greatly benefit from medication. This meeting was especially helpful for my husband who, until that time, had been very hesitant to go the medication route. But seeing the stark contrast in results, her knowledge versus her ability to concentrate, made him understand what a disadvantage she was experiencing.

Q. If medication was prescribed, can you elaborate on your thought process on whether or not to medicate?

Then we met with a psychiatrist who explained the medication process in a great way that further highlighted why it was so crucial for Cindy. She said imagine Cindy was on a hike with friends and they all had small daypacks, but Cindy was forced to carry 10x what everyone else had. She said that medication would help lighten this load and put her on an even playing field.

The first medication she tried was Concerta. Then Focalin. We've landed on Jornay which she takes at night, and it's been such a great fit. She sleeps much better and wakes up right when the medication is taking effect. It takes about 10 hours to start to work because it goes into the blood stream in the colon. It's been a huge game changer.

Q. As you learn more about the neurodivergence of the ADHD brain, can you point to any helpful characteristics or behaviors your daughter has that may be a function of her ADHD?

I believe that ADHD has some benefits as well. Before she was medicated, math homework would take an extremely long time. She would have to re-do problems and correct little errors she'd make in her math but her grit and determination to get the right answer was always inspiring.

She daydreams, but these daydreams lead to fascinating, introspective, philosophical questions far beyond the thoughts of her peers. (Why are we here? Are we all just a collection of memories? etc.) She can hyperfocus on things she's interested in like graphic design, writing, painting etc.

Q. What changes have you made at home that seem to help her days go more smoothly?

We have put more alarms and checklists in place to help remember things. We have tried a variety of calendars, but the alarm app on the iPad works best. We also have a physical checklist in the car and don't leave the driveway in the morning before going through the list (homework, lunch, musical instrument, etc.). Same thing when she gets in the car after school. I ask, what's your homework? (but I already know because I can access it from the school app) and then go through each book to make sure she has it. This year, however, the teachers have given me an extra set of textbooks to keep at home. They also let her listen to audio books when she wants to instead of reading.

Q. What are your biggest concerns about ADHD going forward?

Our biggest concerns are that she will internalize that there is something "wrong" with her. Also, I worry about the long-term effects of being on a medication. Will she always have to be on this medication? I think I had (have) ADHD but have learned or come up with so many coping strategies. Are we doing too much for her? Should she be learning how to clean her locker, keep track of her own assignments, set her own alarms, etc.?

Student Interview

Q. Discuss some of your experiences with teachers and their understanding or lack of understanding of ADHD.

In Spanish I normally forget my book a lot and the teacher would get mad at me. If I left behind a notebook I had to go and get it and wasn't allowed to just take notes on a piece of paper.

Q. If any of your teachers have done things that have really helped you manage your ADHD, can you please share those?

In the beginning of fifth grade I was allowed to use fidgets, but then I realized they didn't help me. Then in math I could use graph paper with bigger squares. One time in math I kept really straight organized notes, and the teacher put them up on the board to show others how to keep organized notes.

When I take tests, I go into another quiet room. During the standardized tests, I can listen to the questions read out loud.

Q. If you take medication, please discuss your experience with it – benefits and side effects if there were any. How does it make you feel? Do you take it on weekends and holidays?

The first medicine hurt my stomach and I didn't eat. It was too strong. The second one hurt my stomach. It wasn't strong but I didn't have any good effects from it. The third medication doesn't hurt my stomach and I don't notice any bad side effects, but it really helps me to focus. It also helps me sleep.

> **Q. Who told you about your diagnosis? Do you remember your initial reaction? How do you feel about it now?**
>
> I remember my initial reaction was "huh, ok." I wasn't that surprised because my mom told me I might have it and that's why I was getting tested. But I was happy to get help.

Home and Community Issues

You know by now that your daughter doesn't leave her ADHD at school. She faces challenges at home, around the neighborhood, and in most activities she pursues because ADHD permeates all areas of a girl's life. It is very common for girls with ADHD to have difficulties when interacting with their siblings and peers.

Helping Her Take Responsibility for Her Actions

Asking your daughter the question, "*Why* did you do that?" after she has caused a problem at home is rarely helpful. I like the advice from Wright (2009), an attorney and parent of two successful boys with ADHD and learning disabilities. He wrote,

> When my children misbehaved or messed up, I never asked them, "Why did you …?" When the parent asks a child "why," the child learns to create good excuses, shifts blame onto others, views himself or herself as a "victim of circumstances" – and does not

learn to take responsibility for his or her behavior. (Wright, 2009)

He suggests asking them what they did, what they are going to do about it, and what consequences would help them remember not to do it again. It is important to help them become responsible for their behavior and believe they have control over it.

Encouraging an Environment of Respect

Consider establishing this primary family rule: "Treat others with respect." This directive must come from parents; after all, you are the head of the family. Your message must be, "We are a family. We treat each other nicely and we support each other." Teaching mutual respect starts with you, the parent. Model it and live it – and that means treating your children with respect and requiring that they treat you and one another with respect as well. Your daughter must know what it looks and feels like. Establish it as a theme in every family talk, especially when that discussion involves conflict. If this message isn't firmly established during the elementary years, adolescent years can be very difficult.

Name-Calling

Name-calling is one type of disrespectful behavior you're likely to have to address with all your children, but your daughter with ADHD may need extra patience in learning that ugly names are absolutely not part of your family's vocabulary. This means you, your daughter, or siblings shouldn't ever call each other a mean or profane name. Agree on consequences and enforce them.

This is one of my colleague's most important family rules. In addition to offering a sincere apology to the offended person who was called a derogatory name, the offending child had to pay that person $1. It simply wasn't to be tolerated, and this consequence really made the "treat each other with respect" rule hit home.

Siblings

If your daughter with ADHD has brothers and sisters, you have experienced times when they fight like cats and dogs and other times they laugh like best friends. Forming solid, civil relationships may not come easily to many girls with ADHD, especially if they have trouble with self-regulation and impulsivity. Home is usually where children with ADHD feel safest because of the unconditional love within a family, so it is the perfect place for them to learn to form appropriate interpersonal relationships.

It is helpful if siblings have some understanding of the obstacles ADHD can bring, like impulsivity, self-regulation difficulties, and disorganization. They need to understand that some activities of daily living that develop automatically for some require more work and coaching for those with ADHD. This understanding will hopefully make them less resentful of the additional time you might need to spend with your daughter with ADHD and more understanding of their sister's behavior, which will probably be annoying at times. When you see your children getting along, don't take it for granted. Make sure to compliment them in hopes of seeing more of it.

Occasionally, sibling disagreements become so intense that the situation requires the help of a mental health counselor, family therapist, or psychologist. Family discord often makes everyone feel miserable, and this feeling spills over into your daughter's life at school and everywhere she goes. Often within a half-dozen or so sessions, a well-trained counselor can help get your family back on the right track. In my experience, the time and money you spend working with a professional is time and money invested in family harmony.

Friendships and Social Situations

Some girls with ADHD are gifted communicators. If your daughter has this talent, continue to develop it, because it will carry her far in life. However, many girls with ADHD have communication and social difficulties because they speak before they think – which tends to get them in hot water. Other girls with ADHD seem to have difficulty processing language, which impacts their social skills. Many girls with ADHD just aren't aware of how others perceive them. They may act as if they have no filters, not thinking about how their questions or remarks will make the other person feel. One time a client said to a bald-headed colleague, "I like your head. How'd you get it so shiny?" Another one asked me, "How did you get so old?" Often, whatever is on their mind just comes out. This lack of inhibition can cause some embarrassing moments. Girls with ADHD often don't have the little voice in their minds that reminds them, "Don't say that, because it could hurt someone's feelings," or they don't pause long enough to listen if they do have that little voice. They don't hold back their automatic thoughts. The words or actions just happen. The next time your daughter gets into trouble by acting before thinking and you ask, "Why did you do that?" and hear her reply, "I don't know," she's probably telling you the truth. It just happened.

Many girls with ADHD benefit from structured play dates with one child at a time where a specific activity is the focus. Depending on the level of your daughter's social skills, it might be helpful to role play some of the situations that might occur. Some children benefit from reading books and stories about how other children interact. As she gains more skills, allow her to help plan social activities with others her age. If you can help her improve her social competency, you will have helped her develop a gift of immeasurable value.

Whenever conflicts with other children arise, you need to listen to your daughter with ADHD. She is often telling you the truth. Over time, you can learn to recognize when she is being honest or when she hasn't perceived the situation in its entirety. As a parent, watch your daughter for nonverbal cues and pay attention to her actions as well as her words.

Believe it or not, lying is not unusual in children with ADHD and doesn't mean they are dishonest. Often children with ADHD can't believe they have actually done what they are being accused of because they certainly didn't intend to do it. Other times, they are too embarrassed to own up to it because it doesn't fit with who they try to be. Or they may be too frightened of the consequences to come clean about it.

Guide your daughter to be accountable for her actions, but if she is impulsive help her understand that sometimes things happen that she didn't intend. The only thing to do then is apologize and problem solve, perhaps with you, how she can avoid a similar situation in the future. We all make mistakes and try to learn to do better next time. If your daughter seems to make more than her share, spend time processing the situations with her and help her come up with alternative solutions.

If you feel your daughter has deficits in the social skills that are affecting her in the community, review the resources for improving social skills mentioned earlier in this chapter in the section on schools entitled "Your Daughter's Peers." Another option is a game called Angry Animals 2 from Creative Therapy Store. It has characters with funny animal names like Mad Mercat, and has the players select cards with scenarios of social situations and choices for how to handle the situation. Children enjoy this game and learn that there are different options for responding to every situation.

Some elementary girls have their own cell phones. Monitoring cell phone use, text messages, or any form of social media for inappropriate contacts or conversations will be important. Cyberbullying, discussed in more detail in the next chapter, can happen even in elementary school. Help your daughter realize how important it is for her to let you know when peers are being inappropriate on the internet. Make sure your daughter understands your position on cell phone and social media use and review them frequently.

Sports

Some girls with ADHD are naturally athletic and excel in physical activities, like dancing, cheerleading, gymnastics, and sports. It becomes a natural outlet for showcasing their talents. Competing in activities may help your daughter with ADHD build a sense of accomplishment that could be missing from academics. These activities provide your daughter with focus, structure, and discipline. One of my colleague's young clients struggled academically throughout elementary and middle school but always excelled in sports. During high school, she was so accomplished that she was the top player on her softball team and landed a college scholarship playing softball. This young woman's motivation to play softball was instrumental in helping her maintain her grade point average for athletic eligibility.

One of my clients had amazing agility and loved climbing on playground equipment. Gymnastics was a natural outlet for excess energy, provided a vehicle for making friends, and kept her interested in school. She knew she didn't like sitting at a desk in class, but her love for recess and physical education made the school day worthwhile in her eyes.

It is becoming increasingly clear that daily physical activity pays big dividends for everyone, but it can be especially important for your daughter's well-being. Even if she is inclined to be a "couch potato" or is not very coordinated, expose her to different sports opportunities from a young age. As soon as she is eligible, enroll her in organized youth activities. Try dance, T-ball, basketball, golf, tennis, roller or ice hockey, swimming, running, or martial arts. Once you find an activity where she has an interest and natural talent, build upon it. It does not matter whether it is a group or individual sport. Many girls I have worked with have been helped tremendously by karate and dance, which stress listening, discipline, respect, and following directions. Compliment your daughter's athletic ability in front of others. Remember to tell her you are proud of her and encourage her to stick with her chosen activities and practice.

An elementary school I served as a school district psychologist has a running club modeled after a national program called Girls on the Run. Girls meet with several faculty members after school and run several miles. Several girls with ADHD benefited tremendously from this burst of activity after school. They were better able to focus later on homework and established camaraderie with other children in the running club.

The tendency for many girls with ADHD is to jump from sport to sport because having a short attention span is part of their disorder. They find a sport and become passionate about it but lose interest just as quickly. You can be the one to help your daughter persevere, at least until the season is over. Although quitting is often the easy way out, it does not build her character. Even if your daughter believes she is the worst player on the team, don't let her bail on her team. Let your daughter earn the feeling of accomplishment and satisfaction that comes from sticking it out until the end of the season. Pushing through tough times goes against everything she naturally wants to do, but she needs to develop this ability for success in school and sports.

Not every girl with ADHD is going to find a sport she is willing to play. If your daughter has tried group and individual sports but still does not have the knack for any of them, then look for talents in other areas to nurture. Even though physical activity may not be a preference, it is still important for her to have some physical outlet in her daily routine, such as walking, swimming, jumping rope, skating, or doing yoga.

Camps

Attending a day or sleep-away camp can build your daughter's confidence. Camps that offer outdoor or hands-on activities during the summer can be a welcome change from the rigor of academics during the school year. Recreational, Scout, and religious camps can all provide good lessons in being organized and keeping up with her belongings. Some girls may not be emotionally ready to sleep away from home or be as independent as sleep-away camps require, so local day camps might be a better idea. Check your local community for opportunities.

When carefully chosen, camps can boost self-esteem by providing opportunities for making new friendships and developing new skills. You know your daughter best and understand the type of camp she'd enjoy most. However, it takes due diligence on your part to locate just the right type of camp for your daughter. Sure, any parent can sign their daughter up for a camp and send her off, but it's different for girls with ADHD. You know her camp must be just the right fit, have the right type of activities, number of children, the best staff, and structure – or it could be a disaster. She'll come home early, say she hates camp, won't want to return, and give you a hard time. You know that if she feels miserable, some of it is going to rub off on you too.

In addition to more typical summer sleep-away camps, some locations offer therapeutic camps for children whose ADHD requires more assistance than the average camp might offer. Bob Field operates the California-based, multisite Quest Therapeutic Camps for children with ADHD and other associated disorders. If you choose a therapeutic camp for your daughter, you want to make sure it offers a process like what Field describes below.

In a personal correspondence, Field explained that his Quest camps are fun for kids. He relies on parental input and an individual screening assessment to develop an individualized treatment plan that helps address a camper's most consequential problematic behaviors. The campers identify and understand specific behavioral goals. Using camp activities, therapy staff can observe difficulties as they occur and provide interventions right then and there. Counselors are advanced college or graduate students trained to help campers gain awareness as behaviors occur. In addition, during each hour of the day, campers receive specific staff feedback about the positive and negative aspects of their behavior. Campers are awarded points each hour based on their effort. As a camper progresses, higher points require increased effort, developing greater success. Combining a cognitive behavioral therapy approach and specially developed neurocognitive strategies, Quest's small-group therapy sessions facilitate the individualized goals of each camper. This model has been proven to successfully address problematic behaviors and help campers develop appropriate social skills.

Before you send your daughter to either a day or sleep-away camp, you need to think about a few important considerations:

1 What is the camper-to-counselor ratio?
2 Do the schedule and activities seem to be a good fit for your daughter?

3 How are discipline and interpersonal conflict between campers handled?

4 What steps are in place to help children who have difficulty making friends?

If you are considering a sleep-away camp, try to talk to the camp director or staff to answer some of these questions:

1 Who keeps and administers her medication?

2 What happens if there is a medical emergency?

3 Are electronics allowed and monitored?

4 How can I communicate with my daughter?

5 What efforts are made to help children make friends?

6 What if she wants to come home early?

In addition to thoroughly researching and selecting the best choice for your daughter, mentally and emotionally prepare her for the experience. As mentioned previously, girls with ADHD do not like unexpected change. Explain what a typical day at camp would be like. If the facility is located close to your home, stop by, and introduce her to the director. Try to anticipate her feelings on the first day of camp and give her words of encouragement that she can replay in her mind through the day. If your daughter is nervous about new situations and does not know any other campers, you might say something like, "On the first day of camp, a lot of kids won't know anyone. They may not look nervous on the outside, but I'll bet they feel nervous inside. Remember that and talk to lots of kids, because they are hoping they meet a good friend like you." These types of simple steps set your daughter up for a successful camp experience.

Phones/Video/Computer/Online Games

While technology makes our life easier in many ways, video games and smart phones add another layer of complexity to parenting. They are often the source of many battles between parents and daughters about proper use and privacy concerns. They can be addictive and an academic distraction. That being said, probably every parent of an elementary-age girl has heard the refrain, "All my friends have them." Navigating this battle requires educating your daughter about the benefits and risks, using parental controls, and consideration of being their friend on social media if she is allowed to use it. If you don't think cell phones are appropriate for your daughter, there is some support from a national campaign called "Wait Until 8th" with a pledge that empowers parents to wait until their child is in eighth grade before giving them a cell phone.

Many girls like virtual online games, some of which have strong parental controls. Games, like Minecraft with virtual LEGO-type figures, offer the opportunity to connect with other users via the Internet in a multiplayer mode or in chat rooms. Games often give children feelings of control and success. They can also allow some children an opportunity to decompress from a hard day at school. The fast-paced stimulation feels great to a child with ADHD but also has the potential to be addictive.

Whether or not girls with ADHD should be allowed to play video or online games is a personal decision. Some parents ban their children from playing all games except those with an "E" rating for "everyone." I do not endorse allowing girls to play without limits or play without some supervision. In this day and time, it is important for you to know what your daughter is playing and with whom she is interacting. Remember that being impulsive and naïve can lead to bad choices.

Research is mixed on the value of video games for children. Many parents allow some time to play video or online games because they can be a great reinforcement for good behavior. There are countless times when I have heard parents say, "If you want to play your game, then I need your help doing so and so," or, "If you finish your homework without arguing, then you can play your game for 30 minutes." As outlined in Table 5.3, video games have pros and cons. Personally, I suggest limiting video game time to a maximum of 2 hours on the

Table 5.3
Pros and Cons of Video Games

Pros	Cons
Can be used as a reinforcement tool.	May hyper-focus on the game.
Some games promote physical or mental exercise.	Some games are violent.
Can develop eye-hand coordination.	May become emotional or defiant when it's time to stop.
May become a hobby that leads to employment.	Video games can be expensive.
May build focus and concentration.	May spend too much time gaming.
May build feelings of success.	May engage in less physical activity and have fewer opportunities for socialization.

Note. From *Raising Boys With ADHD* (p. 137) by J. W. Forgan & M. A. Richey (2012). Copyright 2012 by Prufrock Press. Reprinted with permission.

weekend and 30–60 minutes on weekdays, if at all. I do not endorse allowing children to play without limits.

Clearly defining the amount of game time, rules for stopping, and consequences for arguing about it are important. Children with ADHD don't like new rules or things sprung on them, so with video games, and in everything you do, try to establish guidelines and procedures beforehand.

> *One mother called me out of desperation at trying to manage her 11-year-old daughter. Her bedroom was in the basement of their home, and they had allowed her to have her computer there. Whenever a parent entered*

the daughter's room, she quickly changed screens or interrupted her play. They also noticed her daughter's language had become more aggressive and surlier. Her dad asked if he could play one of the games with her. Of course, she refused. They didn't like what they were seeing and decided to set some strong rules on video gaming.

Luckily their daughter was still young enough that exercising control to make change was not too difficult. She was invited to participate in setting the guidelines for computer usage but did so very grudgingly. When she realized they were very serious about moving her computer from the basement to the first floor family living area, she finally agreed to participate in helping select and set up an area for her computer. Parents established parental controls on all games. She was allowed access to only some online games, which parents were able to view at any time. They helped her understand good online safety rules and limited her play to when homework was done with longer playing times on the weekend. It was a painful process, but they were glad they caught the situation early enough to do something about it.

Children are becoming increasingly savvy about technology. As daunting as it may seem, it is your parental responsibility to stay abreast of the latest trends in social media and how to utilize parental controls to monitor how your daughter is connecting with others. Many handheld devices can limit or time children as they play. It is important to know the passwords your daughter uses on social media or online accounts. Spend time with her making sure she is clear about how to recognize intimidation, bullies, and predators over the Internet.

Physical and Emotional Health

Emotional/Behavioral Developmental Milestones

Along the way, your daughter is maturing a little bit every day, albeit more slowly than children without ADHD. Girls with ADHD often have great difficulty with regulating emotions and with self-control. To keep tabs on your daughter's progress, try to have some awareness of when these developments occur in the general population. Of course, you will want to keep in mind that your daughter may be two to three years behind these milestones in her development. Based on research and child development theory, consider the following stages of development (Teeter, 1998):

▷ **Ages 6–9**: Self-control improves and more internal thinking develops.

▷ **Middle childhood**: Children are influenced by and use standards set by parents.

▷ **Ages 7 and up**: Self-talk guides behavior and enables children to take the perspective of others.

▷ **Ages 6–12**: Children become more adept at regulating emotional reactions to situations.

▷ **Ages 10–12**: Children are better able to control negative feelings and separate actions from feelings.

Metacognition

Metacognition is often described as "thinking about thinking." It can be encouraged in elementary-age children to enable them to monitor their behavior, learning, and impact on others. They use their verbal inner language to accomplish this complex task involving self-reflection. It is a powerful way for them to build resilience by moving from giving up to thinking about how they can accomplish a difficult task.

Stowell explains

> Metacognition allows students to stand back and evaluate their responses and actions so they can consciously change their behavior or make better choices. Students with ADHD tend to be impulsive, reacting first and thinking later. They may be moving so fast physically or mentally that they don't have time to register feedback. As a result, they may be unaware that they are failing a course, have not started a project on time, or have inadvertently hurt someone's feelings. (Stowell, 2021, p. 295)

One way to help develop this is to consciously talk to them about what they are doing and ask questions about their choices, like: "How did you decide which homework assignment to do first?" "Who did you decide to invite to the party?" and "How did that guest list work out?" When they are stuck on a difficult task, ask, "What part of this task is frustrating for you?" "How can you work around it?" "What has helped you in the past when you were feeling like that?" Often when girls give up on tasks, they tend to think they are not smart enough to do it which is an example of a "fixed" mindset. Ideally you want them to develop a "growth" mindset, whereby they don't see the task as a measure of their intelligence but as an opportunity to show what they know at that one point in time. If they feel they have not been successful, they can regroup and try a different strategy next time.

Self-Esteem

Think about your daughter's self-esteem. Does she appear to feel good about herself or is she feeling incapable of doing most things she thinks are expected of her? Sometimes unwittingly, adults and even peers bombard girls with ADHD with negative criticism, thinking they are helping her to do better. This only reinforces her poor self-image, which permeates all areas of her life. When my children brought home graded school papers, I always focused on the things that were marked wrong –thinking I was helping them. Years later, they talked about how it made them feel for me to focus on their mistakes and not even mention all the correct items.

If your daughter's self-esteem appears solid, you are fortunate. Her self-esteem will help provide her with the confidence she needs to navigate life. Continue to nurture her self-esteem, because it can give her a sense of resiliency, which she'll need to bounce back when she has a setback or challenge. Girls who do not develop a strong sense of self in elementary school may become overly sensitive and retiring as teens, making them a target for being ostracized or bullied. Good self-esteem will allow her to stand up, brush herself off, and try again – a key to success. This is an invaluable quality to develop. If you want to learn more about instilling this sense of resiliency in your daughter, I recommend *Raising Resilient Children: Fostering Strength, Hope, and Optimism in Your Child* by Brooks and Goldstein, because it is full of ideas for developing resiliency and self-esteem. *The Girl Guide* by Christine Fonseca is also a valuable resource, written for girls ages 10–14.

If your daughter has low self-esteem, it can stifle her decision-making ability. Some girls with ADHD can't make even the simplest decisions, like what to wear. If your daughter thinks poorly of herself, then over time she may become anxious, frustrated, or depressed. These depressed thoughts create malaise and lack of motivation, which lead to poor performance. Unchecked, it can become a difficult cycle to end.

If your daughter has low self-esteem, her automatic reaction to a new task that appears challenging is probably, "I can't." For many girls with ADHD, this "I can't" attitude turns into what is called "learned helplessness." Your daughter learns that it benefits her to become helpless. This develops over time, because when your daughter automatically says, "I can't," many parents and teachers spring to complete the task for her. What you must do is determine if your daughter's problem is an "*I can't*" or an "*I won't*" type of problem. This allows you to decide how quickly you should step in to help. If it is an "*I won't*" problem, then you need to wait and let her try to work through it on her own. If the problem is "*I can't*," then you should step in, provide instruction or some scaffolding support, and step away to let her try. You want your daughter to develop an "*I can*" and "*I will*" attitude.

You can help strengthen your daughter's self-esteem by giving her honest affirmations in front of others. False or inflated praise isn't helpful because she will probably realize it isn't valid and lose trust in what you say. So often we correct our daughters around other people, but we affirm them much less. Regardless of her age, your daughter needs to hear your encouragement and positive reinforcement, and she needs others to hear you giving it to her. She needs to hear statements like, "I'm proud of you. Your performance was awesome". or "You have a great heart. I love you." If parents don't affirm their daughter in this way, then she may find another way to get that affirmation, possibly from peers or by engaging in dangerous behaviors. Build your child up by telling family or friends a positive story about her, send them an e-mail with a photo or a great story about her, or simply send her a note in her lunch box that she can read.

These are additional suggestions you can use to help develop your daughter's self-esteem:

  ▷ When age appropriate, explain her ADHD, including her strengths and challenges, in a way she can understand it. (If you need some suggestions about what to say, check out Chapter 2 – "Diagnosis for ADHD.")

  ▷ Read age-appropriate books about self-esteem with your daughter. Search online booksellers with keywords such as "self-esteem children." Some good choices might include: *Don't Put Yourself Down in Circus Town* by Frank Sileo (ages 4–8), *Being Me: A Kid's Guide to Boosting Confidence and Self-Esteem* by Wendy Moss (ages 8–13), *Nobody's Perfect* by Ellen Flanagan Burns (ages 9–12), and *My Diary: The Totally True Story of Me!* By Gilles Tibo (ages 8–12).

  ▷ Try to help her have incremental successes and acknowledge her efforts leading to success.

  ▷ Engage her in extracurricular activities (e.g., music, art, drama, sports, computers) where she can find success.

▷ Be aware of your positive-to-negative comment ratio and increase your genuine praise.

▷ Comment on her positive qualities rather than her negative ones.

▷ Try to reduce family conflict by establishing routine, consistency, and structure.

▷ Help her identify and build at least one good friendship.

▷ Try to help her establish a positive relationship with her teacher.

▷ Identify a mentor (e.g., at school, or within a club or other organization) who takes a special interest in your daughter and helps build her up.

▷ Work with a counselor if you feel she would benefit from professional help in building her self-esteem.

Activity/Physical Exercise

Make sure to build in physical exercise daily, if possible, preferably something she would enjoy and find relaxing. Serotonin, a neurotransmitter related to happiness, is boosted through exercise. Some people think that exercise in the morning, prior to school, is important if time and schedule permit.

Healthy Diet

Even girls in elementary school can start to show signs of an eating disorder, so be aware of significant changes over time of your daughter's food intake, increase in food selectiveness, or obsession about exercise. Don't ignore any red flags and bring them to your pediatrician's attention.

References

Forgan, J. W., & Richey, M. A. (2012). *Raising boys with ADHD: Secrets for parenting successful, happy sons.* Prufrock Press.

Goldstein, S. (2004). *What do we want from children with ADHD? Keeping a moving target in mind.* www.samgoldstein.com/cms/index.php/2004/09/what-do-we-want-from-children-with-adhd

Stowell, J. (2021). *Take the stone out of the shoe: A must-have guide to understanding, supporting, and correcting dyslexia, learning, and attention challenges.* Green Dot Press.

Teeter, P. A. (1998). *Interventions for ADHD: Treatment in developmental context.* Guilford Press.

Wright, P. (2009). *Four rules for raising children.* www.wrightslaw.com/nltr/09/nl.0106.htmhttp

Points to Consider

1. You can expect the elementary years to be challenging for you and your daughter. The demands of school shine a new spotlight on her deficits in executive functioning skills and her difficulties with behavior, attention, and social skills. Do you recognize any of these weaknesses?

2. Are you keeping a problem-solving perspective? Seek professional help when necessary and never give up.

3. How involved are you? Your daughter needs you to be involved at school to advocate for her and to work with her teachers to create interventions that will help her succeed at this critical time in her life.

4. Because your daughter is different than every other girl with ADHD, she requires interventions tailored to her needs. What do you have in place for her?

5. Is your daughter in a school and classroom where her needs are being met?

6. Your daughter's challenges spill over into family and community life. Are you helping her be her best self?

7. How is your daughter's self-esteem? What steps are you taking to develop her confidence? Are you providing supports to help her grow in her ability to self-regulate her behavior?

8   Review your self-assessment responses to decide if there are any areas where you still need to learn more.

Action Steps to Take Now

1   If you have not already done so, establish daily or weekly communication with your daughter's teacher.
2   Monitor your daughter's academic progress. Supplement where necessary.
3   Make sure you have a workable homework plan in place.
4   Try some of the techniques in this chapter to create a healthy home and community environment for your daughter.
5   Work on Step 2 and Step 3 in the **Dynamic Action Treatment Plan** in Chapter 9.

Chapter 6

The Middle School Years

SELF-ASSESSMENT: Where Am I Now?

Each self-assessment helps you reflect on your daughter and your parenting practices and is a preview of the chapter's content.

1 When I think about my daughter, and where she is in her physical development, I believe …

   a I have done all I can to prepare her for the changes that will take place in her body.

   b I keep putting off discussions about puberty because I think she won't want to hear it.

   c I think my discomfort with the whole discussion will impact the result.

   d I am going to find some helpful resources and figure out a time to start the discussion.

2 My daughter's social-emotional skills are …
   a immature for her age.
   b one of her strongest areas.
   c definitely impacting her friendships, causing her to be left out often.
   d in need of support from a social skills group or therapist.
3 When I think about the demands on my daughter's organizational skills in middle school …
   a I think she is as prepared as she can be.
   b I know she will need teacher support which we have addressed in a plan. I will stay in close communication with her teachers.
   c I have no idea but haven't heard anything from the school and figure no news is good news.
   d I am currently trying to find an executive functioning coach or a tutor her improve her skills to make her life easier.
4 My daughter's behavior at home …
   a is tolerable.
   b creates havoc on most days.
   c is far better than I imagined given what I know about adolescent girls in today's world.
   d is something we are working on now through family meetings, chore lists, and incentives.
5 When I think about any special interests or passions my daughter may have, I realize …
   a she has not yet found them.
   b they boost her self-esteem immensely and compensate for some of the difficulties she faces in the classroom.
   c I need to expose her to more things to help her find things that capture her attention.
   d she is very resistant to any efforts I make to help her find her interests.

You suddenly realize your daughter is changing. Her body is starting to change. Her emotions are changing, sometimes from minute to minute. She's entering that unfamiliar, oftentimes unsettling phase of life – adolescence. The timeline is variable, but it is happening to most girls at earlier and earlier ages. You're beginning to get more and more frequent glimpses of the young woman your daughter is becoming. She's growing out of her little-girl body, and that's as beautiful as it is unsettling – maybe to both of you. She wants independence, possibly more than you think she can handle. You worry for her well-being, both physically and emotionally, as her world gets bigger.

Your daughter's adolescence will be filled with new experiences and responsibilities. If she is attending a public or private school, imagine her walking down the hall of her new middle school. The hallways are covered with posters for clubs she can join. It's loud. Inside each classroom there's a different teacher, and she knows the work is going to be harder and more challenging. Her interest in friendships and possibly romantic relationships may be growing. She's got a locker, and she must remember where it is, the combination, and which books and notebooks to bring to which class. She's nervous. Or excited. Or scared. Or confused. Or all those things. If she is home schooled or attending virtual school, she will have a different set of challenges. She will have to juggle multiple teachers and assignments. Online and technology temptations can use up her academic time. Loneliness and social isolation may become a factor. However, your adolescent daughter is receiving her education, there will likely be issues to be solved.

Adolescence these days can be extremely challenging on many fronts. On the global front, there is instability among countries and in politics and health care. On an individual front preteens and teens may struggle with family and/or economic instability, the impact of social media, constant bombardment with information, stress of standardized testing and school pressures, insecurities about their future, gender and sexuality issues, and many other concerns.

It goes without saying that it is a critical time for you to stay closely tuned in to your daughter. Because she has ADHD, you already know change can be a challenge for her. This is the time in her life when all her familiar routines may be upset. As schoolwork gets more challenging and demands grow greater, the performance gap between students with ADHD and peers without ADHD tends to widen. She'll need to develop new strategies for success, and she'll need your help and support to guide her toward independence – even though she may not realize it! When she tries to push you away, figure out ways to strengthen your relationship so she will be comfortable confiding in you when she doesn't know where to turn. Hopefully, you and she can form a strong team with open communication to stay ahead of the many challenges that are likely to come her and your way.

You can expect this to be a time of tremendous growth, but not just for your daughter. As she learns to become more independent, your role transitions as well. You'll continue to be her biggest fan, her advisor, and her sounding board. But now, it's also your job to look for ways to start letting go. What a scary thought, right?

If Your Daughter Was Recently Diagnosed

For many girls, ADHD isn't formally diagnosed until their tweens or teens. As you've already learned, girls with ADHD are much more difficult to spot than hyperactive boys because they tend to be quieter and better able to mask the kinds of difficulties ADHD causes.

If your daughter is newly diagnosed, ADHD is a new world for you and her. Neither of you have had years to implement the strategies or routines known to help girls with ADHD in a complex world. She may have a range of emotions that may include being scared or angry because this is the time when she wants to mix in with peers and not stand out or be different. Or she may be relieved to know the root of her challenges. At the debriefing meeting where she received her diagnosis, seventh grader Ellen said, "I always knew there was something. I'm just glad I'm not dumb." The results seemed to validate her inner inkling that she needed more support.

If Your Daughter Is Twice Exceptional – Gifted with ADHD and/or a Learning Disability

In elementary school, many girls who are gifted can stay afloat because their intelligence allows them to compensate for difficulties with attention and academics. They may struggle socially but their academic standing in the classroom could be a self -esteem booster. By middle school, much more focus is required and the demands for organization and the ability to juggle many complex tasks at the same time increase. While they may have considered themselves to be very bright in elementary school, they may now find themselves falling behind peers in classwork and having to work longer and harder for less than stellar results. Now they are no longer viewed as smart by peers and may likely question their ability themselves. They may ask themselves, "If I am so smart, why can't I handle middle school?" So not only do they have to make all the adjustments others have to make to middle school, but they also have to figure out how to shore up their self-esteem so they don't get down on themselves, which could lead to a host of other problems.

Parents I have worked with often don't recognize their gifted daughter could have difficulties with attention and focus or some academic deficits because she had always done so well. If your daughter was successful in elementary school and is floundering in middle school, you and she should begin the search for the root cause. Many times bright girls have amazing insight if given the opportunity to share. Don't hesitate to ask for a meeting with her teachers to gain more insight into her struggles and determine if some more in-depth evaluations are needed. Hopefully, together you can help her get back on the right track.

Girls who are gifted and have ADHD and/or a learning disability are *twice exceptional* (2E). Their cognitive profile may contain very strong areas as well as weak areas, making some *academic* tasks frustrating and difficult for them.

> *Lakisha was at the top of her class in math, a source of pride for her. She knew she wasn't a strong reader but could always use context to make sense of what she was reading. She was easily accepted as a smart kid. Even though she often found herself daydreaming in class, concepts were easy for her to grasp.*
>
> *In middle school, she signed up for advanced math and language arts. She could never finish the long reading assignments because she would lose focus, forget where she left off and need to reread the material. In math she had trouble remembering the sequential steps required to solve complex problems. She failed her first history test because she forgot to study. Luckily, her parents noticed a huge change in her demeanor and sleeping patterns. She confided in them that she had never felt so lost and couldn't understand why she wasn't as smart as she had been in elementary school.*
>
> *Luckily her parents had a trusted pediatrician who was very knowledgeable about the challenges of adolescence. After a talk with Lakisha, she asked Lakisha, her parents and two teachers to complete rating scales. Lakisha was showing signs of depression but also of inability to stay focused in the classroom. Teachers noted her disorganization, need for additional time to complete assignments, and daydreaming in class. Lakisha was diagnosed with ADHD, inattentive presentation. Her parents took the information to the school and asked for a meeting of her*

teachers to discuss her lack of progress and most import-
antly, what could be done to support her as she made this
transition to middle school.

Her teachers were surprised to learn Lakisha was
gifted. Lakisha felt like her intelligence had failed her, but
her nemesis was her previously undiagnosed ADHD. A 504
plan was written which provided for more teacher support
in helping Lakisha with organization, understanding what
was required on her assignments, extended time, and cues
to stay focused when important information was going to
be provided. The guidance counselor invited Lakisha to
join a group of other girls with ADHD, which enabled her
to express her feelings of being overwhelmed and to
meet girls who were also figuring out how to manage
their ADHD in middle school. Her parents, her pediatri-
cian, and teachers continued to monitor her progress with
these accommodations to see if additional treatment was
needed.

ADHD and Executive Function

In elementary school the focus is often on the child with lots of
support from teachers and parents. In middle school the focus moves
away from the student and onto the curriculum with many different
demands from a variety of teachers. Even students without ADHD
often have trouble with the transition. With ADHD it's likely your
daughter may have trouble remembering all the details involved in
her day, paying attention, organizing her time, and/or regulating her
emotions. Middle school and life in general for an adolescent require
lots of executive functioning skills – memory, attention, organization,
planning, self-awareness and self-control – the very things that can be
so difficult when you have ADHD.

Middle school and life in general for an adolescent require lots of executive functioning skills – memory, attention, organization, planning, self-awareness and self-control – the very things that can be so difficult when you have ADHD.

Consider this notion: The act of paying attention is the result of an intricate and complicated interaction among many regions of the brain, like the prefrontal cortex, basal ganglia, central cortex, and anterior cingulate cortex. These areas have been shown to be smaller in size, less active, and less mature in children with ADHD when compared to those without ADHD and are responsible for executive functioning.

As you can imagine, the topic of executive function skills is very complex and the subject of entire books. There is not complete agreement about what skills should be labeled executive functioning skills. It is a dynamic area of study that continues to evolve. Most agree executive functioning skills are those abilities needed to get tasks accomplished. Some people compare them to the conductor of an orchestra who needs to bring in various instruments to work together to produce a musical selection. To pay attention and persevere on a task, your daughter must be able to screen out distractions, regulate her behavior to start and continue a task, organize her materials, use working memory to call up previously learned information, and manage her time – all examples of executive functions. Below is a breakdown of what many consider to be the primary executive functioning skills and very brief suggestions of interventions:

▷ *Defining and setting goals, breaking them down into a plan with manageable steps, activating work, and sustaining effort.* You already know your daughter may have a hard time getting started with … well, you fill in the blank. Completing a science project or her English homework. Emptying the dishwasher. Packing for a sleepover. She may know what she needs to do, and she may really want or intend to get it done. But she has an especially difficult time figuring out which part of the task to do first, and how to proceed once she's gotten started. Organization skills are a key part of this process, and she may find it overwhelming to try to organize her thoughts, possessions, and surroundings.

▷ <u>What to do</u>: Realize she is not being lazy and defiant when she doesn't get started on a task but that she really can't figure out how to approach it. Help her break the task down into manageable steps and even make a checklist if necessary.

▷ *Paying attention and shifting focus as necessary.* It's likely your daughter may be easily distracted and unable to screen out the sounds, sights, smells, and other stimuli that are competing for her attention. Likewise, she may become so focused on one aspect of a project or activity that she can't move on to the next; she gets mired in the details.

▷ <u>What to do</u>: You can try to help her realize when she is losing focus so she can bring herself back to the task at hand. Some girls find it easier to pay attention when they are doing something with their hands while listening to a lecture, like doodling, using a fidget or an elastic band on the chair, etc. If all else fails, she may need medication.

▷ *Managing frustrations and showing emotional flexibility.* In general, girls with ADHD have a low tolerance for frustration and may show deeper sensitivity to emotional events. Their brains just become flooded with emotion, making it a challenge to think about the consequences before engaging in the action. Once her emotions are triggered, your daughter may have an extraordinarily difficult time moving past the incident. It is easy for a girl with ADHD to get down on herself because she encounters so many frustrations. Many girls with ADHD are incredibly sensitive to criticism and negative comments, often because they have been subjected to so many of them.

▷ **What to do**: Help her learn to take a moment to get control of her emotions so she can think clearly and proceed with her "thinking brain" in gear. If she automatically goes to the negative, like catastrophizing, Cognitive Behavior Therapy (CBT) may help.

▷ *Holding back impulses.* Many girls with ADHD blurt out the first thing that comes to mind or constantly interrupt while others are talking. They may jump from one activity to another, without any thought of putting away one thing before pulling out something else.

▷ **What to do**: "Become aware of the times that students have the most impulse control difficulties and build strategies and solutions specific to both your daughter and the circumstance" (Forgan & Richey, 2015, p. 49). For example, if your daughter is constantly interrupting others when they speak, develop a cue to remind her to wait until the person has finished speaking. It could be a finger to your lips or in the air to remind her. Also, having and enforcing firm house rules gives her practice in using self-control and reining in impulses.

▷ *Self-monitoring allows an individual to control her own behavior in socially acceptable ways.* Delaying actions until you have considered many variables, including consequences, impact on others, and other options, is a very complex process. It calls on working memory to recall similar events in the past, ability to shift focus away from the situation momentarily to decide what to do, and to problem-solve. Language, especially the ability to use self-talk, is one of the key elements. It's a function that requires an individual not only to monitor herself, but also to notice the impact she is having on the people around her. Barkley (2020) states, "The mind's brakes (inhibition) and the mind's mirror (self-awareness) interact with each other, giving us the beginnings of that often-heard refrain from parents 'Stop and think before you act!'" (p. 56).

Some girls with ADHD may struggle in social settings because they make inappropriate comments before they have seriously considered the topic of conversation, or they talk nonstop and don't realize how annoyed others are becoming. On the other extreme, they may be so self-conscious that they withdraw from social interactions entirely for fear of making a mistake.

    ▷ <u>What to do</u>: Understand that she may be very defensive about her social presence so approach such a sensitive topic in a non-judgmental way. It will be helpful if she can become a better observer of others' behavior, what causes friendships to fall apart, and how to tell what makes a good friend. Even when watching movies with her, make observations about social interactions and the effects on others. Especially with peer issues, help your daughter realize she doesn't always have to respond immediately but can take the time to consider options. Social skills coaching can be available from speech-language or mental health therapists if you feel she has skill deficits.

▷ *Managing time.* Many girls with ADHD have little awareness of the passage of time and live in the "now." They don't have any idea how long it takes to complete certain tasks and inevitably wait until the last minute to start preparing for something, causing them to be frequently late and frazzled. You have seen this when she is getting ready to leave the house or getting ready for bed at night. Or she may take forever to do a task, especially a school-related assignment. Slow processing speed when writing is very common in girls with ADHD. Not only is it hard for your daughter to stay focused and on task for what seems like a simple assignment like writing a paragraph, but it takes her a long, long time to get her thoughts organized. It can be frustrating, bordering on excruciating, for a parent to watch.

    ▷ <u>What to do</u>: Help her understand that slow processing speed does not mean she is not smart but it can be incredibly frustrating – especially when she doesn't like to do school tasks in the first place and finds it takes her even longer to do assignments than her classmates. Suggest the use of technology, especially voice typing, to brainstorm ideas or make an outline for her writing. Help her take pride in the finished product and commit the time necessary to get it done. If she has accommodation at school, additional time could be one of those. For tasks like getting ready in the morning, help her figure out how long it takes her to do the different tasks and make a visual schedule with times listed for each part of the process. Once the process becomes routine and habit, the chart can be removed.

▷ *Working memory relates to the ability to process, store, and recall information to complete a task.* This is a complex brain function that we rely on nearly every moment of every day; our working memory is like the search engine of the brain. When you're making a telephone call, you need to remember the name of the person you're calling and the reason for the call. If you get the person's voicemail, you need to remember all that information, plus you need to remember how to leave a polite, complete message. Many people with ADHD struggle with working memory and simply can't quickly access information they need to do a job or complete a task, even if they knew that information three minutes ago.

    ▷ <u>What to do</u>: Remind her that focus is critical for information to go into and be stored in one's memory bank. Challenge her to figure out what helps her remember details most effectively. It may be beneficial for her to know whether she is a visual or auditory learner. Using multiple modalities, like verbalizing and visualizing, often helps recall, as do making associations with other things already in memory and frequent review of previously learned information.

You will notice many of these executive functioning skills are dependent on each other. For example, impulse control requires some self-awareness. Organization skills are related to task initiation and persistence. The good news is that these skills respond to practice and routine. They are very related to success in life, so spend time to help your daughter develop any executive functioning skills that might be weak. Now would be a good time to reflect on those that need strengthening and add them to the **Dynamic Action Treatment Plan** at the end of the book.

Back to the science. Because the prefrontal area of the brain is one of the last to mature, it's not unusual for many adolescents to take a while to fully develop the kind of executive functioning abilities mentioned above that help them operate in the real world. In other words, the regions of your daughter's brain that have been affected by delayed or otherwise atypical development are the very same ones that govern impulse control, attention, alertness, focus, recall, and emotional balance. It's the physiological reason she struggles. Some girls need scaffolds and supports until these skills come online, whereas others may always need strategies to help them manage the deficits. Don't worry, there will be many practical interventions and supports throughout the chapter. Turn to the **Dynamic Action Treatment Plan** in Chapter 9 and fill any needs and supports your daughter may have in developing her executive functioning skills.

Looking Ahead

For the rest of this chapter, let's look at how ADHD may show up in your middle schooler's life. It is important for you to be informed parents to guide your daughter as she starts to manage her ADHD on her own. Here's what's ahead:

> ▷ Section 1: School (the challenges, the changes, and the ways you can help your daughter succeed)
> ▷ Section 2: Home and Community Issues (her relationships with family and friends, social media, and independence)
> ▷ Section 3: Your Daughter's Physical and Emotional Health.

Middle School: A Time of Transition

Middle school may be the first time your daughter's delays in executive functioning skills have caused glaring problems in a school setting. Hopefully your daughter has many strengths that she'll take into her middle school experience to offset some of the challenges she will face. Remind her of this and take the time to explore areas you may not have considered before. Is she an especially sharp observer? Does she easily see the "big picture" and make connections that others miss? Is she creative? Does she have an exceptional memory for intricate details? Is she gifted in music or art or math? Does she have an engaging sense of humor?

More and more she'll have opportunities to use and develop her special talents and abilities. Everyone is different but certain strengths have been identified in many individuals with ADHD. Maybe your daughter falls among them. Is she:

- a creative thinker,
- a good negotiator,
- willing to take a risk to achieve a positive outcome,
- intuitive and perceptive, and/or
- able to focus intently on a subject or topic of extreme interest?

As your daughter with ADHD enters middle school, it is easy to dwell on the struggles she's likely to encounter. She is probably aware of those as well. Instead regularly remind your daughter of how she's unique and how far she has come. Encourage her to find ways to use and develop her natural gifts. Make sure you have filled in strengths on the **Dynamic Action Treatment Plan** in Chapter 9.

Middle school will offer a chance for your daughter to grow, to make different friends, and to try interesting things. For many girls, overt hyperactivity will lessen but boredom and restlessness will still be there. Many fidget with their hands, pick at their nails and cuticles, play with their hair, or doodle while trying to pass the time sitting in a desk.

Your daughter probably takes a lot of cues from you. There is no sugar coating the challenges middle school can bring. It's a big step, but if your first response is fear, it's very likely you'll convey that to her, and she'll become worried and nervous, too. If she's experienced frustrations or problems before, it's a chance for her to start fresh. It's true that there will be challenges – there will probably *always* be challenges for a girl with ADHD and for her parents. But do your best to reassure her that solutions can usually be found to most problems and that you're prepared to support her in figuring those out.

Multiple teachers. This may be the first time your daughter is changing classes and having more than one primary teacher. Suddenly, keeping in close communication with your daughter's school just got six or seven times harder. How will you manage it?

Many parents begin planning the transition to middle school many months in advance. You may request to meet with a school administrator and guidance counselor, along with your daughter, to discuss the curriculum and teacher selection. More and more, your daughter needs to be involved in school meetings and speak on her own behalf. This will be easier for some students than others. Still, encourage your daughter to contribute. It's a skill she'll need to practice.

You may find you have less input on teacher selection as your daughter moves into the upper grades. Instead of making specific requests, you may wish to express your preference that your daughter be assigned to a specific "type" of teacher, like a highly organized or an energetic teacher who can keep kids engaged. A good student-teacher match will not only benefit your daughter, but the teacher and the class as well.

Generally, girls with ADHD do better with teachers who are willing to go the extra mile to help a student succeed. It will be important for your daughter to do her part and not take advantage of the support offered. Some characteristics you might look for in a teacher include being:

  ▷ *Flexible.* This teacher may grant extensions occasionally when your daughter misunderstands a homework assignment, leaves her work at home, or simply forgets to do it – if your daughter doesn't overuse these excuses!

  ▷ *Open to modifying assignments.* This teacher understands that the goal is to have the student grasp ideas and concepts. If a student struggles with a long essay but can demonstrate command of the material another way, like making a video or an art project, this teacher is willing to let her do so.

  ▷ *Knowledgeable about ADHD.* Some teachers have far greater understanding of the disability and what to expect of a student with ADHD.

  ▷ *Attentive.* This teacher takes note when students seem to be falling behind and alerts their parents. This is especially important when a student has ADHD and may not remember or is too embarrassed to keep her parents updated when she's having trouble.

  ▷ *Cooperative.* Some teachers are very willing to work with parents. Keeping lines of communication open remains important in middle school. Your daughter with ADHD probably hasn't learned all the skills she needs to be her own advocate. You'll need to stay in close touch with all teachers as much as possible.

Maintaining communication with multiple teachers doesn't have to be an overwhelming task. You will need to do a little homework. Take the time to learn how each of your daughter's teachers prefers to communicate and honor that. One may wish to receive only e-mails or text messages at certain times. Others may ask you to leave a message and a callback number with the school office.

Be sure to establish a courteous, respectful relationship with your daughter's teachers and with the school's administration and guidance staff. Get to know them and show your appreciation for the jobs they do. Together, you can form a powerful partnership on your daughter's behalf.

More classes, more work. In the confusion of changing from one classroom to the next, having to find books, notebooks and papers in her locker and then getting them to the right classes can be an onerous task. How's a girl with ADHD supposed to manage during the day? And what about Thursday night at 9:30, when she mentions the blockbuster science project that's due the next day? Here are a few coping skills:

> ▷ *Establish a routine.* Before school starts, get permission to walk the halls with your daughter, especially if it is her first year at the school. Map out a route for her daily schedule. Together, determine when it makes sense for her stop at her locker to drop off and pick up books. Color-coding books and notebooks can help her know immediately what she needs for each class.

> ▷ *Enlist a "coach."* This could be a very "big" ask, but is there someone at school who may be willing to serve as your daughter's coach or mentor? This could be a favorite teacher, her homeroom teacher, a guidance counselor, or a teacher's aide. This person's role would be to help your daughter stay organized while at school and stay ahead of assignments and coursework. Your daughter and her coach may need to meet in the morning and again before the end of the day, once a day, or weekly. You'll know your daughter will have a little extra help staying on track. You'll also feel more confident that any small problems will be flagged before they become big problems.

> ▷ *Find out about big projects early.* Keeping track of assignments and grades needs to be her job, but she may need support until she develops a routine. Most schools now list course outlines, schedules of assignments, and grades online. Help your daughter set up a routine at the beginning of the year to check this daily. If this is not available, you may want to ask for a heads-up about any larger or more complex projects your daughter will be expected to complete during the semester or year. Girls with ADHD have a more difficult time with

long-term planning and organizing multiple components. Larger school projects are going to require you and your daughter to establish a game plan. For the sake of your family harmony, you want to avoid unpleasant surprises – like learning about a 10-page paper with accompanying 3-D maps and video – the night before they're due.

Setting reasonable expectations. You and your daughter have a right to have expectations of each other. Your daughter isn't perfect. You can't demand more than she's equipped to give. At the same time, don't ever expect complete failure. Most of all, don't assume that the things your daughter does are deliberately designed to drive you crazy. They're not.

What's reasonable to ask of your daughter? As she goes through middle school, you can make it clear that she is required to:

▷ Complete her homework on time, without a huge struggle.
▷ Get acceptable grades. You need to define, together, what acceptable looks like. If she's gifted in one subject, she might earn an A. In other areas, a solid C might represent success. Focus on the effort she puts in, not the grades.

What's reasonable for your daughter to ask of you?

▷ Begin to release control. Allow her to make some mistakes, understanding that children with ADHD tend to take quite a bit longer to learn from their mistakes. Be patient. She will learn.
▷ Trust her. When she demonstrates that she can handle a little responsibility, allow her a little more.

Home and Community

Independence

One of your daughter's responsibilities in adolescence is to develop her independence so expect her to be chomping at the bit to push away from you. It will be a balancing act to figure out what she is responsible enough to do on her own and what still needs oversight. Being independent can go a long way in building her self-confidence, but it will be important to select the right opportunities. Many teens feel omnipotent and take unnecessary risks which can have life-long consequences. Many communities have organized activities for middle schoolers where they can exercise some independence while still having the influence and oversight of adults, like Girl Scouts, sports teams, school-related activities, and religious youth groups.

Guidelines for Behavior

Rules

As much as middle schoolers chafe against rules, they need structure. Dr. Russell Barkley (2020) advocates having what he calls non-negotiable house rules. He states, "Each family has a set of bottom-line rules for living together, which are a function of the parents' values and generalized tenets for civilized living" (p. 229). His wise advice is to keep them succinct and break them down into house rules and street rules. Examples of his suggestions for house rules included not using drugs, smoking, or alcohol (yes, vaping and experimenting with alcohol can start in middle school); treating family members and their property with respect; no violence; and not having friends in the house when no adults were home. His street rules involved keeping parents aware of whereabouts; not using drugs, alcohol, or smoking; and attending school. You might want to add internet usage and social media rules. Include rules that are necessary for you to feel your preteen is safe and that you can have a reasonable family life. Think long and hard about what are non-negotiable rules for your family and be prepared to monitor them often, especially when first starting out. If you have tried this approach in the past and it hasn't worked, today is a new day to try and create the structure your daughter needs. Just be thoughtful about what you can consistently enforce and as always, choose your battles.

Creating Buy-In

Trust your own intuition as to whether your daughter should be involved in the discussion of setting the rules, or if you and your spouse or partner can set them and discuss them with her. My experience has been that girls are more likely to buy in to the structure if they have some role in setting the framework but as noted above, there are some rules you will absolutely have to insist on whether she agrees or not. This is where having a strong, working relationship with your daughter can pay big dividends. If she understands you are coming from a position of love and caring for her, hopefully her pushback will be moderated.

Consistency

Once they are set, posting these rules and going over them frequently are keys to success. If you are lucky enough to have a partner in parenting, it obviously will be critical for you both to be on the same page. Your parenting journey will become much more complicated and unpleasant if your daughter can manipulate one parent. There may be many times you think you are too weary to enforce them, but being consistent is so critical, especially for teens with ADHD.

Notice and Compliment Small Changes Moving in the Right Direction

Ignore low-level behaviors that may be annoying but don't really matter in the scheme of things and notice and comment on the things she does that show a particular behavior is moving in the right direction.

Of course, you want to give positive reinforcement if your daughter is adhering to the rules. There is an old saying that you get more of what you pay attention to in terms of behaviors. Ignore low-level behaviors that may be annoying but don't really matter in the scheme of things and notice and comment on the things she does that show a particular behavior is moving in the right direction. For example, if one of your house rules is respecting property of others and your daughter took a sibling's favorite hat without asking. She later realized what she had done and apologized for taking it and returned it. That shows progress in attempting to follow the rules. Always remember that being cognizant of rules and responsibilities is harder for your daughter with ADHD than neurotypical children. You aren't going to let her use that as an excuse but want to be aware that the struggle may be very real for her.

Incentives

Setting up incentives for following the rules can go a long way to ensure their success. By working with your daughter, you and she can come up with reinforcement that is motivating to her. As Hinshaw (2022) reminds us, "Those with ADHD do not naturally or easily develop intrinsic motivation. Lower brain development, along with aberrations in the flow of the neurotransmitter dopamine through crucial brain circuits, render them dependent on external signs and motivators" (p. 126). The rewards don't have to be monetary or material; they can be for activities or positive comments and praise. Your daughter might choose more screen time, opportunities to have friends over, a restaurant of her choice for a family dinner, a special outing with a parent or relative, or a myriad of other things. It is good to have multiple choices to keep girls motivated because they easily tire of repetition. Some important things about rewards:

> In order to use rewards most effectively, consider the following:
> - ▷ The chosen reward must be effective enough to motivate your daughter to change her behavior and work toward the goals or rules established,
> - ▷ the gap between the behavior and reward must be short enough to keep your daughter motivated,

> ▷ lots of positive reinforcement and encouraging words must be thrown in along the way to keep her moving the right direction, and
>
> ▷ her patience must be observed and noted in waiting for the ultimate reward.

You can monitor progress through checklists, family meetings, or daily or weekly ratings of her success in adhering to the rules or working toward the desired behavior. If one rule is more difficult, work with her to figure out how to help her follow it. She may need support in learning how to comply. Any behavior changes your daughter is making will require a lot more monitoring and support on your part but think how much better it will be in the long run.

Consequences

It goes without saying that there will be times when you will have to take a hard line and impose consequences. It will be an important part of your behavior plan to lay out consequences clearly in advance so they can be administered judiciously. Hinshaw (2022) advises:

> Then, when an infraction occurs, there can be no bickering or negotiating related to these consequences. In fact, stalling and prolonged negotiations will send a message that your daughter can get away with almost anything and get plenty of attention for it! Furthermore, you must deliver the negative consequences without resorting to yelling, scolding, or castigating. In fact the progression of such hostile interchanges, related to parental caving in, failing to follow through, and eventual sarcasm/bitterness, must be avoided at all costs. They are a clear step on the pathway from ADHD to more frankly aggressive or self-destructive behavior. (Hinshaw, 2022, p. 127)

Natural consequences can be the best teachers, but only if they resonate with your daughter and/or don't cause devastating consequences. If your preteen does try vaping and feels physically ill afterwards, that result should make her think twice before doing it again. It would be up to you to determine if she also needs the consequence specified in your behavior plan. Obviously, this is a serious behavior that could develop into an addiction, so you want to handle it carefully. If she is particularly rude to her sibling, she may be reminded of that the next time she wants some cooperation or favor from him or her. In some cases, the natural consequences can be too dire and can hurt you as much as your daughter. For example, failing her classes would be a natural consequence of not turning in assignments but could send her into a tailspin and impact her life for years to come. In those cases, it would be important to step in and help her manage her life more effectively. It will be up to you to determine if the natural consequence of a behavior is a "safe" and effective deterrent, or if other consequences for the behavior are required in addition to support in figuring out a better way to handle the situation.

Parent and Student Interview

Background

This middle school student was diagnosed with anorexia, ADHD, and anxiety. She is now doing well in middle school, has found a passionate interest in an afterschool activity, and continues to see a therapist and take medication.

Parent Interview

Q. What are your biggest worries related to your daughter's ADHD? What has helped you the most in managing them?

My biggest worry had always been school and being up to grade level on everything. But now with an eating disorder,

I worry more about the medication and the side effects on lack of appetite. I just make sure to pay attention to her intake each day. I thank God for making her healthy again and ask for that to continue.

> **Q. I know you have had experience with comorbid disorders like anxiety and anorexia. What do you wish you had known at the time of these diagnoses? What can you share about your experience that might help other parents?**

Early on in her diagnosis of anorexia, I was told that the signs had been there for a couple of years. She wanted to be vegetarian in fourth grade. I didn't think much of it, just that she didn't like the consistency of meat. But I learned later that was an initial sign of restricting. The anxiety was harder to accept. Looking back now I suppose there were signs – problems with teachers, upset stomach, and not getting work done. The combination of anorexia, depression, and anxiety all went together, and it was devastating to feel so helpless.

My best advice to parents is TRUST YOUR GUT! I knew something wasn't right at her annual 11-year-old physical. I discussed my concern with our pediatrician, but at the time her height and weight were perfectly normal. In 6 weeks she lost 13 more pounds, and I knew then we needed help. It was hard to navigate because the depression made her non-compliant. My husband and I kept asking questions, didn't believe everything we were told, and kept searching for the right answers. Thankfully we found the right team of physicians, therapists, and a nutritionist to help us to get our daughter back. She was down to 80 pounds at her lowest; she had a very low heart rate causing her to pass out and risk of causing heart damage.

Q. How important do you think a comprehensive treatment plan is for your daughter?

Very important. At such a young age nothing can be taken lightly. She went downhill so rapidly that I was told if we had waited a few more weeks/months for help, the conversation would have been very different.

Q. What steps have you taken that have helped your daughter the most?

Finding the right doctor has been a very special gift to our family. My daughter calls him "Dr. Awesome." He listened to her, my husband, and me and got to the root of the issues and prescribed the right medications. In the past I would have been against prescription medications at such a young age. I was the mom who would think she could help with diet. Sometimes it is beyond that, and you have to find a physician you trust.

Q. How have relatives reacted to the various diagnoses? How have you handled their suggestions if they were off base?

Ha, well ... with the anorexia diagnosis I was offered several "suggestions" on how to get her to eat. What you would expect, "have you tried protein shakes?" "you know she always liked (fill in the blank) have you tried that?" etc. I would get very defensive (and feel very judged). I am her mother, "Gee no I didn't think of ways to get my child to eat…" (sarcasm) I found myself shutting off from family and friends because I couldn't handle it. Looking back, they just didn't understand. I did have to educate our families. There was resistance to the medications from both sets of grandparents, but I just said this is what the doctor has said, we trust him, THE END. I did feel very isolated; this was the first time I had experienced something that I didn't know ANYONE to ask for help or advice.

I don't know if it's the stigma of mental health that no one wants to discuss. But post COVID and with social media, sadly I think this may be an issue more young children and their parents are faced with. I want to advocate and help as much as I can. My husband and I (and my son) are so incredibly thankful that we got the help we needed for our daughter and are in a good place. But although it is in our "rearview," we must be conscious. I am very open with friends with female daughters about things to pay attention to, like weighing themselves constantly.

We do not have a scale. I had to talk to family members about not talking about their recent "dieting" programs, how much they have gained, how much they have lost ... I didn't realize how much of that went on until I had to look at everything in order to protect my daughter.

Student Interview

Q. Do you remember how you felt when you found out about your ADHD diagnosis?

I was 11 turning 12. The doctor I was seeing for my eating disorder diagnosed me because he said I was moving a lot. I was sick at that time from the eating disorder so I didn't really feel anything at that point. Later I was relieved that there was a name for what I had. Before that I used to make up weird names for it like "my jittery problem."

Q. ADHD affects everyone differently. How do you think it has impacted you?

It has definitely impacted me socially. I was at a new school that year. When my medication wore off in the afternoons, I was in art class. I would start tapping my pencil. The girls next to me would make fun of me and say, "Why don't you stop?" I would tell them I couldn't stop. When they kept bothering me, I said, "No, I can't stop. Mind your own business."

I have trouble following long conversations, especially about teenage drama. I lose focus and ask, "What are you talking about?" Other times, I would hear a name and think, "Oh, that is what we were talking about." Then I would add a comment. They would say things like, "Oh, I thought you weren't listening."

Q. What are the benefits of your medication? Are there any side effects and if so, how do you manage them?

I am more focused, get better results on schoolwork, am more social, and am not moving around as much. When it wears off, I am in history class, and I just sit there and don't do my work. I am just thinking of everything in the world. I talked to my doctor and my medicine was increased. If I don't take my medication, it is hard to explain how I feel, but it is like I feel every muscle in my body. "One of the side effects is I don't feel hunger. I know my body won't tell me when to eat, but I know I must eat so I do."

Q. You mentioned you do well on tests, but your grades are impacted because you don't always turn in homework. Since you are such a good problem-solver, do you have any ideas on how to correct that?

Last year was such a bad year that I just didn't know what to do. Now starting this year, my plan is to start my homework in my support class, do more when I get home before I go to an activity, and then finish when I get home.

Q. What are your best tips for a girl diagnosed with ADHD who also has anxiety?

Don't take girls seriously – In my school, I found that most girls are clueless about eating disorders, ADHD, and anxiety. For example, when I told a group of girls that I had ADHD they said, "No, you don't." I said, "You mean I take medication for nothing?" They said, "We have never seen you do any ADHD stuff." I said, "That is why I take medicine."

Be careful about social media – For many in my school, social media is what they do in their spare time. Many of them post videos of themselves on Tik Tok, YouTube, and Instagram. I do want to say that social media is not all bad, there are some good things about it. When I was sick with anorexia, I watched videos that showed new ways to get better like distracting yourself by watching tv while eating.

Try to find friends who will stand by you – Once I was sick and threw up in the bathroom. Some girls said I had bulimia because they didn't know the difference between anorexia and bulimia, but others stuck up for me. Now I try to be the one to stick up for people.

Talk openly about your feelings and not keep them inside. In fifth grade I had feelings about eating but kept it balled up inside. Now I am more honest, like telling a friend when I am feeling insecure.

Try to find a teacher at school that you connect with and who cares about you.

Try to find a way to get your energy out and get engaged when bored in the classroom. One of my doctors taught me to take a break when I am bored by putting my thumb to my index finger, take a deep breath; then do it to the remaining three fingers. When you have finished, try to focus. In social studies, I love maps and hands-on projects but get bored and lose focus

> when teachers are just talking. Then I start reading the text-book because I like reading and I get the same information the teacher is giving but in a form I can pay attention to.
>   **Try not to overthink things**. If you think people are looking at you, take a deep breath, sit with someone and chill, or go to the bathroom for a minute and then come back.

Communication

If you are like most parents of preteen girls with ADHD, you have realized that your daughter doesn't value what you say as much as she used to when she was younger. Try to keep in mind her struggle for independence juxtaposed against a history of struggle in so many areas that may have impacted her self-confidence, her delayed maturation in many areas, and the complex societal envir-onment she faces. Open, honest communication is so important. Let her know and understand mistakes will happen. You must make the most of your opportunities to communicate with her and be clear about your most important messages and how they are delivered. Remember tone of voice always matters. Make sure she feels listened to and respected. It may be a tall order but try to main-tain your calm and walk away when you cannot. Giving yourself a moment can be just as important as giving her one when tempers start to flare. Revisit the conversation later when both of you have had some time to reflect.

You must make the most of your opportunities to communicate with her and be clear about your most important messages and how they are delivered.

Peers

Peers are important on many levels, emotionally and developmentally. "Peer interactions allow children to learn to cooperate and negotiate with parties of equal status" (Nadeau et al., 2016, p. 107). They provide a sense of belonging and if supportive, can be a buffer for some of the turmoil of adolescence.

These preteen years are critical as your daughter begins to get a better read on who she truly is. She must balance this against the overriding importance of finding group acceptance. This can be especially daunting for a girl with ADHD who may not be able to follow the complex interchanges that take place among adolescents, misinterpret social cues, or may constantly interrupt. Relational aggression, which can involve teasing, exclusion, or trashing a reputation, are mine fields in middle school.

If your daughter is already two to three years behind in maturation of social and executive functioning skills, she is already at a huge disadvantage. If she still likes pretend play, building things, creating crafts, and even dolls, she may feel disconnected when her peers are constantly talking about boys, fashion, and popular music groups. You can just imagine the stress and anxiety this puts on a girl with ADHD as she struggles to stay focused on fast-paced conversations that don't even interest her. If she slips up and says or does something very awkward, it could be all over social media instantly and remain there for a long time. In previous generations, faux pas would be quickly forgotten but not today. If your daughter happens to be highly sensitive to criticism as most girls with ADHD are, then her antenna may always be up for signals she is not meeting expectations, further complicating her social relationships.

Another risk is how conforming middle school girls tend to be in terms of following the crowd. Going along with the mores of the crowd in lieu of staying true to themselves can be a blow to self-esteem and lead to daily anxiety wondering when they might say or do something outside of group norms, leaving them open to ridicule or bullying. Since peer acceptance is so critical for preteen girls, some create and present a "false self" which can put them on a slippery slope to anxiety, depression, and eating disorders. Instead, you want your daughter to find her own voice and be on a path to developing her own strengths and finding her own passions.

It is critical for you to know her friends, which can be a challenge, as your daughter may continually try to keep you "out of her business." Even though entertaining adolescents may not be your cup of tea, it can pay big dividends to have her friends at your house. You will get to know her friends and have a finger on the pulse of what is happening. As you may already know, you can't trust all parents to provide adequate supervision and may find that some allow their preteens to entertain friends when no adult is home. If your daughter is going to others' homes, don't be shy about finding out the details. Your daughter may be mortified but you can figure out a way to do it which will seem perfectly fine.

Even though entertaining adolescents may not be your cup of tea, it can pay big dividends to have her friends at your house.

Peer experiences may vary depending on your daughter's diagnosis, whether she is inattentive, hyperactive, or the combined type. Some inattentive girls shut down and withdraw rather than try to compete in a stressful social environment. In *Understanding Girls with ADHD*, authors Nadeau et al. (2016) state:

> … More impulsive girls with ADHD are more prone to rule-breaking, feeling confined and limited by the rules rather than structured and supported by them. More oppositional and aggressive than the

inattentive girls, the impulsive girls may come to identify themselves as belonging amongst those who violate social norms. (Nadeau et al., 2016, p. 114)

Unfortunately, these days, the consequences can be dire if your daughter starts running with the wrong crew. Do what you can to keep those relationships from forming as they can lead to earlier experimentation with substances, risky online presence, and early sexuality. If your daughter moves away from an established peer group to a more alternative one, be on the alert if she becomes more secretive, belligerent, or changes the way she dresses. These could be perfectly normal preteen behavior or on the other hand, they could also signal trouble ahead. Believe me, I am not trying to scare you but help you be vigilant and aware. Girls are exposed to so much at an early age, sometimes as early as 11 or 12.

Having a loving home where she feels valued and accepted for who she is can lessen the sting of peer issues and provide a safe haven where she can be herself. A supportive adult, especially a mother or father, who is willing to listen without critical judgement can be a game changer. It doesn't mean you have to accept or agree with stances you know aren't appropriate but that you will hear her out and provide a forum for her to explore her feelings. It can be heart-breaking at times but hopefully you can help them put things in perspective. The truth of the matter is that often the coolest kids in middle school don't end up being the most successful and happiest in life.

Having at least one quality friendship is another important factor that helps teen girls navigate adolescence. The quality of the friendship seems to matter more than the quantity of friends.

If your daughter is struggling to find that friend, continue exposing her to different community activities based on interests, such as a theater or music group, athletic team, Girl Scouts, or religious or social service group. She may find some like-minded friends and will have less time on her hands to ruminate about her problems or engage in riskier activities.

Some girls who aren't successful with actual friendships develop online personas. To me, this could be concerning if it takes the place of face-to-face friendships and attending social gatherings.

All Things Internet

Most parents I work with agree that the internet has added a mountain of problems to parenting a teen. The current generation is much more tech savvy than most parents. One parent told me, "As soon as I implement parental controls, my daughter finds a way around them." As you know, the internet is full of misinformation, negative messages (especially for girls), pornography, and stalkers. The algorithms on social media are designed to keep people coming back over and over, and video games are also designed to hook kids. It is no wonder that internet addictions for adolescents are becoming more prevalent.

Children and teens are posting questionable photos and videos online, some of which have serious repercussions. Even though they have grown up in a tech savvy world, most of them don't understand how quickly things can go viral and cause ridicule and heartache and how posted items may stay on the internet for years to come. The rate of depression and anxiety in teens has never been higher, and many of teens' problems are linked to social media. The "fear of missing out" (FOMO) is almost unavoidable when teens see posts about gatherings they were not invited to but their friends are attending.

How do parents manage? As you already know, there is a wide range of the types of internet usage and video games parents allow. It comes down to a personal preference. The American Academy of Pediatrics has backed away from suggesting time limits because teens use technology in such different ways. They recommend focusing on the quality of the time the teen spends on line. If you see screen time taking the place of other important developmental activities, like getting proper exercise or face-to-face social contact, place strict limits on the amount of time they can spend online. If you suspect an addiction is developing, seek professional help early. Most professionals who deal with children recommend that you limit sites they can visit and games they can play, have access to their sites, and keep a close eye on postings. Currently, there are so many alluring things on the internet that can lead to harm. Privacy takes a back seat to the need for parental oversite and guidance. The American Academy of Pediatrics (2021) states, "When it comes to household rules around technology use, there is evidence that rules focusing on content, co-viewing and communication are associated with better well-being outcomes than rules focused on screen time."

Dealing with cyberbullying. Today parents must deal with a relatively new danger requiring attention and vigilance – cyberbullying. It is defined as sending or posting mean, embarrassing, or threatening texts or images over the Internet via computer, cell phone, or iPads/tablets. It can happen on social networking sites, in chat rooms, on message boards, via text message or Twitter, or on Snap Chat – the most difficult of all to monitor.

It can happen to anyone, but risk factors include vulnerable, socially naïve, or unpopular teens; youth who have impaired relations with parents and/or peers; and those who suffer from depression, anxiety, or are fearful (Feinberg & Robey, 2009). Many girls are reluctant to report the incident out of fear, embarrassment, or guilt that they may have brought it on themselves or out of concern that their phones or online activities will be curtailed. If it happens to your daughter, your support and understanding will be important.

Keep abreast of trends and new developments by visiting social media safety centers, such as Stop Bullying, a governmental website (www.stopbullying.gov), and Pacer's National Bullying Prevention Center at www.pacer.org/BULLYING. These provide steps that should be followed if you feel your daughter is the victim of cyberbullying.

Physical and Emotional Health

Puberty

Puberty and its many physical and emotional components are like a seismic shift in a girl's life. It is like the carefree life of a little girl is over as there are now a myriad of things to contend with like menstruation, breast development, body hair, possibly acne, and body odor. Factor in that girls with ADHD may be two to three years delayed in their emotional development and executive functioning and still have to deal with all those changes, and it can seem overwhelming. Many feel they are just not ready for it. Nadeau et al. (2016) said, "Managing the heightened emotional and physiological sensitivities of puberty and integrating them into their developing sense of self makes this upheaval one of the defining challenges of the middle school years for girls with ADHD" (p. 111).

Don't underestimate the challenges dealing with menstruation and other changes in the body can bring. Again, this is where having a good relationship with your daughter can be very important. You can prepare her gradually for the changes that are about to occur. If your daughter is resistant to change in general, this time may be particularly hard on her. Do your best to provide plenty of opportunities for her to come to you with concerns or questions and be a good listener. With all the misinformation floating around, you want to make sure she gets correct information coming from you.

The awakening of sexual urges can be potent for any girl, but especially one with ADHD. If your daughter has a history of poor impulse control and difficulty with peer relations, her head can be turned easily by attention from boys. She may be more prone to engage in early sexual experimentation.

Unfortunately, girls with ADHD can easily get in over their heads, and parents should be vigilant about providing oversight during parties, private online chats, and text messaging. The combination of high stimulation, hormonal changes, and social rewards can lead to an addictive involvement in sexual acting out. (Nadeau et al., 2016, p. 119)

Again, this information is not presented to make you paranoid or over-reactive, but to reinforce the importance of helping your daughter make wise decisions as her delayed executive functioning skills and maturity catch up to her body.

Gender Issues

If your daughter is struggling with gender issues, it may be shocking to you. However, you want her to rely on you for support and information, not peers or unreliable sources on the internet. It will be important for you to educate yourself, so you feel you have a solid knowledge base and understanding of all the new terminology surrounding gender choices. If you want her to continue to confide in you, it will be important for you to be non-judgmental and an excellent listener. It is not easy for girls to navigate all the complexities involved. Your daughter's ADHD, which may include impulsiveness, social difficulties, emotional reactiveness, and tendency to hyperfocus on issues, can come into play and complicate the process. Finding trusted professionals can be helpful. Remember, she needs you as this can be a complex and highly emotional journey.

Internalizing Problems

The rate of internalizing disorders, like anxiety, depression, and eating disorders, has been increasing at alarming rates. As you know, girls with ADHD are known to have higher rates of these disorders than girls without ADHD. It is important for parents to be aware of subtle changes in behavior or affect that could signal the onset of mental health issues. If your daughter changes her eating habits, becomes overly concerned or is secretive about what she is eating, or gains or loses weight for no apparent reason, be very observant. If you are concerned, consult your pediatrician or a therapist who deals with eating disorders. If she becomes more withdrawn, moodier than usual, doesn't want to participate in her normal activities, or worries more than usual, reach out to her guidance counselor to find out how she is at school. Some schools offer mental health counseling, or you may prefer to use a private therapist. The bottom line is that you want to seek professional help to ward off more serious problems in the future. See the next chapter about high school girls for more information about comorbid disorders.

Protective Factors

Amid all the minefields of puberty, girls with ADHD who have proper treatment and a supportive home environment do come through it and move on to create wonderful lives.

Protective factors for your daughter with ADHD include:
- ▷ A loving family who understands the challenges of ADHD but holds her accountable.
- ▷ A home she sees as a "safe haven" from the complexities of daily life.
- ▷ A strong trusting relationship with at least one adult who is "always in her corner."
- ▷ Structure and support both at home and school to help her manage responsibilities.
- ▷ Participation in organized activities that keep her busy with less time to engage in risky activities.
- ▷ Discovering her passions and interests.
- ▷ Understanding her strengths and weaknesses.
- ▷ Support in developing her own voice.

References

American Academy of Pediatrics. (2021, April 6). *Media and children.* www.aap.org/en/patient-care/media-and-children/

Barkley, R. A. (2020). *Taking charge of ADHD: The complete, authoritative guide for parents* (4th ed.). Guilford Press.

Feinberg, T., & Robey, N. (2009). Cyberbullying: Intervention and prevention strategies. *Communique*, 38, 21–23.

Forgan, J. W., & Richey, M. A. (2015). *The impulsive, disorganized child – Solutions for parenting kids with executive functioning difficulties.* Prufrock Press.

Hinshaw, S. P. (2022). *Straight talk about ADHD in girl: How to help your daughter thrive.* Guilford Press.

Nadeau, K. G., Littman, E. B., & Quinn, P. O. (2016). *Understanding girls with ADHD: How they feel and why they do what they do* (2nd ed.). Advantage Books.

Points to Consider

1   Remind yourself of the significant changes your daughter's body is going through.
2   Middle school can be quite a challenge but remind her to take one challenge at a time and look at it as problem with a solution.
3   Notice positive steps your daughter is making in getting along with siblings or other family members.
4   Are there ways to support her friendships, such as allowing her to have a sleepover or a cookout?

Action Steps to Take Now

1   If your daughter is falling apart in middle school, make an appointment to meet with her guidance counselor to see what supports can be provided for her. Then ask for a meeting with her teachers to discuss implementation of a plan.

2   On **the Dynamic Action Treatment Plan**, add one or more strengths to Step 1 – Strengths and Needs and work on Step 4 – Support and Step 5 – Roadblocks with your daughter. Make sure to communicate that strength(s) to her tomorrow. (Remember, the **Dynamic Action Treatment Plan** can be found in Chapter 9.)

3   Plan a special outing for just you and your preteen daughter to begin building better communication.

4   Decide on one behavioral strategy you can apply or try again.

5   Make it a point today to say one positive statement to your daughter.

Chapter 7

The Teenage Years

Each self-assessment helps you reflect on your daughter and your parenting practices and is a preview of the chapter's content.

1 When I think about my teenage daughter, I believe …
  a she acts older than her chronological age.
  b she acts younger than her chronological age.
  c she acts her age.
  d her actions vary from day to day.
2 My daughter's organizational skills are …
  a in need of a lot of work.
  b good enough to get by but could use some strengthening.
  c one of her strong points.
  d I don't know.

3 When I think about my daughter's school …
   a we have her schedule optimized for the way ADHD affects her and accommodations in place.
   b she has an OK schedule, but we need to review her accommodations.
   c we need to have a school meeting ASAP to review everything.
   d my daughter does not want me involved in her school life.

4 My daughter's study skills …
   a are one of her strengths.
   b are OK but could be improved.
   c are non-existent.
   d are something we are working on now.

5 My daughter's mood is …
   a consistent.
   b typical for a teenage girl.
   c ever changing.
   d out of control.

You blink and you have a daughter in high school! No matter how great a girl she is, her teenage years will likely test your limits and fortitude. Remember the Terrible Twos? With a scowl and a stamp of her little foot, she'd defy you with a pouty, "NO!" You can expect the teen years to be a bit like that – but even with more complexities. Her snippy attitude (maybe you've noticed it) is her way of saying, "I'm not a child. I can think for myself, and I want the freedom to make my own choices." At the same time, though, she's still unsteady and uncertain. She needs you to be consistent, fair, and compassionate, even if she's inconsistent, reactive, and insensitive. You're going to need to help her learn to navigate everything – school, mean girls, hormones, sexuality, dating, driving, social media – all within the context of her ADHD. It is critical for her to know she can always count on you to be in her corner. That doesn't mean you accept inappropriate behavior or that you won't make decisions she strongly disagrees with, but that she can trust you to want the best for her.

As with the previous chapters on preschool, elementary, and middle school, this chapter is divided into:

> ▷ Section 1: School (the challenges, the changes, and the ways you can help your daughter succeed).
> ▷ Section 2: Community Issues (her relationships with family and friends, dating, driving, money, jobs).
> ▷ Section 3: Your Daughter's Physical and Emotional Health.

I hope you'll find all three sections valuable, but I'm hoping you pay special attention to the final section because teenage girls are showing an alarming uptick in rates of sadness, sexual violence, and suicidality in CDC's recent release of data. They report, "In 2021, almost 60% of female students experienced persistent feelings of sadness or hopelessness during the past year" (Centers for Disease Control and Prevention, 2023). It further reported that 30% of girls surveyed reported seriously considering attempting suicide. Of course, the risks could be even higher for girls with ADHD with their rates of experiencing depression, anxiety, eating disorders, self-injury, and/or low self-esteem.

While this is alarming, it is not a given for your daughter but alerts you to be vigilant and focused on protective factors. Research specifically on girls with ADHD suggests, "Minimizing parenting stress and dysfunctional mother–daughter interactions during ado-lescence might reduce the risk of adverse adult outcomes for girls with ADHD" (Gordon & Hinshaw, 2017). In this study, less-than-optimal parenting practices mentioned included ineffective monitoring, inconsistent discipline, and withdrawal of parental support. So never underestimate the impact your relationship, understanding of her ADHD, and support has on your daughter.

Your daughter is undergoing profound physical changes as her body matures. Often burdened by acceptance issues and impulse-control problems, girls with ADHD may engage in risky sexual behavior that you'll want to help your daughter avoid. Some adverse outcomes may be out of your control, but by educating yourself about ADHD and its impact and working on your relationship with your daughter, you are doing what you can do to minimize the negative effects.

As a community, we're just starting to understand the complex nature of ADHD in young women. Research consistently shows that ADHD in girls is a persistent disorder with symptoms that can carry into adulthood The importance of a comprehensive treatment plan cannot be overstated.

High School

Much of what I've written about middle school holds true for high school as well. She will be forced to take subjects that she thinks have little relevance for her. The academic and social challenges continue to increase year by year. By this point, hormonal and physical changes are in full swing. Right before your eyes, your daughter is a young woman. Don't lose sight of the fact that certain skills and abilities haven't caught up to her physical changes. It is easy to expect more than she can do based on her appearance. ADHD will be impacting her functioning in many ways, some subtle and others more glaring. It is clear you love your daughter or you wouldn't be reading this book. Most parents realize teens can close doors for themselves that will negatively affect their future by poor choices and just want the best for them, but teens don't often see that. It is a fine balance to help them develop their skills but not put too much pressure on them.

These are the years when a young person should be striving for independence and self-reliance. It's no different for a teen with ADHD, just more challenging in many ways. In fact, it may be even *more* crucial that your daughter be aware of supports she needs to be successful and learn to advocate for herself. This will be a major step for both of you, one of many during the teen years. But remember, your primary job as a parent isn't just to get your daughter with ADHD through school. It's to prepare her to be a strong, self-assured young woman who can make a go of life on her own.

Self-Advocacy

From the time they enter high school, students should be present at all meetings that concern their disability. There may be obvious exceptions, such as when other students' privacy is at issue. But your daughter is now old enough to be part of the discussion, and you need to encourage her to answer the questions that pertain to her. Resist the urge to answer for her. As girls gain more insight into their functioning, they sometimes come up with the most helpful accommodations.

It is appropriate for your daughter to initiate discussions with her teachers about her ADHD but not always a comfortable thing for her to do. Many teachers respond well when a student approaches them directly about her disability. High school teachers today have so many students that it takes months to learn about each one, so it makes their lives much easier if your daughter helps them understand her learning style and needs. She should be prepared to describe what ADHD means for her – what it might look like in the classroom, the kinds of assignments that have been hard for her in the past, and what's helped her succeed. She could talk to the teacher privately between classes or communicate via e-mail. It might go something like this:

> *Mrs. Nelson? Can I talk to you for a couple minutes? I don't know if you know this, but I have ADHD-inattentive type. For me that means I have trouble paying attention and remembering things. Sometimes in class you might see me daydreaming, and it's sometimes hard for me to remember what we've*

already learned. It's not because I'm not interested or because I don't want to learn. It's because I have a really hard time focusing and holding on to information. I have a 504 plan with accommodations that help me. For example, last year in history, Mrs. Williams gave me a copy of her notes before every class. That helped me focus on her lectures rather than frantically trying to take down notes because I write so slowly. When we had a test, she also let me stay after school and answer my essay questions out loud. That really helped a lot because writing out long answers is hard for me. I don't mind talking about it if I can answer any questions. I hope we can work together so my ADHD doesn't get in the way.

I'm not suggesting you abandon your daughter and let her figure out everything on her own. As you may know, that can lead to a very bad outcome. A school staff that ignores accommodations or the severity of your daughter's ADHD with comorbid learning disabilities may require your more active involvement. I'm simply advising you to step back when it's appropriate to do so and see how your daughter does when she gets the chance to take the reins. This will build skills for college and the workplace.

Jennifer explained how she helped her teenage daughter, Kali. "At the beginning of the year we asked for a meeting with all the teachers to explain her IEP (Individualized Education Plan) accommodations and highlight the most important ones. We reminded Kali during the school year to use these accommodations and ask her teachers about them if they forgot. Kali also sat in on a recent IEP meeting to talk about what she believes she needs to succeed."

Extracurricular Activities and Sports

Extracurricular activities are a valuable part of the high school experience. Surrounded by teens with similar interests, your daughter will have the chance to make new friends. This can be especially important for girls with ADHD who struggle in social situations. She'll gain a sense of belonging and have an outlet for the energy and frustration that may have built up during the day. Her life can become more balanced as she gets to turn her focus temporarily from the challenges of school and homework. Girls with ADHD, especially those with the hyperactive or combined type, often need to be busy all the time, and extracurricular activities are a great, positive way to respond to that need.

Let your daughter explore a wide range of activities, though not all at once. Try new things one or two at a time and see what works for her and your family. If a particular activity, group, or sport isn't a good fit, require that your daughter fulfill her commitment and then move on to something else. Some guidelines for you and your daughter to consider:

▷ Many girls with ADHD love to draw, paint, sing, or act. These are wonderful activities that encourage self-expression and help keep her emotions from getting bottled up inside. You can be her biggest fan in creative pursuits, displaying her work or taking her to galleries, plays, and concerts. Sharing a common love of the arts can be a powerful relationship builder.

▷ Remember that every added activity is one more thing for your daughter's daily planner and for her to remember. You probably already know that overloading a girl with ADHD is a bad idea. Remember this when you're thumbing through her school's activity booklet or reading your city's online recreation flyer.

▷ Every child is different, and your daughter may be an exceptional athlete. But hand-eye coordination often tends to be less developed in girls with ADHD. This can make some team sports – like softball or volleyball – a challenge because they require agility in catching, throwing, and hitting. Your daughter may have more success in sports that emphasize gross motor skills – swimming or running, for instance.

▷ If your daughter's ADHD is severe, she may still have difficulty paying attention to the rules of a game or instructions of her coach. Talk through choices of sports and encourage her to choose sports and positions that are engaging. She might be a good soccer player but might not fare well at playing goalie, where there's a lot of downtime.

▷ If your daughter's ADHD is likely to impact her during an activity or sport, be honest with adult leaders and coaches. This can be a very touchy subject for teens, so you'll have to use your judgement about how to handle it. The best case scenario would be for you and your daughter to talk to the adult together, but most teens I have worked with are very opposed to bringing it up. Many coaches and leaders will be unfamiliar with ADHD and would benefit from knowing what to expect from your daughter and what might help her if problems occur.

Homework

Think for a minute of the executive functioning skills required for efficient homework management:

▷ organizing large projects into smaller steps
▷ getting started and staying with the task until it is completed
▷ gathering the materials needed
▷ retaining focus on work that may be uninteresting and difficult
▷ storing, recalling, and processing information she's already learned
▷ managing time
▷ evaluating her performance

These are the very same functions that are often compromised in a girl with ADHD. If she has struggled in school all day, the last thing she will want to do is sit down and do more boring work. Boredom is often her nemesis, and homework can be at the top of that list. In the families I see, homework causes an immense amount of frustration and aggravation. It leads to fights, nagging, exasperation, anger, and tears and often takes a toll on parent–child relationships. It is important for your daughter to realize homework isn't meant to be a punishment but further reinforcement for the skills she has been learning and a necessary part of her education. Your daughter may not be a good test taker and her test grades may reflect that. Homework is something she does have control over. Turning it in can only help her grades.

If you've already spent years sitting beside your daughter at homework time, you're ready to turn the responsibility over to her. You're eager to help her develop a study routine that works. This may be a gradual transition, but the goal is to have your daughter be as self-directed as possible.

Getting Her Off to a Good Start with Homework

Helping your daughter get organized is the first step toward breaking bad homework habits. You could devise a great organization system and study area that is just perfect for homework, but she must be the one to decide what ultimately works for her. By now she probably knows where she can do her best work – whether it is at the kitchen table with someone within reach to ask for help or in her room where it is totally quiet. Some girls work better with quiet music playing in the background or earphones with white noise or other calming sounds. After some of the decisions are made, work with her to gather all the supplies she'll need.

Spend some time brainstorming about an age-appropriate planner system she finds workable and interesting. Far more than their friends without ADHD, teens with ADHD need a way to keep track of every assignment, every report, every project, every swim meet, and every band rehearsal. Go shopping together and see what makes sense to both of you, based on her needs. If she thinks a new iPad would be just the thing, but tends to lose electronic gadgets, you're well within your rights to suggest a less pricey alternative. You can even download an app for her phone to help her track assignments. *What* you get is far less important than *how* she uses it and *how faithfully* she uses it.

Help her set up a schedule that can become routine and be followed. As you well know, girls with ADHD tend to procrastinate. But to her, it won't seem like procrastination at all. She'll be very busy trying to create some sense of order in the mass of papers in her backpack and on her desk, or even just clearing a space to work. She calls a friend to get a homework assignment and they talk for a half-hour. She does an online search for a definition, which leads her to a cool website on the subject, which eventually leads her to YouTube. An hour has passed, and she's no closer to finishing her work. You and she need to collaborate on creating a system, so she won't have to spend a lot of time thinking about how to get started on homework – she'll just do it. Here are some guidelines:

> ▷ Let her set the time she's going to do her homework every day. Help her find a way to stick to it, whether by using an alarm on her watch, a computer alert, or some other reminder.
> ▷ Remind her to use the homework area she has chosen.
> ▷ Encourage your daughter to tackle her more difficult (or least favorite) homework assignments first.
> ▷ Help her learn to prioritize assignments in terms of their importance in the overall grade. If she can't get everything done, a project that is 50% of her grade is more important than something that is 5%. Sometimes girls need help in seeing the big picture of how their overall grade is established.
> ▷ Have her build in short breaks if that helps her focus. It may be effective for your daughter to set small goals for herself (e.g., read one section, do ten problems) and then assess whether she's fresh enough to continue. If she is, she sets another small goal. If not, she takes a short, timed break.
> ▷ Reinforce the concept that homework is her responsibility. You are not to do your daughter's work for her. Make yourself

available if she has questions but do not correct her work when she's done as this can lead to unnecessary arguments. Simply check to see that it's finished.

▷ Work to eliminate the "I forgot the textbook or the assignment excuse." Investigate whether you can borrow or buy an extra set of textbooks for your home if your daughter's school isn't using digital versions. Encourage your daughter to identify a fellow student in each class, preferably one without ADHD, she can contact for help with forgotten information.

Studying

Often, girls with ADHD will confuse preparing with studying. An example: Your daughter may be very proud of the flashcards she painstakingly prepared for her geometry class. But if she doesn't then study the flashcards and learn the material, those cards really haven't served their purpose. The older your daughter, the more she needs to be involved in working with her teachers to understand what she needs to study and in what depth. Here are some suggestions I've found helpful:

▷ *Ask the teacher for a study guide.* This can include a reading schedule and which content is to be covered in every class, and it will help keep her from falling behind if she uses it.

▷ *When possible, find out the format for upcoming tests and quizzes.* Your daughter will need to study differently for an essay test than she will for a multiple-choice test. Some girls are extremely hesitant to approach a teacher for this information but remind her that it's an important part of self-advocacy. She's not asking for the answers. She's asking for information about testing procedures.

▷ *Working in groups can be effective for many girls with ADHD.* See if your daughter can organize a study group of friends. They can help remind her of work requirements, and participating in discussions of the material will help her learn.

The following suggestions can help your daughter maximize her study time:

> ▷ Research shows that studying material for short periods over several days prior to a test produces better results than trying to learn everything the night before a test.
> ▷ Only study one subject at a time to avoid confusion.
> ▷ Review notes before beginning an assignment.
> ▷ Avoid the temptation to study with social media sites open on the computer. Distractions like these can prolong study time and interfere with concentration.

Extra Help

Organization and routine still may not be enough. If your daughter continues to have trouble grasping course content or needs hours and hours to finish her homework, it may be time to bring in supports. You want to be her loving parent, not a sentry who keeps her locked in her room at night slaving over her desk. Some solutions include:

> ▷ *A tutor.* If you can afford it, this is often a wonderful option for a student with ADHD. The one-on-one attention helps her maintain focus, and talking through the material is an effective learning method. Teachers are obvious choices, but sometimes a special neighbor or college student can make a great tutor. A gifted tutor can build a strong relationship with your daughter and will see her value and help her realize her abilities. No less important, if there are struggles over homework, then they're on someone else's watch. You're not the bad guy anymore.
> ▷ *An accommodation plan.* If your daughter is laboring for hours every night over the sheer amount of homework she is given, then ask her teachers about reducing her workload. With the appropriate paperwork (discussed in Chapter 8 – "When School Problems Escalate"), she may be eligible for an accommodation plan. If producing material in writing is laborious, she may be allowed to use voice typing for some assignments. Or it may be acceptable for her to complete only the even-numbered math problems if she can demonstrate mastery of the concepts. If your daughter's work is reduced,

make sure she still has enough practice to solidify the skill in her memory. Some teachers are very resistant to this but remind them how much longer it takes your daughter to complete assignments than those without ADHD.

▷ *A deadline extension.* Occasionally, your daughter may need to ask for additional days to complete an assignment. If this is part of her accommodation plan, then it's already available for her to use. I stress that this should be the exception, rather than the rule. Many students with ADHD tend to put things off, and being given an extension on the due date simply means their work piles up even more.

School Attendance

There are many reasons being in class every day is critical for your daughter. For one thing, it teaches her important skills for life – show up when you are scheduled. Secondly, missing classes only makes keeping up with the work more difficult. Thirdly, missing classes can easily become a habit and part of a bigger problem. It is especially important for the school to notify you when your daughter is missing classes without an excuse.

> *Susan, diagnosed with ADHD in fifth grade, initially started skipping a few classes here and there in middle school. On one occasion, she was caught vaping in the bathroom. Her father had recently passed away, so everyone gave her some slack because she was a grieving adolescent. Her mother and the school set up counseling, but she continued to be defiant. In her early years of high school, the problem of school attendance would come and go as would problems with her peer group. Then in her junior year, her mother found out in February that Susan had not been in one class since October. Of course, it was irresponsible on Susan's part and negligence on the part*

> *of her teacher and school. Unfortunately, by then school attendance was minor compared to other problems she had with drugs and alcohol.*

The scenario with Susan shows why attending to problems when they first appear is critical. When red flags start flying, they usually don't go away on their own and can morph into much bigger problems.

Teaching Her to Fail Forward

At one point or another, everyone fails. It's especially important for high school girls with ADHD to develop resiliency and learn from mistakes. As a parent, praise her efforts rather than the outcome. On a test, if she studied appropriately and gave it her best effort but failed the test, appreciate the effort she put in and help her figure out how to prepare for the next one. Even if she fails a test, it does not mean *she* is a failure. Help her recall all the times she was successful and use positive self-talk like, "Even though I didn't do well on my geometry test, I have passed many similar tests in the past and will figure out what I can do better next time."

> *It's especially important for high school girls with ADHD to develop resiliency and learn from mistakes. As a parent, praise her efforts rather than the outcome.*

Failure is temporarily uncomfortable, but it is important to let it go and move on to the next challenge. You want your daughter to understand that failure is an opportunity to learn, adjust, and try again. Help her resist the urge to internalize her failure and beat herself up over it. To encourage resiliency, help her:

> ▷ try new things and take risks,
> ▷ set realistic goals and break them down into small steps, and
> ▷ ask for help when needed.

Student and Parent Interview

Background

Lucy is a 19-year-old who has just successfully completed her first year of college. She was diagnosed with ADHD at 6 or 7 years old and has taken medication periodically.

Parent Interview

Q. How hard was it to accept the ADHD diagnosis? Did you share it with her right away?

I was initially ok with the diagnosis, actually relieved – knowing neither she nor I was crazy wondering "Why can't she function like others?" I didn't use the word ADHD until a few years later when she was around 10. I always told her it was a mild case. It wasn't until she was 19 when she realized she did not have a mild case of ADHD, she was a full-blown ADHD girl.

We discussed my strategy of claiming she was only mildly ADHD, and she thinks it was ok – this took away the victim role. She said it can be easy for a child to manipulate the parent with the ADHD card. It is important to know:

1. your child's strengths and weaknesses,
2. what they need help with and how much help, and
3. to identify tiredness vs. executive function skill deficits.

Q. What do you wish you had known about ADHD at the time of her diagnosis? What would you have done differently in terms of managing it?

There are two main "wish I had knowns." First, the impact of the struggle of girlfriends. Second, the importance of routine. I consciously did not have a routine because that is not reality. However, it is the foundation for growth, confidence, and keeping calmness in a child's mind. I would have focused more on a homework and weekend routines and eased up (a lot) on the yelling. Yelling does not help anyone or the situation. The child is not "misbehaving" but struggling. As a parent, knowing how to help the child would allow a successful outcome rather than tears and trauma.

Q. Do you feel ADHD has impacted your daughter socially? If so, how?

Unfortunately, yes! My biggest regret is not knowing about the social awkwardness and difficulties girls with ADHD have with making and keeping friends. If I had known, I would have had conversations with my child about how she is being a good friend and encouraged her to be aware of her behavior/ social cues around other girls. I would have also stayed in the background. I was a very involved mother, which caused a bit of helicopter parenting. When we reflected on the social and friendship relations, neither of us know exactly what she did, but the isolation was real.

Q. Have you observed that hormones seem to impact your daughter's ADHD in any way?

No, I believe my daughter transitioned with her hormones like any other girl. However, we had very hard rules:
- ▷ no boyfriends or dating boys until 16 years old
- ▷ very limited posting on social media and no bathing suit photos
- ▷ curfews

As my daughter is now 19 years old, these were the best decisions my husband and I made for her. She learned it's okay to be "alone" with herself which built confidence and personal awareness.

Q. What would be your advice on how to approach schools and teachers about children with ADHD?

I personally believe educators are inundated with students with ADHD and training has been provided. I would educate schools and teachers, if they are not aware, of the differences between boys and girls with ADHD.

Q. What has her transition to college been like? Does she have accommodations there and if so, what are they?

Transitioning into college was stressful for my daughter because she was going to a school out of state where she did not know anyone. However, she managed the first semester well because we knew what to expect from our older daughter. To buffer the transition we:

1. had her sign up for a lighter class load – 12 credit hours first semester;
2. reached out to the students with disabilities office requesting accommodations – they provided extra time on exams, not homework;
3. developed a weekly schedule/routine;
4. stocked her dorm room for the first semester, so there would be no pressure to run to the store for something – to remove stress (tampons, toilet paper, soap, shampoo, protein bars, protein powder mixes, school supplies and medications/vitamins).

Additional Topics that Might Be Helpful to Parents

Medication – Pediatricians can prescribe ADHD medications up to the age of 18. After that, psychiatrists prescribe. This was the biggest surprise to me. It was the second semester of freshman year of college, and her medication was running low with exams a few weeks away. We experienced a bit of a meltdown. My first line of defense is homeopathic options, and we tried multiple ones. Today my daughter will turn toward homeopathic choices first; however, for the larger projects, homework, and exams, she says, "The prescription meds are the only thing that truly work."

Open Dialogue – I found the most helpful tool was establishing a rapport with my daughter. I believed she understood herself and her needs. Once I removed my stubbornness and my helicopter behavior and started listening to her, I was able to meet her needs. One simple example: She struggles with getting things started. Her bedroom would look like a cyclone hit it. She could not start the cleaning process and still cannot at 19. We are now at the point where I will ask if I can help get the process started. You might think, as I once did, this is ridiculous, but accepting and understanding her capabilities allowed me to calmly communicate with her as we work toward a goal of adulthood and independence. Moreover, if I had established a routine when she was a child, the bedroom issue may not have been such a big deal.

Should have, Could have, Would have:

▷ Broken tasks down into steps with a calm voice and supportive heart

▷ Listened with open ears and observed with open eyes to determine her needs

▷ Given more love and support, hugs, positive talks because the struggle is real!

Pet Therapy

Having a dog helped my daughter in a few ways. It helped soothe her during those meltdowns from homework, when feeling overwhelmed, and when lonely because of the friendship struggles. (Please be realistic, you will be the primary caretaker of the pet, but the benefits for your child are worth it.)

Love Language Quiz

I did have my daughter take the Love Language Quiz when she was a teenager. (https://5lovelanguage.com/quizzes/love-language) This helped me know what I could do to let her know she is loved and was a way to strengthen our connection.

Student Interview

Q. What has helped you manage your ADHD?

When I was younger, I was in a smaller private school where the teachers kept a close eye on you. You couldn't get away with a whole lot. Being held accountable helped in a positive way. I attended the same school in middle school. It was challenging, but comfortable because everyone knew you. I started high school in a private school where there were many opportunities, but I wasn't happy there. All I really wanted from high school was my degree, so I transferred to my local public high school.

There was more room to fall behind there. When COVD-19 hit, I had to do three quarters online which was really hard for me to stay focused, but I managed.

Q. Has ADHD impacted your friendships? If so, how?

Yes, it did. When I was younger, it was hard to realize I had ADHD. I was told about it once or twice but forgot about it. I was quiet and aloof and did not add energy to a group. I was not invited to things and felt left out a lot. My friends were mostly my parents' friends' kids. In the private high school, I had trouble connecting to groups but had one close friend. In the public high school, I also had one friend. I think I was inattentive and just didn't seek out friends. In college, I am making much more of an effort to be more social. I was invited to join a sorority. I am learning to get along with a group of girls, and think I have matured. I try to stay aware of my body language.

Q. Have you found technology to be useful?

Yes and no. I decided to delete apps like Tik Tok and Instagram because I was wasting way too much time on them. I put timers on some of my other apps. I need to find an online schedule that really works for me.

Q. Thinking back, what would you have done differently in managing your ADHD?

I wish I had been coached on how to be more self-aware and form relationships with others at a younger age.

Q. Did you ever feel stigmatized or discriminated against because of your ADHD?

No, just the opposite. I love to claim my ADHD and don't take it as a disability. I feel like everyone has something. In high school I randomly used the accommodations, sometimes needing more help and sitting in front of the class. Now in college, you choose where to sit. So many of my classmates complain about running out of time on exams, so I feel lucky to have a different testing location and extended time. Most of my professors are understanding and helpful.

Q. Anything else you would like to add?

It would have been easy to use ADHD as a crutch if I had known more about it. I am used to putting in the hard work whereas lots of kids coast. I think knowing you must put in effort is better in the long run.

Planning for College or Post High School Training and Career

Your daughter's high school years are the time for both of you to shift your focus from what's immediately before you to the future – college or additional career training, career, or other life plans. It's a time for the boundaries to expand again.

In high school, your daughter will be given the opportunity to choose the classes and electives she wants to take. She'll start to consider where – and whether – to go to college. She'll think about what she wants to do for a living. She'll need your guidance, along with the input from others. Many successful adults with ADHD point to the importance of identifying strengths and passions and following those into a career.

Encourage your daughter to think about college early if that is a possibility for her, even during her freshman year. She'll feel your support, and it will help keep her focused on her goals and understand why she needs to work so hard in high school. One of my young clients offered this advice to other teens:

> Use college as a goal for motivation. You have one part of your brain that says give up, but the other half says you'll feel worse if you give up, so you have to try your best. You must identify where you are, decide what you want, and figure out how you are going to get there. Think of it as having a master plan.

Tools for Identifying Interests

There are two web-based tools you can use with your daughter for a fee if she is uncertain about her interests and future career possibilities. One is the Self-Directed Search, 5th edition by PAR Industries SDS (parinc.com/products/pkey509). This is a tool to help your daughter discover the majors, fields of study, and potential jobs that match her interests. After completing the survey, you'll instantly receive a written report that matches her personality type to potential occupations. Each occupation is linked to the *Occupational Information Network* database, which lists specific details about education, job requirements, employment outlook, and salary. This information is useful for researching a career in greater detail.

If your daughter needs help identifying her natural strengths and talents, a second web-based tool is the Kolbe A Index for Youth (www.kolbe.com). This is an online survey that also produces a written report for the student and parent. Once completed, you daughter can learn how to use her natural talents to excel in school and life. Ideally, parents and teens would discuss the results together from either of these and then incorporate them into the **Dynamic Action Treatment Plan** in Chapter 9.

College

Have her make a list of target and/or dream colleges. Not 20 schools. A half-dozen, maybe, and talk about why she's interested in them. Be objective and realistic. For instance, going to school near the beach is a legitimate draw for a young person, but it might not quite match what you're looking for in a curriculum. Going to a college 1,000 miles away from home is a legitimate draw for a young woman seeking independence, but it may not be affordable or wise to be that far away. Remind her that a college with small class sizes, academic support, engaged professors, and an active Office for Students with Disabilities is much more important than the athletic teams or where her friends are going.

If you and your daughter feel she may need a moderate level of support in college, two colleges specifically for students who have learning differences and need support are Landmark College in Putney, VT, and Beacon College in Leesburg, FL. Many other colleges welcome students with ADHD and provide significant support, such as:

▷ Northeastern University in Boston, MA, pairs students with expert counselors,

▷ Auburn University in Auburn, AL, has a semester-long SKILL Program that helps students adapt to college and involves weekly meetings with the counselor,

▷ University of Arizona in Tucson, AZ, features a Strategic Alternative Learning Technique Center (SALT) that provides ADHD coaches for a fee, and

▷ St. Louis University in St. Louis, MO, offers student success coaching.

Other resources include:

> ▷ *The KW Guide to Colleges for Students with Learning Differences*, 16th Edition, published by The Princeton Review in 2023.
> ▷ *ADDitude* magazine's "Questions to Ask Yourself Before You Choose a College," available at www.additudemag.com/adhd-college-accommodations-school-decision.

After you have done some research on your own, make an appointment for the two of you to sit down with your daughter's high school guidance counselor and talk about her choices and her likelihood of being admitted to her target colleges. This will be a great opportunity for her to practice advocating for herself, something she will have to do in college. Even practice questions beforehand and help her be prepared with a list of potential colleges and questions for her counselor. Hopefully she will walk away with a realistic list of colleges.

Visit as many schools as possible. Just being on campus, sitting in on classes, and talking to students will help your daughter see that college isn't just an extension of high school. It's a different world. She'll need different, new skills.

Begin to coach her on the life skills she'll need. If she doesn't already know how, teach her to do her own laundry. Let her begin to navigate bureaucracy herself. One great way to teach her life skills is by planning a trip together and teaching her the responsibility of taking care of details.

Help her stay on track with her classes. Teens with ADHD sometimes make impulsive choices. A student with ADHD might decide to take a class not because she's interested in it, but because her best friend is going to be in the class. In high school, the choices your daughter makes about her curriculum will start to affect her potential for admission to college in general, and to the colleges of her choice. If getting her work done requires additional time, encourage her to sign up for a light schedule. She needs to understand what goes into wise, long-term decision-making.

> *Darlene was so excited to be admitted to her first-choice college. Unbeknownst to her parents, she started procrastinating on her classwork for the last semester of her senior year and ended up failing three of her classes and was unable to graduate. Of course, her admission was rescinded. She was ultimately able to graduate, went on to a different college, and ultimately got a law degree but definitely paid a price for her poor decision-making in her senior year in high school.*

Technical, Career, or Military Training

As we all know, college isn't the answer for everyone's future. Many girls I know with ADHD have developed very successful careers by following their passions and interest in areas like the culinary arts, medical field, business, beauty industry, horticulture, and coding to name a few. There are many certification and diploma programs for training in various fields. Apprenticeships offer opportunities for on the job training and mentorship. Many students I have known who need structure have benefitted from being in the military. The most important thing for your girl's future is that she finds an area where she can thrive and be successful, happy, and independent.

Gap Year

If your daughter doesn't know what she wants to do after high school, taking a gap year can be a good solution. This extra year can have benefits for girls with ADHD, some of which include:

- ▷ providing more opportunity for maturation,
- ▷ getting more experience in managing time, money, and responsibilities,
- ▷ creating opportunities to explore different career options,
- ▷ allowing her to clarify her goals and discover new interests,
- ▷ reducing stress of having to make big decisions when she isn't ready.

Career Options

There are no careers that a woman with ADHD can't do. *ADDitude* magazine regularly publishes profiles of highly successful women with ADHD across a range of industries, from medicine to law to business to entertainment and the arts. Your daughter needs to understand that fulfilling careers result from a combination of talent, dedication, passion, and a great deal of hard work.

Home and Community Issues

As young people mature, society looks for them to take responsibility for themselves, their actions, and the choices they make. This extends across an ever-widening arc, from their social lives to the workplaces and on to the roadways. Remember that most girls with ADHD are still experiencing delays in impulse control, attention to detail, decision-making ability, problem solving, and social skills. In fact they may be months or years behind their peers without ADHD. Your daughter still needs time, tools, and tactics to succeed.

Remember that most girls with ADHD are still experiencing delays in impulse control, attention to detail, decision-making ability, problem solving, and social skills.

In *Understanding Girls With ADHD*, Nadeau et al. (2016) write, "The internal experience of a girl with ADHD is frequently one of chaotic disorganization, a whirling barrage of thoughts and feelings from within, as well as a relentless stream of unfiltered external stimuli" (p. 67). It's exhausting to be her, but it's also exhausting to be you. Her chaos spills over into your home and into your relationship. Of course, you love your daughter. But living with her is unbelievably stressful at times? (Trust me, living with *you* drives *her* crazy, too at times.) How do you manage?

In the Home

Parents

Research has shown us that families of children with ADHD have more negative, stressful, and intense interactions. Not surprisingly, it seems to be the relationship with Mom that is affected most drastically. Part of that is a practical matter – Mom is typically the one who manages the day-to-day events. Mothers have more contact, and from that results the potential for more conflict. Sometimes it's the daughter who initiates the dispute, but it can also be a frustrated, exhausted, or insensitive mother. Fathers tend to argue with teens about clothes, loud music, and fighting with their brothers and sisters. Mothers report those same arguments, but also tend to take over an "enforcer" role when it comes to grades, bedtime, homework, and choice of friends. Remember, life in your family is going to be more conflicted simply because you have a child with ADHD. As the adult, do your best to maintain balance and have structure that helps everyone co-exist together in the best way possible.

> *A colleague once tested a 14-year-old girl with ADHD who showed very strong visual spatial abilities for remembering pictures, as well as understanding how puzzle pieces fit together. He tried to build this up as one of her natural areas of strength by telling her she might be naturally good at design, graphics, or photography. Her eyes lit up. "I love taking pictures!" she exclaimed. "I asked for a camera for my birthday, but I didn't get it." At the end of the evaluation, the girl's mother came in to pick her up. The young lady reported her natural ability for seeing things spatially and mentioned again that she'd hoped for a camera. Her mother answered, "For the amount I had to pay for this testing, I could have bought one."*

Those words hurt. The girl's mood immediately changed, and she became sullen and withdrawn. It's just one example of the tumultuous relationship between mother and daughter, and it shows how one sentence can make a big difference in how you relate to one another. What if, instead, the mother congratulated her daughter for possessing such a special gift, and agreed to help her figure out a way to earn her camera?

Parents, for the next few days, take note of how you speak to your daughter. Because most girls with ADHD have the inattentive presentation, they'll often seem daydreamy, mentally checking out in the middle of a conversation. That's how she's wired, even though it may seem disrespectful. If you constantly voice your frustration with her in negative terms, your daughter may start to view her entire being in negative terms as well. Remember, her tendency is to internalize behaviors and interactions. As much as you're able, try to keep your communication respectful. If your daughter doesn't think you're in her corner, it's not a big leap for her to assume the rest of the world will be mean to her, too.

Siblings

If your daughter has siblings, keep an eye on how they relate to each other as well. A young person with ADHD can be entertaining, talkative, and engaging, but endless chatter can easily become annoying to her brothers and sisters. Help your children get a break from one another, so that annoyance doesn't escalate. Also – and it's not new advice – try to give your non-ADHD children the individual attention they deserve. That goes a long way toward alleviating any resentments they feel toward their sister. Try to level the playing field as much as possible, so you treat all your children equally. Make sure house rules – like obeying curfews, showing respect, and doing chores – are enforced uniformly. Communicate some of the challenges your daughter faces with ADHD to siblings in a respectful manner.

Discipline that Works

Just as many of your other parenting strategies have evolved, you also need to find discipline techniques that are appropriate and effective for the teenage years. Hinshaw (2022) has noted that many scientists and professionals consider authoritative parenting – not to be confused with authoritarian parenting which can be punitive and rigid – to be an excellent style because parents' firm limits (those non-negotiable rules) are "balanced by a democratic stance, through which the child comes to understand and learn the value of the limits" (p. 107) and ultimately becomes part of the negotiation over the course of development. Your approach needs to respect your daughter's increasing maturity and preserve your relationship with her while still building in the monitoring you may feel is necessary. Tall order? Maybe. But you may have been juggling life with ADHD for a long time. You can do this, too.

Many professionals recommend contracts whereby parents state their expectations of their children (like treat family members with respect, use no drugs or alcohol, follow curfews, and adhere to driving rules) with consequences and meaningful rewards attached. Girls would also add their reasonable expectations of parents, like not embarrassing them in front of friends etc. (Put teen contracts in a search engine for many examples.)

When situations arise causing conflict in the family, the goal would be for you and your daughter to look at those situations as simply another problem with a solution.

When situations arise causing conflict in the family, the goal would be for you and your daughter to look at those situations as simply another problem with a solution. By taking a problem-solving perspective, hopefully you and your daughter can develop a collaborative approach to solving many discipline problems. For example if she is constantly rude to a sibling, explore reasons that may be behind her negative feelings and what can be done to reduce the conflict. Perhaps the sibling is egging her on by purposely annoying her in a covert way – known to happen, right? Or perhaps one of her siblings breezes through life, so your daughter with ADHD may feel jealous. Help her understand that at some point, everyone has things that are not easy for them. She is ahead of the game because she has already learned to work hard and be flexible in searching for solutions to problems. Help her examine situations clearly and figure out ways to resolve them. If, for example, she suggests trying to think of a funny response when her siblings bug her rather than losing her temper, she can try that. Let her know that if that doesn't work, she will have to come up with another plan because disrespect and anger just aren't part of your family's way of operating. You will ultimately be the one in charge but having her initiate or even "buy into" the solution increases the likelihood of its success.

You are preparing your daughter for independence while still recognizing her need for monitoring and limits. It is a tricky dance and sometimes, it is helpful to have a family therapist intervene, especially if your daughter is defiant about rules made for her safety Below are a handful of discipline strategies that can be effective with teen girls with ADHD. Try them out and "rent to own" any that resonate with you and your daughter.

Natural Consequences

Natural consequences can be a great teacher and can prevent parents from becoming the "bad guys." For example, if she leaves her new tennis racket in the rain, it will likely be ruined. She will have to do without one for a while, borrow one, or use her own money to get a new one. But other examples may have more severe consequences: If she neglects her homework, she'll fail her classes. If she annoys her classmates, she'll struggle to make friends. Sometimes the cost of these can just be too high, especially for girls with ADHD who are typically much more easily discouraged. If she fails her classes or struggles with making friends, she may convince herself that she'll never succeed at anything. She needs more encouragement and support than this form of discipline typically provides in more important matters like school performance.

Consistent, Mild Consequences

This tactic can be a more effective solution to chronic discipline problems for a young person with ADHD. Instead of seeking a harsh punishment, start with the least restrictive, most lenient punishment possible. Many teenagers with ADHD remember one thing – that they were punished. They don't tend to remember how long they were punished. Lengthy punishments often end up hurting the entire family without any additional benefit. Teens with ADHD often repeat the unacceptable behavior, even when they've been punished. You may have to take away your daughter's iPod or cell phone for 20 two-day periods over the course of a year, but eventually she'll get the point.

Never threaten consequences you aren't prepared to impose.

Never threaten consequences you aren't prepared to impose. When you do that, your daughter will quickly learn that you don't mean what you say. She will continue to argue and test your limits, which is never a good thing for parents or teens.

Grounding

It's rare for any teenager to escape getting grounded. Proceed with caution if you're going down this road. Grounding your daughter will take her out of activities for a week, two weeks, a month – whatever sentence you've pronounced. That's a long time for a girl whose social network may already be fragile and whose social skills need daily practice. If you isolate her, the effects could range from rebellion to depression. If a situation calls for it, try grounding for short periods of time (a day or two). Warn your daughter ahead of time that this is the consequence she'll face for a particular rule violation, so she is ultimately choosing this for herself when she breaks the rule.

Losing Car or Electronic Privileges

Neither of these are given rights, much to your teenager's surprise! It's perfectly reasonable to refuse her the right to use her phone or social media for a period if she is not using it responsibly. If she's old enough and mature enough to drive, you can also take the car keys for a week if she's chronically late getting home and it's become a major inconvenience. But don't take away car privileges for two months if her room is messy. That's an overreaction.

Communication and Reasoning

There should be room in your relationship for both of you to express your opinions about whatever you feel she did wrong. You both need to speak respectfully and calmly. For a girl with ADHD, this can be an empowering way to build conflict-resolution skills in a nonthreatening environment. It will be most helpful if she can understand the problems her behaviors might have caused or the implications they may have for the future. If the two of you can view the occurrence as a situation that needs a solution and then work toward that end, your daughter's follow-through will probably be much better.

Second Chances

Far more than other kids, teens with ADHD need plenty of second (and third and fourth) chances to regain your trust and prove they have learned whatever lesson you've meant to teach. If your daughter messes up, discipline her. But after a while, give her another chance along with a hearty dose of forgiveness and encouragement.

The Last Word on the Last Word

Your daughter may argue every point. Some teens with ADHD do. It can be a tremendous source of stimulation for her and next to impossible for her to resist. But it's a no-win situation for you. Try not to let yourself get drawn into pointless arguments with your daughter. If you do, either let her have the last word or simply refuse to discuss the matter until she stops arguing.

In the Community

Her First Job

Much like an extracurricular activity, finding a part-time or summer job can give your daughter a place where she can excel. There are many valuable skills and lessons she can learn in the workplace:
  ▷ employer, coworker, and customer relations;
  ▷ the importance of being on time;
  ▷ remembering and following directions;
  ▷ a sense of independence;
  ▷ money management; and
  ▷ building a resumé for future positions.

If you and your daughter decide the time is right for her to find a job, talk through the commitment it takes to be a dedicated employee. There are any number of entry-level jobs well-suited to a creative, enthusiastic teen with ADHD, so take the time to help her find the right kind of job. Remind your daughter that she has what it takes to pursue jobs in many different areas, but selecting areas she is passionate about which utilize her strengths will bring greater commitment and job satisfaction.

Because working, even part-time, will be a new challenge, be prepared to help your daughter succeed. She'll need to establish a new routine and may need to practice some new skills. For instance, you can help her:

▷ Learn how to fill out a job application. Help her collect and keep data often required on applications at her fingertips, such as important telephone numbers and information about her school. She might benefit from filling out a practice application with you.

▷ Understand the interview process. If conducting a two-way conversation is difficult for your daughter, practice this at home. She needs to be comfortable answering questions about herself, but also needs to know when to stop talking and listen. Together, you could role-play through a typical interview scenario: Why are you interested in this job? Can you tell me about your strengths? What experiences have you had working on a team? Your daughter should also be ready to ask some basic questions about the job. This indicates her interest level to a potential supervisor.

▷ Pointers in communicating with her boss, especially if she has difficulties with relationships. It will be especially important for her to let her boss know what she needs to be successful. For example, she may need to practice a new skill a few times to gain her confidence before she is expected to do it independently.

▷ Be on time. Before it becomes an ingrained habit, you may need to wake her up, or remind her it's time to leave for work. It could mean setting two alarm clocks, leaving reminder notes on her mirror, or having someone call or text her when it's time to get ready for work. You don't want her to lose the job because of being late. Arriving at the job 5–10 minutes early should become part of her routine.

▷ Manage her clothing and work-related items. Develop a routine to make sure her work clothes get laundered, and the other items she needs daily are ready to go when she is. A teen with ADHD is just as likely to misplace her plastic nametag as her homework. Having a specific place where these items are kept is a good habit to develop.

> ▷ Work on her manners. No matter where she goes, your daughter will need to have adult, appropriate interactions with people. If she blurts out inappropriate remarks, interrupts people, or chatters endlessly to her coworkers, she'll jeopardize her job. Employers need to see the same kinds of self-control she's been working to develop in other areas of life.

> ▷ Show her how to be a team player. It's unlikely your daughter will be working alone. Having a job will be a wonderful experience for her to bring her unique perspective to a group effort, but she also must be willing to consider others' ideas and figure out how to work with people she might not like.

> ▷ Explain the value of extra effort. By nature, your daughter may be a people-pleaser, so this might come naturally to her. But when she is being paid to do a job, she should try to do it in the best way she can. It may be a confidence booster to receive compliments on her effort.

Having a "Work-for-It" Attitude

Some kids believe that showing up to a job is really all that should be required of them. Young people get into trouble when they feel certain work is "beneath them." An attitude of entitlement is dangerous and unrealistic, and you need to make sure your daughter doesn't buy into that kind of thinking. Any job is worth doing well. But developing that kind of determination can be tricky for kids with ADHD, who not only have trouble thinking in the long-term, but are easily bored with the kinds of mundane tasks that require ongoing, sustained effort.

It will be great if your daughter can find a summer job that sparks her interest. But she needs to practice her ability to work steadily no matter what the circumstances. You can help her develop this patience by assigning her chores that she does not do for pay, but for the gratification of a job well done. It's a great way to give her a sense of success and mastery, and she'll get used to doing what's required of her.

Money Management

Once your daughter has an income (or if you give her an allowance), she'll need your guidance in learning to manage her money. Together, you can begin to explore basic financial principles such as:

▷ how a checking account works and how to balance it,

▷ how compound interest works, and

▷ how to pay bills and expenses on time. This is a little like homework. But in this case, if she fails to do it (or forgets), the penalty isn't a failing grade. The consequences will be additional fees and eventually, a poor credit score. A thousand reminders from you may not be as effective as the first $35 late fee that comes out of her own pocket. Today there are many apps that make transfer of money so easy, like Zelle and Venmo, to name a few, but it is important to understand security issues unique to these services.

People with ADHD are especially vulnerable to spending their money impulsively. Saving is a very difficult concept for them to grasp because it's so abstract. Saving her money to buy something later is not nearly as stimulating as buying something – almost anything – right now. As she matures, she needs to understand that the concepts of self-control and delayed gratification apply to her finances as well. Depending on the severity of your daughter's ADHD, she might be months or years behind her peers in her ability to handle money soundly.

It's a simple coping strategy, but if your daughter is saving for a big purchase, she should not take a wallet full of cash every time she goes with her friends to the movies or the mall. Restricted-access accounts, like long-term CDs, are a great place to park money meant for a car or savings for a goal.

If you feel your daughter needs to carry a credit card for emergencies, a card with a prepaid balance or a debit card you monitor carefully may be the way to go. Show your daughter that you trust her with a small amount. You can increase her access as she shows that she can handle it.

Driving

Another major milestone for your daughter will be when she slides behind the wheel of a car. It represents freedom, independence, and being on the brink of adulthood. For you, it represents a major loss of control and untold worries! Unlike many of the other obstacles you've navigated, this one truly is a matter of life and death.

You may have a sense that your daughter is not ready to handle the responsibility of driving when her friends without ADHD begin getting their licenses. This is common feeling among parents of girls with ADHD, so you are on firm footing if your gut feeling tells you she is not yet ready to get her license. As you could guess, studies have not been focused on large clinical samples of girls but have documented risks associated between ADHD and traffic violations for teens – both boys and girls – with ADHD. Barkley (2020) states, "… on average drivers with ADHD often do not get their licenses until 20–21 years of age while drivers who don't have ADHD get theirs between 17 and 18 years of age" (p. 256). He notes that the teen years form the peak ages of risk for drivers. He says, "And the typical cause of most crashes is driver inattention, especially at higher speeds, followed by being highly impulsive (willing to take risks others wouldn't). If your teen has ADHD, magnify those risks two to five times" (p. 257).

One of the reasons Barkley is such a proponent of limiting nighttime driving for teens with ADHD is that accident rates spike late at night and early in the morning. If your daughter is driving and takes medication to manage her ADHD, you need to be aware of the times that her medication begins to wear off. Take precautions to see that she avoids driving when she may be more distracted or impulsive.

When the timing is right, the day she earns her license is a day she'll never forget. Celebrate this moment together. But also emphasize that driving is a privilege, not a right. She needs to earn and continue to earn the privilege of driving a car.

Rules for operating a motor vehicle are essential, as is taking her ADHD medication as prescribed. Especially in the case of a young driver with ADHD, it's important to see those rules every time she gets behind the wheel. A contract agreeing to follow the rules is essential. One can be downloaded at *ADDitude* magazine: www.additudemag.com/driving-contract-adhd-teen-driver-safety-rules. Her responsibilities might include:

▷ Absolutely NO alcohol or drugs.

▷ Keep music low.

▷ No wearing headphones or ear buds.

▷ No texting. There are mobile apps you can download to your daughter's phone to disable it when she is driving.

▷ No talking on the cell phone, unless it's a parent calling. Then she should wait until she can pull off the road safely before she takes or returns your call.

▷ No other teens in the car until she has driven for six months. After your daughter has earned your trust, you could allow her to drive one friend providing she can stay focused on the road.

▷ Obey the speed limit and all traffic rules.

Your part of the contract might include promising to give her calm and respectful feedback on her driving and agreeing not to punish her if she calls you for a ride home because she's under the influence of drugs or alcohol.

You must have immediate, preestablished consequences for violating rules associated with her use of the car, and they need to be reasonable and proportionate to the offense. It's not reasonable to remove her car privileges altogether if she's a half-hour late getting home one day or if she forgets to fill the gas tank. That kind of offense might warrant loss of driving privileges for a week. But if you find she's been drinking and driving or driving recklessly, the penalty needs to be strict and severe. She needs to know this.

Beyond these basic rules, there are several additional precautionary measures recommended for teen drivers with ADHD:

▷ Figure out an "essential documents" system – like her driver's license, registration, and insurance card for whatever car she's driving. Together, devise a routine to help her remember these each time she drives.

▷ Ensure she gets plenty of practice, with you or another responsible adult in the car. Don't give her permission to take her driver's test until you are convinced she meets the criteria for being a safe driver.

▷ Be sure she understands the long-term consequences of reckless driving. This includes death or injury to herself or others, property damage, and loss of her driver's license.

▷ Make sure your daughter knows what to do in case of emergency. Does she know how to handle an accident? When a police car pulls her over? A flat tire or other mechanical breakdown? How should she respond to a stranger who has pulled over to offer help? Does your family have a roadside assistance program? Go over the scenarios with her, not to frighten her, but to help her be prepared.

▷ Consider having your daughter pay for her auto insurance if she has a job. The greater the risk she becomes, the more her insurance will cost. She'll have a financial incentive to stay safe.

▷ Remember the "other stuff." One mom told the story about her daughter, a new driver who had ADHD. The girl pulled into a service station to get gas. She put the nozzle into the tank and began to pump the fuel before deciding to run into the convenience store for a snack. She paid for her food, returned to her car and sped off – forgetting all about the gasoline that was still pumping away. Another girl with ADHD put diesel fuel in a car designed for regular gas, causing a huge repair bill. Help your young driver remember that she must pay attention all the time, not just when she's behind the wheel.

▷ Set a good example for her. If you want her to drive safely, make sure she sees you driving safely. Your behavior will always have a powerful impact on your daughter.

Your Daughter's Physical and Emotional Health

Teen girls with ADHD are going to need extra help and guidance in several areas – developing a healthy lifestyle, understanding their own bodies, dating, emotions, and maintaining a healthy, positive self-image.

Sleep and the High School Student

Most current research shows that a typical teenager's body is designed to stay up late into the night and sleep well into the morning. Our school systems, on the other hand, still run on up-with-the-chickens time. In many parts of the country, high school students are in class by 7:30 a.m. Studies suggest that half of all teens with ADHD have additional sleep challenges. Many girls with ADHD report finding it hard to quiet their brains. Their sleep can be restless, or they may wake frequently in the night. They often feel tired in the morning.

Your daughter can't learn effectively if she can't get proper rest. In addition to trying common-sense procedures at bedtime (e.g., no caffeine, no cell phones or texting, no video games right before bed), you might explore the following:

▷ *Establish a reasonable bedtime.* Talk this through. For instance, your daughter may observe that she usually feels tired at about 10 but gets a "second wind" after 11. An optimal bedtime for her would be 10:30 to 10:45.

▷ *Don't start projects after a certain time.* Whether they're school-related or just for fun, big projects can make a person with ADHD lose track of time. If she becomes absorbed, she might look up to see that it's 3 a.m.

▷ *Get plenty of exercise.* There's a lot to be said for taking a bike ride, a swim, or a run after school. A tired body sleeps better.

▷ *If possible, arrange the school schedule to avoid your daughter's typical groggy times.* It may be possible to set up her school day so her heaviest academic classes are scheduled when she is most alert with non-academic classes (e.g., P.E., art, music) when she tends to run out of steam.

Her Hormones

Your daughter already may feel awkward and out of place among her peers because of her ADHD, and puberty can make those feelings more pronounced. Make sure your daughter understands what's happening to her body.

The hormones that regulate her menstrual cycle can affect her mood and functioning. During the first two weeks of the menstrual cycle (starting with the first day of the period), levels of estrogen are on the rise. This elevates the levels of serotonin and dopamine, the feel-good neurotransmitters in the brain. During weeks three and four, progesterone levels rise and diminish those feel-good effects. These fluctuating hormone levels can affect your daughter with ADHD, on both an emotional and a functional level.

Sexual Behavior

During adolescence, your daughter will probably start to feel the sexual fluttering that is normal for any teenager. For teens with ADHD, the line between dating and sexuality is a fine one. Barkley (2020) has conducted exhaustive studies of children, adolescents, and teens with ADHD. His research is often shocking and showed that girls with ADHD are "far more likely than other girls to get into sexually compromising situations and to be victimized or assaulted sexually than typical girls of the same age" (p. 254). He also found that teens with ADHD (both boys and girls) "started having sexual intercourse a year ahead of typical teens and were likely to change partners more often" (p. 254). They were also less likely to use contraception and were "10 times (!) more likely to get pregnant" (p. 254).

Parents, sit up and take notice. You already know that girls with ADHD have little self-control. They can be impulsive. They find it difficult to delay gratification. So from physical and psychological perspectives, the temptation to have sex is powerful. Girls with ADHD often feel socially rejected and may seek affirmation through sexual relationships. Remember that the drive to "fit in" during the teen years is a huge one. Because she has trouble projecting long-term consequences of her actions, your daughter may not be affected by fear of getting pregnant or the threat of contracting a sexually transmitted disease.

I urge you not to turn a blind eye to the possibility that your daughter is acting on her strong sexual urges. Here are some tools and guidelines to help her:

 ▷ Talk to her about the rest of her life. If she becomes pregnant, it will forever change her, no matter the outcome. Taking care of a baby is a full-time commitment. She may not understand that millions of teens contract STDs every year and that for some of them, like HIV and herpes, there are no cures.

 ▷ Don't rely on school sex-education classes alone. Anticipate the physical changes she's experiencing and discuss them openly. If this is impossible or difficult for you or her, make sure she has access to good resources she can read or watch. Just because your daughter has ADHD and may have difficulty with reading material, don't presume she won't read a book about sex.

 ▷ Make sure she knows your family's moral code. Reinforce how loved and valued she is, so she does not feel the need to go outside of your home to experience love and affection.

 ▷ Many parents presume their daughters know how to say "no" to a boy. That can be a dangerous and false assumption. Make sure she understands that she has the right to say no to sexual activity and to be respected.

▷ Decide how you are going to handle the issue of birth control. This is highly personal and can be put on the back burner because parents find birth control uncomfortable to discuss. However, it's a conversation you'll want to have with your daughter so that she's not left wondering. Let her know your stance on birth control, and make sure she understands exactly how it is used correctly, if that is a decision you make.

Mostly importantly, be available to discuss – calmly and thoughtfully – any issues of sexuality that come up. Remember, you *want* her to come to you.

Gender Exploration

Today is a new day in terms of teens questioning their gender identity and how it will be expressed. If your daughter isn't comfortable with her internal sense of being female, you and she may have many questions. It is important to listen to your daughter's feelings without judgement and keep lines of communication open. Make sure you have a respectful and knowledgeable health care provider and seek additional support if needed. As difficult as it may be to accept your child's choices, it is important to assure her of your love and support because she may not experience that in the community. Remember how critical it is for her to be able to come to you with issues and questions.

Dating

It is important to discuss your family's dating rules before she starts to have romantic relationships. This will help her know what to expect when the time comes. These include:

▷ When she can go on dates and how often. Rules may differ for the school year, school holidays, and summertime.

▷ Who can she date? What if you don't know the person? Typically, your daughter will date a friend from school or the community. But she might wish to date someone you don't know. It is important to make sure you meet anyone you don't know.

▷ Where they're going, what they'll be doing, and whom they'll be with. If you would not permit your daughter to attend unsupervised parties alone, she shouldn't be allowed to go to one on a date.

▷ Guidelines for when her boyfriend comes to your house. Her boyfriend should be welcome in your home. Whether you approve of him or not, make him feel comfortable. If he's not the person for her, she'll figure it out eventually. But she's never to have him over when she's home alone, and you'll want to limit the time they're alone together in a room with closed doors.

▷ What if she breaks a rule? Your daughter needs to know in advance that she will face consequences for breaking one of your rules about dating. They have been put in place for her well-being, even though she will likely not see that. Dating is a privilege that shows you trust her. If she loses that trust, take away that privilege for a week or two, and then return it for a trial period.

Comorbid Mental Health Concerns

As mentioned throughout the book, your daughter is at risk for developing additional comorbid disorders by virtue to having ADHD. For example, an article published in *Pediatrics* in 2016 by Tung et al. compared the incidence rates of externalizing behavior disorders and anxiety and depression between girls with ADHD and those without over multiple studies. They found that "compared with girls without

ADHD, girls with ADHD were most likely to have comorbid CD (conduct disorder) (9.4 times) and ODD (oppositional defiant disorder) (5.6 times), followed by depression (4.2 times) and anxiety (3.2 times)." These disorders can seriously impact a girl's and her family's lives.

Below is a brief discussion of some of those disorders to begin to build your awareness. Clearly if your daughter experiences any of these you should get professional help sooner rather than later. They can be very tricky to diagnose because of so many overlapping symptoms with ADHD, so take care to seek out very perceptive and thorough professionals, especially psychiatrists, neuropsychologists, and mental health therapists.

Disruptive Behavior Disorders

The hallmarks of externalizing conditions like conduct disorder and oppositional defiant disorder are defiance, disregard for rules and cultural norms, and aggression. Most teenage girls show some defiance in their rush to independence, but these disorders take defiance to a whole different level. Hinshaw notes that conduct disorders and oppositional defiant disorders are more prevalent in girls with ADHD, combined presentation than in inattentive or hyperactive presentations. He has observed that females' show of aggressive behavior is often through "relational aggression. That is, instead of physically confronting their peers, they may attempt to ruin reputations through the spreading of rumors or 'backstabbing' via other means" (p. 24). There is some thinking that oppositional defiant disorder can morph into the more serious conduct disorder at older ages. Behavioral therapy involving the family is critical to learn how to respond to this level of defiance.

Depression

Depression can be debilitating with its hall mark dark moods, loss of motivation, lethargy, social withdrawal, and sleep and appetite disturbance. It is linked to the high suicide rate in teens, so immediate and comprehensive treatment is necessary. Medication is often needed to lift the depression so the person can benefit from Cognitive Behavior Therapy.

Anxiety

It is understandable how girls with ADHD can experience some level of anxiousness. It can start with worry about what people think, questions about whether they can meet expectations, how they can fit in socially, and a host of other concerns. Some teens develop physical symptoms, such as rapid heartbeats or stomach aches. When these worries are out of proportion to the situation and impair functioning, it could be an anxiety disorder. As with depression, Cognitive Behavior Therapy and sometimes medication are treatments.

Bipolar Disorder

Bipolar disorder is often characterized by symptoms of mania and depression. It has many overlapping symptoms with ADHD, like difficulty concentrating, disturbances of sleep, racing thoughts, distractibility, and impulsivity. In my experience with clients with bipolar disorder, medication is a crucial part of treatment and will require a psychiatrist expert at balancing medication needs, which could include mood stabilizers, antipsychotics, or an antidepressant.

Cutting and Self-Harm

These behaviors provide a means to express deep emotional distress. Those who injure themselves feel as though they have no choice, and injuring themselves can make them feel better – but only temporarily. Self-harm is accompanied by feelings of shame, guilt, and loneliness. The sufferers are usually unable to share their feelings and actions with family or friends. They aren't trying to get attention. In fact, they will usually make it a priority to keep the act a secret.

Because young women with ADHD tend to internalize their pain, some turn to self-harm to cope with the vastness of their emotions.

Red flags include unexplained wounds, usually on the wrists, arms, thighs, or chest; bloodstains on clothing or linens; withdrawal; irritability; and an unwillingness to reveal arms or legs even in hot weather. Hinshaw et al. (2012) reported "suicide attempts and self-injury … were highly concentrated" in ADHD-combined presentation. Immediate professional help is warranted in these young women.

One brave father shared his experience with his daughter's cutting.

The day I found out that she had cut, I was heart-broken. I quickly scanned the Internet for articles about cutting, why girls did it, and fear washed over me. Although I saw causes that fit (stuffing feelings and a rocky relationship with Mom), I also saw a few that scared me (abuse and other harms of that nature). Not wanting to put words in her mouth, I approached her room with love and understanding and confronted her about it. I told her that I knew and asked if she wanted to talk about it. She was scared that I knew but seemed to be truthful in her answers. I left feeling confident that the reasons were an inability to express her emotions and an inability to please Mom. I let my daughter know that she could talk to me about anything. I would never judge her. I wanted to be available to teach her to express her emotions in a healthy way.

I also worked with her mom to encourage her to communicate in a more positive way. We began to restrict time away from home with friends that seemed to have a negative influence, opting for time at our house with these friends. At the time, we felt absolute restriction from friends would be more destructive as this was one of her issues and would leave her with no friends. This also gave us an opportunity to invest in the friend's life as well. We also arranged a counselor, but our daughter didn't connect with the first person we saw. So, while searching for a new one, the counseling was left to us. Increased Daddy–daughter time seemed to help. Over time, it seems she is getting better and better at expressing herself, and honestly, we are getting better at accepting who she is rather than what we might want her to be. The cutting stopped, although the emotional outbursts have not. We are currently searching for a new counselor. It is a constant teaching and learning process to battle the lies that so abundantly exist in our culture. She is an incredibly gifted and wonderful child! I just have to never miss an opportunity to tell her that because the world around her tells her differently.

Eating Disorders

These disorders include anorexia (the inability to consume enough calories to maintain a healthy body weight); bulimia (cycling between eating and purging using vomiting, laxatives, or excessive exercise); binge eating; and compulsive overeating. Puberty is a common time for the onset of eating disorders, which can be fatal or cause long-term physical injury. Girls with ADHD are susceptible to begin self-medicating with food, especially sugar, chocolate, and carbohydrates. That behavior can become addictive and when coupled with our society's preoccupation with weight and physical beauty, can lead a girl to follow those comforting binges with purges to try to achieve "perfection."

Other Addictive Behaviors

Girls with ADHD are often plagued with the feeling that they don't fit in. Girls in general have a far greater need than boys for relationships and emotional connection. Girls with ADHD may be willing to risk substance abuse so they can achieve a kind of peer acceptance they may never have had. They want to belong, even if they must smoke, drink, or do drugs to make that happen. I have seen this firsthand in one of the girls I have worked with who was caught using drugs by her parents. She told them, "Using drugs is the first time in my life that I have felt like I was really cool." Luckily, they were able to intervene in the early stages and found a drug addiction counselor who was able to help their daughter.

Importance of Being Connected, Aware, and Proactive

Please be clear that my intention is not to scare you. Although the research suggests an increased rate of these disorders in girls diagnosed with ADHD, it does not mean it will automatically happen to your daughter. I want only to stress how important it will be for you to monitor her behavior, observe her, listen to her, and support her. If she is faced with any of these issues, there is a great chance that she's feeling shame and guilt. Please do your very best not to judge, lecture, or criticize. Instead, understand that these can be deeply rooted psychopathologies that require serious, compassionate, and often immediate treatment.

If you have the sense that something is wrong, seek professional help for your daughter. Don't be afraid to seek a second opinion and keep digging until you can get at the root of the problem. Often a team approach is the best means of identifying and treating coexisting conditions, and that could include input from a psychiatrist, clinical psychologist, physician, or university-affiliated hospital. The most important thing is to get her the help she needs.

Self-Esteem

The teen years can be rough on any girl's self-confidence. As a girl grows and matures, she may experience moments of pure awkwardness she is sure no adult can comprehend. She may feel her peers are so much more successful and so unapproachable. She wants to be seen as cool, as fitting in – but how? Her own body betrays her: her face may break out, her arms and legs may seem too long, or her hips too wide. If only she could be taller, shorter, more athletic, or funnier, or have better hair. She's overflowing with emotions, but she doesn't have the inclination or the words to express them. So those feelings get stuffed inside, making her feel crazy at times. Then factor in ADHD.

If your daughter has been struggling with ADHD since she was a little girl, there's a chance her self-esteem may already have taken a hard hit. She may have been called disruptive, uncooperative, reactive, unfocused, or belligerent to name a few, and she may still carry the hurt from them. Is it any wonder that by the time they're in their early teens, some girls find it impossible to list even one of their strengths? And if her diagnosis is relatively recent, she may look at it as a crushing blow, something to set her apart from her peers. But hopefully, she will find relief to know the difficulties she has been having have a name and strategies to make management easier.

Indeed, when you ask your daughter about how she feels, a lot of the time her answer will be, "different." Adolescence is a time when fitting in becomes as important to a young person as almost anything, and that is particularly true for girls. More relational by nature than boys, girls are also more likely to define themselves by how other people feel about them – whether they have ADHD or not. By the time she reaches high school, your daughter may have been feeling left out or misunderstood for a very long time.

See if you could apply any of these traits to your daughter (Teach, 2012):

> ▷ She is anxious, eager to please.
> ▷ She is very reactive to even a hint of criticism.
> ▷ She is a perfectionist.
> ▷ She is easily wounded in social situations.
> ▷ She feels isolated.
> ▷ She is verbally impulsive (e.g., interrupting, talking too loudly, speaking before thinking).
> ▷ She is bullied, either physically or emotionally.

Every one of these characteristics can impact the quality of your daughter's relationships, and the quality of your daughter's relationships can have a direct impact on her self-esteem. Whereas boys with ADHD tend to be more active and physically aggressive, girls with ADHD tend to turn that energy inward – and it can create havoc with their self-esteem. Girls' friendships are more complex. They are held to a stricter code socially, from the way they look, to the way they dress, to the way they act. Because girls with ADHD have so much difficulty picking up on social clues and navigating relationships, they suffer. But they often suffer in silence.

As a caring parent, you can take measures to restore or protect your daughter's self-confidence. In fact, it's essential that you do so. Her self-esteem is closely linked to her likelihood for success now and into adulthood.

Components of Self-Esteem

An individual builds self-esteem bit by bit, by being valued by those around her and by developing her strengths which can allow her to find success in a variety of areas in life, at school, with friends, and/or in relationships. True positive self-worth, particularly in the case of a young woman with ADHD, needs to include a number of elements:

▷ She sees herself as valuable.

▷ She believes she can identify and fix what's wrong. Your daughter already knows that life with ADHD is challenging. If her self-esteem is healthy, she has begun to develop the ability to identify when there's a problem and to have confidence that she can, with effort, work toward a solution. If her grades have slipped, she's aware of the steps she needs to take and follows through. If she's had an argument with a buddy, she doesn't give up on the friendship. She figures out what went wrong and works it out. The key to this aspect of self-esteem is her belief that her efforts can be productive.

▷ She tries. Some teens with ADHD have become the unwitting victims of "learned helplessness." It's often quicker and easier for adults to do something for a girl with ADHD than it is to teach her to do it for herself. Sadly, when she grows up, she may come to believe there are many things she's incapable of doing on her own. That can result in an extremely low sense of self-worth. On the other hand, a young woman who's willing to take a risk and attempt to figure things out – even if she's not successful all the time – is likely to have higher self-esteem. She will believe that trying may result in success, at least sometimes.

▷ She views her ADHD not as a problem but as something that makes her different and special. Believing that she's unique in a positive way is a key component to healthy self-esteem. As she grows older, your daughter may begin to see that there are components of her ADHD that can help her succeed. Encourage this sort of thinking, and she'll feel good about who she is and how she's wired. Maybe she is a big picture thinker and doesn't get mired in the details, or perhaps she can hyperfocus on something of interest to her. Some girls with ADHD are friendly and outgoing or are great problem-solvers because they see things in a different way. Make sure she knows about the long list of influential, tal- ented, and often brilliant people who have (or were believed to have had) ADHD. Some of these include Simone Biles, gym- nast; Katherine Ellison, journalist and Pulitzer Prize winner; Michelle Rodriguez, actress; Cynthia Gerdes, owner of Hell's Kitchen Restaurant; Patricia Quinn, pediatrician and author; Evelyn Polk Green, educator; Marta Bot, makeup artist to the stars; Margaux Joffe, producer; and Caitlin D'Aprano, entrepreneur.

▷ She develops and maintains self-control. Your daughter needs to know that ADHD is not in charge of her. A person with high self-esteem is learning to exert control over herself, her feelings, and her reactions. Although this ability may be naturally delayed in a girl with ADHD, it's a crucial part of self-confidence to know that she can trust herself to stay in control.

▷ She acknowledges her own efforts and rewards herself. If your daughter feels valued and confident, then she'll understand it's OK to give herself a pat on the back when she really tries hard at something. If she's feeling good about herself, then she'll realize that it's the effort that earns the reward, not the outcome. She's not after perfection, which is unhealthy. She's rewarding persistence.

▷ She has a parent or parents who support, praise, and love her for who she is. Time and again, adults with ADHD report that their parents were their most consistent encouragers. As children and teens, they knew home was a safe place. They never doubted their self-worth because they always felt loved by the people who mattered most in their lives.

Believing that she's unique in a positive way is a key component to healthy self-esteem.

So what does healthy self-esteem look like? In this case, that may be better answered by discussing what it doesn't look like. Your daughter shouldn't be walking around feeling inferior every day of her life. But it's also a warning sign if she constantly brags that she's better than everybody else. That kind of false bravado can be a red flag for real difficulty with self-confidence lurking beneath the surface of her big talk. She should know that she has strengths and weaknesses; that she's wonderfully flawed just like the rest of us. Like everything in your walk with ADHD, the pursuit of healthy self-esteem is about balance.

Self-Esteem-Building Strategies for Teen Girls

As your daughter matures, she becomes more capable of understanding how her own actions and thought patterns contribute to her self-esteem. Encourage her to boost her own self-esteem by:

▷ *learning how to make and keep friends.* Friendships are an important defense against the tumult of adolescent life. The good news? She doesn't have to have dozens of friends to get a boost. One study found that the presence of just one friend reduced the likelihood that a girl with ADHD would be mistreated by other girls (Cardoos & Hinshaw, 2011).

▷ *developing "islands of competence."* This concept comes from Dr. Robert Brooks, educator and faculty member at Harvard Medical School. Everyone has some special gift, and some people have many. Your daughter needs to have at least one special area in which she can shine. It could be in art, sports, music, computer programming, salesmanship, teaching, or other areas.

▷ *identifying life skills that will serve her well as an adult.* Ironically, the same qualities that are considered a drawback in a child with ADHD can be beneficial to an adult in the workplace. It can be an eye-opening exercise to look at your daughter's individual characteristics and define which ones might be extremely valuable to her later in life. For example, her high energy level is frustrating when she's expected to sit still all day in school, but it will serve her very well if she decides to pursue a career in sales or as an engineer in charge of a production facility. Challenge her to brainstorm ways her gifts will help her in the future. You might also arrange to have her take an online inventory like the Keirsey Temperament Sorter at www.keirsey.com or the Myers-Briggs Type Indicator® (MBTI®) | Official Myers-Briggs Personality Test (themyersbriggs.com) to help her determine her skills and personality strengths. Magazines are full of stories about successful surgeons, educators, artists, and entrepreneurs – women often diagnosed in adolescence or as young adults.

▷ *realizing good is great.* In many cases, girls with ADHD aren't striving to be the stars of the team or a standout student. They just want to know they're good. This is healthy thinking. Knowing she's good in at least one area will help her realize she can be good at many other things.

▷ *setting small goals.* It can be self-defeating to look at an overwhelming challenge or lofty goal, particularly for a teenage girl with ADHD. It's far gentler on her self-confidence to set smaller goals and feel the confidence boost that comes from achieving each one. Imagine your daughter thinking about saving enough money to buy a car. Now help her break that down into small, manageable pieces: $25 a month, for instance. Maybe you'll even match all (or a portion) of it if she's faithful to her goal. By overcoming the challenge bit by bit, her confidence will build and she'll see she *can* do it.

▷ *having hope.* Things tend to happen just a little later for people with ADHD. Encourage her not to lose sight of the fact that good things will still happen for her, even if she feels like ADHD has really messed up her life. She might try keeping a "gratitude journal" so she can remember the times things went right for her. It's easy to forget.

Your daughter may relate to and find the following books helpful.

▷ *You Grow Girl!: A Self-Empowering Workbook for Tweens and Teens* by Kim Dever-Johnson

▷ *The Self-Esteem Workbook for Teens: Activities to Help You Build Confidence and Achieve Your Goals* by Lisa M. Schab

▷ *The Anxiety Workbook for Teens: Activities to Help You Deal with Anxiety and Worry* by Lisa M. Schab

▷ *The Girl Guide: Finding Your Place in a Mixed-Up World* by Christine Fonseca

Strategies for Parents

She needs to know she's precious to you, not a bother, despite the wild ride you and she have experienced with her ADHD.

▷ Don't for a minute forget the influence *you* continue to have in building and nurturing your daughter's feelings of self-worth. Remember, the most effective support she'll ever get comes from you, when you say and believe with your whole heart, "I know you can do it."

▷ Love her unconditionally. Love your daughter exactly as she is – her gifts, her talents, her quirks, and her faults. She needs to know she's precious to you, not a bother, despite the wild ride you and she have experienced with her ADHD. When a girl is accepted and cherished in her own family, what other kids think of her tends to matter a whole lot less. Your love goes a long way to offset the actions and words of mean-spirited peers.

▷ Make a list of her strengths. Begin to list all your daughter's gifts and talents. Find a quiet time to share your list with her, and make sure she has a copy of it. It may become one of her most cherished possessions.

▷ Help her build on those strengths you just listed. As a parent of a young woman with ADHD, you need to keep her engaged and growing. Once her eyes have been opened to her many gifts, explore together how she can build upon them. Find seminars she can attend, books she can read, or volunteer opportunities she can pursue.

▷ Have fun with her. Make sure to laugh together. Enjoy each other. Create memories.

▷ Stay engaged. As your daughter matures, continue teaching her the skills she needs to feel confident in life. She's old enough now to really grasp the consequences of her actions on herself and others, and you can coach her.

▷ Teach by example. You cannot simply bestow self-esteem upon someone. You need to demonstrate how your choices and actions produce your own feelings of self-worth. Talk with your daughter about the beginnings of your own self-esteem.

▷ Praise her. But do so genuinely. Like all kids, your daughter has a finely tuned "fake praise" meter. She'll know when she deserves praise and when she doesn't. If you gush with praise over trivial things, your true admiration will become meaningless. (And remember to praise effort, not outcome.)

▷ Don't let your fears become her fears. Some parents of girls with ADHD develop a "worst-case" mindset. They end up envisioning the darkest possible future for their daughters. Watch the words you use, your tone of voice, the looks you give. You can tell her a lot without ever saying a word.

▷ Listen when she speaks. She needs to know you're willing to put down what you're doing, look her in the eye, and hear what she has to say without interrupting her. Problem-solve with her, and look for win-win solutions. Involve her in decisions. This goes a long way toward making her feel valued.

You've spent a lifetime – your daughter's lifetime – helping her in countless ways, large and small. Now you're in the strange and uneasy position of needing to pull back a little here, a lot there. How will you know when to stop helping? One wise mom said, "I don't do things for my daughter she can do for herself to build her self-esteem. If I step in and do things for her, she gets the idea that I don't have confidence in her or that she isn't able to handle things on her own."

References

Barkley, R. A. (2020). *Taking charge of ADHD: The complete, authoritative guide for parents.* Guilford Press.

Cardoos, S. L., & Hinshaw, S. P. (2011). Friendship as protection from peer victimization for girls with and without ADHD. *Journal of Abnormal Child Psychology*, 39, 1035–1045.

Centers for Disease Control and Prevention. (2023). *Youth risk behavior survey data summary and trends report 2011–2021.* cdc.gov/healthyyouth/data/yrbs/pdf/YRBS_Data-Summary-Trends_Report2023_508.pdf

Gordon, C. T., & Hinshaw, S. P. (2017). Parenting stress as a mediator between childhood ADHD and early adult female outcomes. *Journal of Clinical Child and Adolescent Psychology,* 46(4), 588–599. doi: 10.1080/15374416.2015.1041595. Epub 2015 Jun 4. PMID: 26042524; PMCID: PMC4670298.

Hinshaw, S. (2022). *Straight talk about ADHD in Girls: How to help your daughter thrive.* Guilford Press.

Hinshaw, S., Owens, E., Zalecki, C., Montenegro-Nevado, A., Huggins, S., Schrodek, E., & Swanson, E. (2012). Prospective follow-up of girls with attention-deficit/hyperactivity disorder into early adulthood: Continuing impairment includes elevated risk for suicide attempt and self-injury. *Journal of Consulting and Clinical Psychology,* 80, 1041–1051.

Nadeau, K. G., Litman, E. B., & Quinn, P. O. (2016). *Understanding girls with ADHD: How they feel and why they do what they do.* Advantage Books.

Teach, J. K. (2012, November 9). Lost and unidentified: The plight of the ADHD inattentive female. Presented at the 24th Annual International Conference on ADHD, San Francisco, CA.

Tung, I., Li, J. J, Meza, J. I., Jezior, K. L., Kianmahd, J. S., Hentschel, P. G., O'Neil, P. M., & Lee, S. S. (2016). Patterns of comorbidity among girls with ADHD: A meta-analysis. *Pediatrics,* 138(4), e20160430. doi: 10.1542/peds.2016-0430. Epub 2016 Sep 21. PMID: 27694280; PMCID: PMC9923580.

Points to Consider

1 Remember to nurture the relationship you have with your daughter. Nearly everything else is secondary.

2 There are no careers a person with ADHD can't pursue, and no jobs a person with ADHD can't do. Remind your child she has what it takes to succeed in any area she's passionate about, gifted in, and dedicated to.

3 Be cautious how you speak to and about your daughter, and what your expressions and body language say to her. She needs to know you see her value. Children who do best in overcoming the challenges of ADHD are the ones who can say, "Somebody believes in me." Are you that person for your daughter?

4 Review your self-assessment responses to decide if there are any areas where you still need to learn more.

Action Steps to Take Now

1 Complete Step 4 in the **Dynamic Action Treatment Plan**.

2 Set reasonable expectations for your daughter's performance at school, at home, and in the community.

3 Together with your daughter, explore clubs, activities, sports, volunteer work, and part-time job opportunities that are interesting and appealing to her.

4 Be sure you understand the significance of your daughter's ADHD as it relates to issues of sexuality and impulse control. Have open and honest discussions with her about dating, sex, and pregnancy.

5 Stay actively involved in your daughter's life, and watch carefully for signs of depression, anxiety, bipolar disorder, self-injury, eating disorders, or addictive behavior.

6 Praise your daughter when she tries, listen when she speaks, and love her all the time.

Chapter 8

When School Problems Escalate

Each self-assessment helps you reflect on your daughter and your parenting practices and is a preview of the chapter's content.

1 When I think about my daughter's struggles in school, I ...
   a realize I need to learn more about the types of eligibilities that might be available to help her.
   b had no idea additional help could be available.
   c am totally opposed to my daughter being labeled as having a disability.
   d am going to talk to her teacher to determine what is currently being done and what else might be available to her in her current school.
2 When thinking about eligibilities for my daughter, I ...
   a have never heard of a 504 plan or IEP eligibility.

   b have talked to parents who have felt an eligibility was helpful for their child.

   c need to find out more about a 504 and an IEP eligibility.

   d have a good understanding of both plans, their benefits and limitations.

3 When looking into the future for high school and college, I …

   a am afraid to think about it.

   b feel she is on a good path to acquire the skills she will need.

   c think I need to get serious about identifying potential problems and getting her remediation or assistance in those areas.

   d feel completely incapable of figuring that out for myself and need to find someone who can guide me and assist in locating supports.

4 When thinking about virtual or home school options, I …

   a would never consider either.

   b need to learn more about them – both their benefits and limitations.

   c know people who have had good experiences with them.

   d am seriously considering it as a good educational option for my daughter.

5 I think my child will qualify for a 504 plan or an IEP, and I …

   a have no idea what kinds of accommodations or services are allowed or provided.

   b have to research the school district's website or the Internet to find out more about which accommodations would be most helpful.

   c need to talk to other parents to gain knowledge about their experience.

   d am confident I can count on her school to determine the most appropriate services and accommodations.

Sometimes even your most effective parenting tools and your daughter's best efforts are not enough to enable her to succeed in the classroom without interventions. Many girls try to mask their difficulties at great cost to themselves. ADHD is a recognized disability so asking for help to level the playing field in the classroom when needed could be very important to her well-being.

ADHD is a recognized disability so asking for help to level the playing field in the classroom when needed could be very important to her well-being.

Does your daughter need additional time on tests, frequent cueing to stay focused, assignments presented in smaller chunks, or a behavior plan? If so, how do you go about advocating for your daughter? Becoming informed about accommodations and services the school can provide is critical. It can be complicated and time-consuming but well worth your effort to educate yourself about them, so get ready to dive into the details.

If your daughter attends a public school and ADHD **significantly impacts her life at school**, one of two federal laws could enable her to receive assistance if she meets the qualifications. These two laws are:

▷ **Section 504** of the Rehabilitation Act of 1973 (referred to as Section 504) and its companion federal laws – Americans with Disabilities Act (ADA) and Americans with Disabilities Act Amendments Act of 2008 (ADAAA); and/or

▷ **Individuals with Disabilities Educational Improvement Act of 2004 (called IDEA)**, which began as Public Law 94–142, the Education of All Handicapped Children's Act in 1975. It has been amended multiple times with the last one in 2017, which liberalized some of the standards for eligibility. An Individualized Education Plan (IEP) is associated with this law.

My experience as a school psychologist in public schools is that most children with ADHD who need interventions can be served through a 504 plan. Exceptions would be those with severe ADHD or other comorbid conditions like a Specific Learning Disability or an Emotional Behavioral Disorder which may require the intervention of a special education teacher.

If your daughter attends a private school receiving federal funds, Section 504 still applies but the school would not have to meet the same standards as a public school. The accommodations vary significantly with many private schools providing accommodations like extra time on tests while others make more extensive accommodations, dependent on staffing and their willingness to serve neurodivergent students.

Private schools are not covered under IDEA and do not accept or implement IEPs from public schools. Many of them will write their own accommodation plan based on their staffing and philosophy, but few of them are equipped to provide a significant level of service. If your child enters a private school with an IEP and was receiving direct services from a specialist in a public school, like speech-language therapy or occupational therapy, you may be able to continue receiving those services if you transport your child back to the public school to receive those.

Sometimes the public school will initiate the process for services and accommodations. Often, however, parents need to take the leadership role. In either case, it will be important for you to understand the parameters of both Section 504 and IDEA to help you determine which best fits your daughter's needs. As a parent, you can influence the outcome. The following sections give you the information you will need to have a basic understanding of both 504 and IDEA.

Section 504

What Is Section 504?

Section 504 is a federal civil rights law that protects a child from ages 3–21 with a record of impairment or who is regarded as having an impairment against *discrimination* in public and nonreligious schools, including colleges and technical schools, receiving federal funds. A student with a disability, like ADHD, is protected against discrimination but is only eligible for accommodations under Section 504 if the student is determined to have a physical or mental impairment that substantially limits one or more major life activities, which in a child's case would be school functioning. However, Section 504 does not provide funding; it simply mandates accommodations and some services. The intent is to provide a level playing field so the student's disability will not interfere with her access to education. Section 504 states:

> No qualified individual with a disability shall, on the basis of disability, be excluded from participation in or be denied the benefits of the services, programs or activities of a public entity, or be subjected to discrimination by any public entity. (35.130, Subpart B, p. 549)

According to the Americans with Disabilities Act of 1990 (ADA),

> The term "disability" means, with respect to an individual – a physical or mental impairment that substantially limits one or more major life activities a record of such impairment being regarded as having such impairment. (*HR 3195 RH*, Americans with Disabilities Act of 1990)

To clarify, your child can be diagnosed with ADHD by an outside source or can be suspected of having ADHD and receive the protection against discrimination *but* still not be determined eligible for services and/or accommodations through a 504 plan because she does not demonstrate a substantial impairment in the school setting. A team of personnel from the school, which isn't tightly defined by 504 and doesn't always include parents, must determine if the ADHD *substantially limits* your child's access to an education on a case-by-case basis.

If your daughter's ADHD is causing her to get in trouble at school, do poorly on her schoolwork or on standardized tests, or have to spend hours at home completing work she should have been able to complete in school, she could be considered to be *substantially limited* by her disability. In some districts, a referral to the 504 team must be made for all children receiving medication at school to determine if they meet eligibility requirements or not.

The impact of American with Disabilities Act Amendments Act of 2008 (ADAAA) included the following changes:

▷ broadened the definition of "disability" under Section 504 to include "learning, reading, concentrating, thinking, communicating, and working" (Section 2A);

▷ clarified that an impairment could limit one major activity but not others and could be episodic but should not be transitory, meaning it should have been present and last for at least 6 months or more;

▷ stated that effects of medication and other forms of assistance should not be considered when determining if impairment substantially limits a major activity (that means that if your daughter is receiving medication, the team should consider what her performance would be like without the medication. Why? If this support was withdrawn, your daughter's performance might decline significantly); and

▷ provided broader interpretation to the term "substantially limits."

What Does the 504 Process Look Like?

Most schools will follow similar steps as outlined below to determine if your daughter is eligible under Section 504 but it can be very individual with each school:

1 The school will gather information about your daughter's classroom performance, which might include teacher observations, grades, results of standardized assessments, and any outside history, medical, or psychological information you might provide.

2 The school team may or may not require additional evaluation. If your daughter is below grade level in reading, math, or written language, an evaluation could be very important. As a parent, you have the right to request an evaluation through the school district. Once permission is signed for the evaluation, it must be completed within 60 school days.

3 An eligibility determination will be made by the 504 team. If the team determines that your daughter's ADHD *substantially limits* her academic performance, functioning, or behavior at school, it would determine her eligible for a formal 504 plan.

4 A written 504 plan will be developed to delineate services and accommodations. It is reviewed annually but can be revisited at any time and is kept in place as long as needed. Even though a 504 plan includes strategies and assistance that an effective teacher would often implement without a plan in place, it is always important to have it in writing. Without it, one year you may have a teacher who makes accommodations, and the next year you may have one who does not, or you could move to a different school and have no written record of accommodations. Going forward, you want to ensure your daughter has the accommodations she needs and that they are provided consistently from classroom to classroom.

Tom's daughter, Juanita, has a 504 plan for her ADHD established at the end of her second grade year. Tom and his wife had their daughter privately evaluated by a psychologist and brought the paperwork to school. After reviewing the report, the school met with the Rivieras and determined Juanita was eligible for a 504 plan. Because she was struggling to follow the classroom routine, there was no resistance from the school. Some of the accommodations written on her third-grade 504 plan included:

> ▷ *not taking away recess for unfinished work,*
> ▷ *allowing reduced homework if she worked diligently but didn't complete it,*
> ▷ *providing spelling words on Friday instead of Monday,*
> ▷ *allowing frequent breaks, and*
> ▷ *frequent cuing when she was off task.*

IDEA

What Is IDEA?

IDEA is the federal law that states that a free and appropriate education must be provided to all students who:

> ▷ have a disability,
> ▷ meet their state's eligibility criteria, and
> ▷ have an *educational need* for special education services.

IDEA provides funding for instruction addressing your child's unique needs, usually from a special education teacher, and can provide related services like occupational therapy when criteria for those services is met. The federal law specifies 13 disability categories. Other Health Impairment is the eligibility category most often considered for children with ADHD. Other disability categories could be considered, depending on your daughter's specific difficulties. If she has academic problems, she may qualify under Specific Learning Disabilities. If your daughter has serious behavioral or emotional problems, she may qualify under Emotional Behavioral Disorder, although the number of girls labeled with this eligibility is far less than boys because boys' disruptive and externalizing behaviors come to the attention of school personnel far more readily than girls', who generally have more internalizing behaviors. If you are considering this option, it is very important to make sure that the programming and services offered would meet your daughter's needs.

If a child is considered for services under the Other Health Impairment eligibility, she would have a disability (such as ADHD) that *significantly impacts* her ability to learn and perform in the classroom to the extent that she would require special education services. Factors other than her test scores should be considered. Those factors might include "grades, homework completion, independent work habits, alertness, sleeping in class, class participation and attendance, ability to complete schoolwork and tests within specified time frames, relationships with peers, and compliance with rules" (Durheim & Zeigler Dendy, 2006, p. 128).

How Is the Disability Category "Other Health Impaired" Defined Under IDEA?

IDEA, 2004, Section 300.8©(9) law defines Other Health Impairment as:

> having limited strength, vitality or alertness, including a heightened alertness to environmental stimuli, that results in limited alertness with respect to the educational environment, that:

i. Is due to chronic or acute health problems such as asthma, attention deficit disorder, or attention deficit hyperactivity disorder, diabetes, epilepsy, a heart condition, hemophilia, lead poisoning, leukemia, nephritis, rheumatic fever, and sickle cell anemia; and

ii. Adversely affects a child's educational performance.

If your daughter qualifies as having a disability under IDEA, then the school staff meets with you to write an IEP. IDEA requires that your child must be educated in the least restrictive environment (LRE) that will enable her to progress in the general curriculum to the maximum extent possible, meaning that she must be educated in a general education classroom setting as much as possible. Schools have different options for delivering educational services. Many have inclusion classrooms where a special education teacher comes into a regular classroom for part of the day or the general education teacher is trained in techniques for instructing children with disabilities. In other service models, the child leaves the general education classroom and goes to a different classroom or office for a portion of the day to receive instruction in areas where she needs extra help.

What Would the IDEA Process Look Like?

The school may follow steps like those listed below in determining if your child qualifies under IDEA:

1 The school would gather information about your daughter's classroom performance, which might include teacher observations, grades, results of standardized assessments, and any outside medical or psychological information you might provide.

2 A formal evaluation is required, either done through the school district or provided by you from an acceptable outside source or a combination of the above. As a parent, you have the right to

request an evaluation of your child to be done through the public school system, even if your child is in a private school. Schools often have limited personnel to conduct these evaluations, so you may have to push hard to get the school to agree to provide one. Once permission is signed for the evaluation, it must be completed within 60 school days in which the child is in attendance.

3 Once all the documentation is obtained, an eligibility determination will be made by the IEP team, which includes you, the parent, as a member. Sometimes parents invite advocates, lawyers, or other outside personnel, such as a therapist, executive skills coach, or psychologist to the meeting, but must notice the school in advance that an outside person has been invited. If the team determines that your daughter's ADHD is a disability that requires special education services, then it would determine her eligible for a disability category.

4 A written IEP would be developed to delineate services and accommodations. It is reviewed annually, and a re-evaluation is considered every three years but doesn't have to include a formal evaluation.

What Determines Whether 504 or IDEA Is Most Appropriate for My Daughter?

The decision will be based on the needs of your daughter and how those needs can be met, so the extent of her impairment will be a key factor. If she needs individualized instruction from a special education teacher, eligibility under IDEA should be considered.

Girls with ADHD are often made eligible for services under the Other Health Impairment. If your daughter is doing relatively well, she may only need accommodations in the classroom, such as being reminded to pay attention, permissible movement, or extended time, so her needs could be met through a 504 plan. If there are comorbid conditions, like a Specific Learning Disability or an Emotional/

Table 8.1
How IDEA and Section 504 Differ

IDEA	504
Office of Special Education of the U.S. Department of Education responsible for enforcement	Office for Civil Rights of the U.S. Department of Education responsible for enforcement
Students generally more impaired and require more service	Students generally don't require services from a special education teacher
Funding provided based on disability category	No funding provided to schools, but schools receiving IDEA funds must meet 504 requirements
More stringent qualification procedure	Less stringent qualification procedure
Individualized Education Plan (IEP) developed	504 plan written
Members of IEP team specified by law	504 team may vary by school district
Formal evaluation necessary	Some documentation of difficulties necessary
Re-evaluation to be considered every 3 years	No re-evaluation specified
Specific parental rights are outlined	Parent rights provided but not as stringent as IDEA
Official IEP meeting and parent permission required before change in placement can occur	No meeting required, but parent should be informed

Note: From *Raising boys with ADHD* (p. 198) by J. W. Forgan and M. A. Richey (2012). Copyright 2012 by Prufrock Press. Reprinted with permission.

Behavioral Disorder, her IEP might reflect those eligibilities. See Table 8.1 above, detailing how Section 504 and IDEA Differ for a comparison of the two plans.

Informed Parent Participation Can Make Difference

When I worked for the school district in my area, I felt like many parents felt powerless when attending meetings with school staff. Being informed about your rights as parents can be empowering. It is critical for you to advocate for your child because if you don't, who will? And who knows your child better than you? It is important for the staff to realize you are intent on helping your child in the best way you can and you need their support to do it. Try to:

▷ make every effort to maintain good communication with your daughter's teacher(s).

▷ provide any outside documentation that might help the team.

▷ request an evaluation through the school if more information is needed. Put your request in writing and keep a copy.

▷ try to understand the eligibility process and parental rights for your school district, often addressed on its website.

▷ make sure the school staff is aware of all you are doing on the outside to help your daughter, whether it is providing medication, tutoring, counseling, or spending hours reinforcing school work.

▷ be reasonable and understand teachers are responsible for many students, not just yours.

▷ make sure accommodations the school offers don't mask the need for actual services, such as a behavior-management plan or training in executive functioning skills.

▷ work as a team with the school staff to figure out appropriate supports. Don't feel compelled to agree with the school if what is recommended does not address her

347

needs. If you need support, check with your school district to see if parent advocates are available. Some parents bring attorneys to the table, but my experience as a school psychologist has been that this is usually unnecessary. Parents always have the option to request mediation or a due process hearing if necessary.

What if I Don't Want to Label My Child?

Some parents are reluctant to create a "paper trail" and formalize their daughter's disability in the school's records, but it is better for your daughter's chronic problems to be understood for what they are – deficits in neurocognitive processes that affect her day-to-day functioning.

Some parents are reluctant to create a "paper trail" and formalize their daughter's disability in the school's records, but it is better for your daughter's chronic problems to be understood for what they are – deficits in neurocognitive processes that affect her day-to-day functioning. It's not laziness, lack of ability, or obstinacy.

At times, early intervention provided through accommodations on a 504 plan could prevent the need for special education services later. The goal of a 504 plan or IDEA eligibility is not to provide a crutch or an easy out for your daughter, but to enable her to receive the support she needs to be as successful as possible when she's at school. Recognizing a disability is no longer the stigma that it used to be.

Jenny was having significantly more difficulty in her third-grade classroom than in any of her previous grades. When her parents attempted to help her with homework, they felt as if she had not heard one thing taught in the classroom that day. A conference with her teacher was an eye-opener for the parents. Her teacher observed that Jenny was often daydreaming, especially when reading long passages or completing difficult, multistep math problems. She frequently failed to turn in homework her parents had spent hours helping her complete. Her teacher questioned Jenny's organizational skills, observing she seemed to have great difficulty getting out the correct materials for each subject. Her parents felt they could not possibly help Jenny any more than they were currently doing and asked for Jenny to be discussed at the school-based team meeting to come up with additional ideas. The school implemented a Response to Intervention (RtI) plan targeting specific reading skills, one of the first steps in most states to look at whether a child has a learning disability. Her RtI plan involved additional time spent during the school day on reading comprehension. Jenny was taught additional research-based strategies for comprehension in a small-group setting. Her teacher noted she was more able to concentrate on what she was reading in a small setting where there were fewer distractions. Her progress was monitored weekly over a 6–8-week period. With the additional assistance on reading, she showed improvement and seemed more engaged in the reading process as her skill level increased.

Because Jenny seemed to be making progress, the school did not pursue formalized testing to determine if she had a learning disability. However, she was still having difficulty staying focused on the teacher, doing her best work, and finishing assignments in the large classroom setting. Her parents brought Jenny to a psychologist for an evaluation. She was not found to have a learning disability, but tests of neurocognitive functioning suggested deficits in attention and working memory, commonly seen in children with ADHD. Rating scales completed by her parents and teachers showed significantly more inattentive and disorganized behaviors than would be expected given her age. She was diagnosed with ADHD, inattentive type.

The school initiated a meeting to discuss her eligibility for a 504 plan. Her parents brought in documentation of her ADHD diagnosis (not required but helpful), and the team developed a 504 plan. It included an individualized task-monitoring plan, which her teacher used to help Jenny keep track of her responsibilities. She received a star for each item completed and turned in, for checking her work, and for self-monitoring her reading. She was able to earn special privileges, such as additional time on the computer, with the stars she received. In addition, she received frequent cueing on tasks by her teacher and opportunities to move about the classroom to different stations when her work was completed. She showed progress and benefited from the provisions of her 504 plan. If her difficulties had been ignored, she may have fallen further and further behind in her academics.

School Accommodations
and Supports

As your daughter's advocate, you should be familiar with the options that could be available to her. Listed on the following pages are examples of some of the accommodations that can be made with either a 504 plan or an IEP (take note that it is not an all-inclusive list). It is important to be realistic about what a teacher can be expected to do for your child and still manage an entire classroom. The best advice is to focus on the accommodations that you feel would be most beneficial to your daughter. The quality of interventions will likely be more effective than the quantity. Even though teachers have written documentation of the interventions, my experience has been that they can only effectively implement a reasonable number of interventions. The teacher may have the best intentions but the pressure of dealing with so many students and all the demands placed on teachers these days frequently get in the way of consistently implementing the accommodations. You and your daughter will likely have to monitor whether the agreed-upon accommodations are being implemented. As discussed later in this chapter, there is little to no research about the effectiveness of these interventions so don't mistakenly think they will be a panacea for your daughter's problems. Support, whether provided at school or outside of school, to help develop skills that she is missing will be critical to her success.

Support, whether provided at school or outside of school, to help develop skills that she is missing will be critical to her success.

Suggestions for accommodations are listed below. Select only those you feel would be most important for your daughter.

Classroom Structure

▷ Warnings should be provided before transitions if that is an area of difficulty. For example, the teacher gives your daughter a 5-minute warning before she must put away her work and begin a new task. It is helpful for some children to be allowed to begin cleaning up a few minutes before the rest of the class, allowing extra time to improve organizational skills.

▷ Placement of your child's desk in an area that is as free of distraction as possible – not in a high-traffic area or near a noisy air conditioner.

▷ A clean and clutter-free workspace to limit distractions.

▷ Provision of a quiet workspace, such as a study carrel or quiet corner of the room, where your daughter could take her work if she is too distracted.

▷ Placement near a positive role model.

▷ Demanding classes, like reading or math, scheduled earlier in the day and including some activity, such as physical education or recess, during the middle of the day.

▷ A routine for turning in homework or the ability to e-mail homework.

▷ Permissible movement, such as being allowed to stand by her desk and work or go to another area of the classroom for a specific purpose, if she does not bother others.

▷ Ignoring movement behaviors, like twirling a pencil, that do not interfere with classroom instruction.

▷ Specific classroom routines and consistent structure.

▷ Eye contact established with the student when providing important information.

Assignments

▷ Extended time for assignments and tests – 1.5 times additional time is common. (Especially important on long, standardized testing. If extra time is granted on the ACT or SAT, the testing company expects your daughter must be using extended time in the classroom.)

▷ Reduction in the amount of work to be completed. For example, in math, your daughter could complete the even-numbered problems rather than doing all the problems *if* she had demonstrated she understood the concept being taught. A caveat here is to make sure she has enough practice to cement the skill being taught.

▷ Large assignments presented in manageable chunks so she isn't overwhelmed by the volume of work. Ultimately you want her to learn to break the assignment down herself.

▷ Masking her papers using a plain sheet of paper to cover up a portion of the page to minimize distraction from so much information on a page.

▷ A monitoring plan to check work for careless mistakes before submitting it.

▷ Leniency in grading papers, such as marking but not deducting points for misspelled words on written assignments.

▷ Use of highlighter for key words in reading or for mathematical operational signs.

▷ Frequent checks by the teacher to ensure directions are understood and provision of extra instruction if necessary. It may be helpful for your daughter to repeat directions to the teacher or silently to herself.

▷ An example of what the finished product should look like.

▷ Multimodal instructions – visual and auditory instructions paired with hands-on learning when possible.

▷ Use of technology such as computer programs for additional skill practice.

▷ Study guides in writing when possible, as well as copies of notes or board work.

▷ Use of word-processing programs or voice-to-text dictation apps to produce written work.

Self-Regulatory Skills

▷ Training in turn-taking, waiting in line, remaining seated, and identifying cause and effect of behaviors, especially important in kindergarten and first grade.

▷ Opportunities to regain self-control by removing herself from overwhelming situations.

▷ Holding "stress" balls or fidget toys, especially if they enhance concentration.

▷ Assistance in organizational strategies such as writing items in an agenda and keeping papers in their proper place.

▷ Opportunities to self-manage behavior. For example, your daughter counts and records a specific behavior (an example would be the number of times she caught herself daydreaming and regained attention) with teacher assistance and receives positive feedback and some reward such as verbal praise or a tangible item.

▷ Placement on an individualized behavior-management plan where the teacher monitors behavior in specific areas and your daughter earns tickets or points which can be redeemed for something rewarding such as additional computer time, lunch with the teacher or a special friend, or some special activity with a parent. These are most effective when the system carries over to the home with parental involvement.

Memory

▷ Frequent repetition and review of previously learned material.

▷ Provision of cue cards that would outline steps that may be hard to remember, especially important in solving math problems requiring sequential steps like long division.

▷ Use of a calculator in higher grades.

▷ Assistance in attaching new learning to previously learned material.

▷ Use of memory techniques such as mnemonics, jingles, rhymes, or pictures.

▷ Overlearning until it becomes firmly embedded in long-term memory. This may require intensive practice, repetition, and review.

▷ Assistance in organizing information into meaningful categories.

▷ Using verbal rehearsal (repeating information to herself) or using visual imagery to assist with recall.

During her school-age years, Jolanda, who was diagnosed with ADHD inattentive type, never required a 504 plan or special education eligibility. There were times she could have benefited from some accommodations, such as being allowed to make up tests she had missed in a quiet environment or receiving extended time on complex testing, but her intelligence and strong self-regulation skills helped her do well. Her organizational skills improved over time with help from an executive skills coach, and even though it was often a scramble at the end, she was always able to produce projects on time. Her parents made sure she had a quiet place to work and tools that she needed, and worked with her to learn how to break large assignments into manageable components well ahead of the due date. However, she seemed to work more effectively under the pressure of time.

When attending college, she found the academic demands were much greater than in high school, and she needed the accommodation of extended time on classroom tests, which was allowed after an updated psychological evaluation documented the need.

What the Research Suggests about the Effectiveness of Accommodations

Many parents fight hard to get accommodations for their daughter with ADHD and think that after those have been granted and documented, things will go more smoothly. In some cases, these interventions do seem helpful. For example, if a girl with slow processing speed is granted extended time and actually uses that time to its best advantage, the result of the testing may show the benefit.

Research on results of these accommodations is sparse. Lovett and Nelson (2020) reviewed 68 studies about the effectiveness of accommodations for ADHD. They found the studies "often fail to show any efficacy in the sense of improving students' performance, and it is even rarer that they are found to have benefits that are specific to students with ADHD (as opposed to raising all students' performance, potentially lowering standards)" (Lovett & Nelson, 2020). An exception was having directions read aloud to younger students with ADHD, which showed documented benefits.

In his review of the Lovett and Nelson's article, Hinshaw (2020, p. 159) said, "Accommodations may in many cases take the place of actual behavioral interventions (for example, for organizational skills and time management, or specific academic remediation, or even medication)." He noted that lowered expectations for students with ADHD might replace interventions that could enhance skills.

As a school psychologist, I have seen interventions administered with fidelity improve outcomes in the short run. However, it is important to see some of them as temporary supports while addressing other ways to actually build skills. For example, having her assignments broken down into smaller units may be helpful, but your daughter should also be receiving instruction in how to do that for herself. Slow processing speed can have multiple causes. Some children have legitimately slow processing speed which will be difficult to change, but others may be able to improve their speed with work on time-management skills, developing more efficient ways to approach tasks, or improving their fluency in reading, writing, or math. Remember that accommodations may be provided in school and college but not often on the job.

The take away is not to discourage you from seeking accommodations and supports for your daughter, because they can be helpful in the short run. It is important to advocate for training or academic remediation to address the *need* for those accommodations so ultimately your daughter may learn to manage some aspects of the deficit on her own. As it stands now, much more research needs to be done on effectiveness of accommodations so widely prescribed in 504 and IEP plans.

Student Interview

Background

Jennifer is a ninth grader at a large public high school, having attended public school since kindergarten. She was diagnosed with ADHD in fourth grade, had a 504 plan written, and has been taking medication since.

Q. How has ADHD impacted you and how have you managed the symptoms?

Besides having difficulty with focus and sitting still, some of my biggest challenges have been related to sensory issues. I am still easily overwhelmed and can go into "freak out" mode. For example, I joined the high school swim team but found getting into the very tight bathing suit in a hot, crowded locker room to be stress inducing. I cried and thought, "Why did I sign up for this?" At the end of the day, I realized I am a better person for learning how to push through those experiences and refusing to give up. Even though it is hard in

---

the moment, I know it will help me in the future. I think by having ADHD, I have learned more about how to control my mindset and focus on small parts of tasks I can control when I get overwhelmed.

I can also look at the big picture. For example, I am enthusiastic about protecting the environment but am bored in class when the teacher is talking about the molecular structure of water. I know sitting through that is what I have to do to be able to study environmental science.

I am very visual and can help troubleshoot coding problems kids may be having and help them. In geometry, I can visualize the figures and get my work done very quickly.

I procrastinate, so I use color-coded lists and check off completed tasks. I am very indecisive when I am overwhelmed, so have to take things one step at a time.

I have extended time as one of the accommodations on my 504 plan. The main value of that is the sense of calm it gives me so I don't get stressed out worrying about time. I usually always finish without using it.

Q. What has transitioning to high school been like for you?

It has been easier and harder in a different way. I find my high school to be more accommodating than my middle school where teachers had super high expectations. However, the crowds in high school are a challenge since I have sensory issues. It is easy to become overwhelmed in the packed hallways with 18-year-olds around. The key is to try to make a big school seem smaller. In the halls, I try to be observant about kids around me. If I know someone is a slow walker, I don't get behind that person. Figuring out who is going where helps me know what to expect. Also, before school started, I went to school and practiced following my schedule.

Q. How does medication impact you?

It helps with focus but also, I feel more regulated. I take the medication during school days and during summer if I am going to a new summer camp and think it might be stressful.

Q. Do you advocate for yourself?

If I need to, I do. I do get extended time which helps my anxiety about being able to finish on time. I work quickly, so don't actually need the additional time but it is a comforting safety net for me.

If I am sitting in an area of the room with distractions like bright colors or too much stimuli, I will ask the teacher to move me to a quieter area.

In sixth grade, my teacher complained that I was doodling in class, but my mom asked the teacher if I could still follow the lesson. She realized I could, so I was allowed to continue doodling.

Thinking Ahead to College or Post-Secondary Training

Accommodations for SAT and ACT

Requirements for receiving accommodations on the SAT and ACT for students with ADHD have become more stringent in recent years. Independent testing groups like those providing the SAT and ACT are governed by the Americans with Disabilities Act in terms of providing a level playing field.

In addition to a diagnosis, the student must provide a comprehensive psychoeducational evaluation that was completed by a licensed professional documenting the diagnosis and reasons accommodations are needed. If a student is requesting additional time on the tests, she is expected to be using extended time on other school tests and assignments. It is always good to have accommodations in place well before requesting them on an important test in their junior or senior year.

Accommodations for College

Many girls benefit from the structure provided at home and the efforts of elementary and secondary school faculties to foster success. When they get to college and the demands on their executive functioning escalate, they sometimes fall apart without those supports. It is important for them not to overload their schedule that first year.

If you suspect your daughter's ADHD might cause her significant difficulty in college, then it is important to establish eligibility for 504 or IDEA before she leaves secondary school, so her needs and accommodations will already be documented. The eligibilities don't transfer to the college setting, but the paper trail can be helpful. The law which provides for IEPs, the Individuals with Disabilities Education Act (IDEA), doesn't apply after high school. The law providing for 504 plans, Section 504 of the Rehabilitation Act, is a civil rights law that prohibits discrimination against individuals with disabilities in many settings, including colleges. The college does not have to follow your daughter's 504 plan but may use that information in determining what accommodations and services they will provide.

Colleges provide accommodations and services but generally require updated testing completed within three years and school history of needing accommodations. Most colleges have a designated disability coordinator. In my experience, one of the most valuable services the coordinator can offer is helping your daughter with her schedule, especially selecting professors who work well with children with disabilities.

Options When the Current School Isn't Working

In some cases, girls with ADHD cannot function in a public school even with special education eligibility or 504 accommodations. Other alternatives can include: private schools; charter schools; private day schools specializing in ADHD, learning disabilities, behavioral difficulties, or all three; specialized boarding schools; home schooling; or virtual school. All of these options will require extensive research to ensure your daughter's educational needs will be met while preparing her for a successful future. It will be especially important to ensure that there is an adequate and robust curriculum, accountability, evidence-based instructional practices, a well-trained and certified faculty, and a positive environment dedicated to developing your daughter's strengths and fostering her self-esteem.

Home Schooling

Home schooling is legal in all 50 states, so if you are interested in your state's specific requirements, contact your state's Department of Education or check with your local school district. Homes schooling may be an option if a parent can commit the time, patience, and knowledge necessary or hire a teacher or find a co-op to assist with the effort. Whichever option you choose, it would require registering with your local school district, many of which have a separate office to handle home schooling. There, you would be informed about state requirements, which usually entail annual evaluations to assess progress, and documentation of the programs you will be using. Make sure you have a firm, comprehensive plan before you choose home schooling for your daughter, which should include:

    ▷ a structured and comprehensive curriculum,

    ▷ a method of monitoring and documenting progress,

    ▷ where and how instruction will be delivered,

    ▷ adequate supervision, and

    ▷ social opportunities with peers.

The home school movement is continuing to expand, and more resources are becoming available to support homeschooled students. There are national, state, local, and online home school groups for you to investigate.

There are many models for home schooling which include the parents as teacher, virtual school where the student would take all or some of their classes online with a teacher, home school co-ops where parents share responsibilities, and private schools offering specific classes home schooled students can join, like science or math labs. If your child has an IEP and is receiving various therapies, like speech-language, occupational, physical, or behavioral, you have the right to continue to access those at her home school by providing transportation to and from the therapies.

Latoya had an IEP for Other Health Impaired and Speech-Language Impaired. Her parents were very concerned that Latoya's ADHD would make it very difficult for her to transition to six different teachers in middle school. Furthermore, they knew she was a follower and were concerned about the influences in a large middle school. They were able to find a small private school which offered a combination of in-person as well as home school options. Latoya continued to need speech-language therapy so her parents arranged transportation to her assigned middle school. She was a strong athlete and wanted to participate in sports at the public middle school, so they were able to schedule her language therapy at the end of the school day. When school was over, Latoya met

> *up with team members for her sport with parent pickup at the end of the session.*
>
> *Latoya had her challenges with the school so her parents had to put in extra effort to problem-solve and figure out how to make it work. Much to their surprise, Latoya was generally co-operative with online learning for part of her curriculum. Her parents felt like they had the best of both worlds – small pupil to teacher ratio for classroom learning, virtual learning for some classes, continuation of her speech therapy, and opportunities to play competitive sports. Arranging all the transportation and overseeing Latoya's schedule made for a hectic life but they felt they were managing on most days.*

Of course, a prime secret for a successful home schooling experience when the parent serves as teacher is having a good working relationship between the home schooling parent and daughter. I use the term *working relationship* to emphasize your daughter must be able and willing to complete schoolwork for you. You should have good organizational skills and the time to plan your instruction. It can be like a full-time job to adequately home school your daughter. When you are deciding on a home school curriculum, look for key features that include quality instructor resources for you, engaging learning activities, availability of computer-aided instruction, and the quality of the tracking system for recording your daughter's progress.

It is a myth that home schooling is isolating and does not allow your daughter to have social interactions. Home schooling affords your daughter the flexibility to interact with others as little or as much as needed but requires planning and coordination.

Although home schooling is not for everyone, it works for many. It provides parents with the ability to give their daughter an individualized curriculum, no homework, opportunities for hands-on learning, and the flexibility to be more active in non-academic areas like sports, the arts, or volunteering. Some families home school their daughters because it does not require participation in high-stakes testing and/or they don't agree with positions of the school board. If done properly, home schooling can allow your child to gain academic confidence and build self-esteem. Be realistic in determining whether you and your daughter can handle the responsibilities.

Virtual School

Virtual schooling had been around long before the COVID-19 pandemic, but during that time it grew in importance out of necessity. Today the virtual learning offered varies widely. Some systems were very organized in presenting teacher-led lessons throughout much of the day with teachers accessible for questions. Others offered programming that almost ensured a parent would have to be heavily involved, such as having second graders do check-ins with their teacher at specific times, like 9:20 AM.

Virtual school offerings have expanded. Some enroll in virtual school full time or elect to take specific courses, either for remediation or advancement, while attending regular school or during the summer with approval of their school counselor or principal. I have known students who have taken calculus or even physical education virtually. Students interact with the teacher online and do the majority of their work on the computer.

Some students with ADHD are successful with computerized instruction because it can be faster paced than traditional classroom instruction, and much of the monotonous repetition can be eliminated. Others I have known have an incredibly hard time staying focused without a teacher near them to reinforce attention and oversee work quality and completion. It is usually more effective with children in the upper elementary grades, middle schoolers, and secondary students. Attending a virtual school can require parental supervision and access to a computer with dependable Internet access. Contact your local school district.

Private Schools

Private schools can be expensive but some offer a more innovative curriculum with less emphasis on standardized testing and smaller class sizes. My experience has been that private schools vary widely so it will be important to do your research if you are in the market for one. There are accrediting agencies for private schools, such as the National Independent Private Schools Association and the National Council for Private School Accreditation, who review policies, curriculum, facilities, faculty, etc. If you are looking at a private school, ask to see their curriculum for the grade your daughter will be in, talk to parents of other students enrolled in the school if you can, ask about discipline policies, how medication may be dispensed if needed, and see if you can schedule a visit. Some states have scholarships or grants to help support students with and without disabilities to attend a private school. Check with your local public school or state Department of Education to see if your state has any options.

Charter Schools

Charter schools are public schools that charge no tuition. They are granted a charter to operate as a school of choice and must adhere to educational objectives but are exempt from operational and budgetary regulations that govern public schools. The idea was conceived to encourage innovative solutions for meeting the needs of underserved students. To date the large majority of the states and the District of Columbia have charter schools.

The charter schools I have been involved with honor IEPs and 504 plans and have some services for students with disabilities. Many have good outcomes but the quality of the school may vary so doing your own research will be important.

Specialized Day Schools

For some families, there comes a point when their daughter's academic and/or behavioral difficulties approach the disaster level. Your daughter's ADHD or comorbid learning disabilities may be so severe that she needs more than you or her current school can offer. Or her behavior and emotionality may have escalated to the point that neither you nor the school knows how to help her. In some larger metropolitan areas and even in some smaller towns there are private or charter schools that are designed to serve children with ADHD and/or comorbid learning disabilities like dyslexia and dysgraphia. Some of these schools have very good track records of helping girls improve their executive functioning and academic skills while building their self-confidence. Some of the specialized schools for children with learning disabilities do an excellent job of adhering to research-based interventions and instruction geared to a girl's particular deficit. It will be important to investigate their success rate, visit the school, and hopefully talk to parents who have sent their children to the school.

Boarding Schools

Despite your best efforts and the efforts of the school staff, your daughter may require a more therapeutic setting because she needs an overwhelming amount of support that is all consuming and plays havoc on your family's well-being. Attachment to a negative peer group can be another reason to consider a change of venue.

There are boarding schools around the country providing additional support for girls with ADHD and their accompanying academic or behavior problems. In some large metropolitan areas, there are educational consultants who specialize in boarding school placement for girls with ADHD who can make your search much easier.

It can be a highly emotional process requiring exhaustive research and visits to the campus but can pay big dividends if it is the right setting for your daughter. Once the decision is made that she would benefit from a boarding school, try to involve her in the process of researching and making a final school selection. She should definitely attend the campus visit with you. Seeing the campus in person and talking to students and other parents will help finalize your decision.

Summing It Up

No doubt, getting the best education for your daughter will be challenging but well worth it. Hopefully, along the way you will find some teachers, tutors, or coaches who will take a real interest in her and thereby remove some of the pressure on you. It will be critical to maintain frequent contact with them so you can deal with problems early before things go completely off the rails. Remember that school can be especially trying for a girl with ADHD because she will likely have to take many classes she finds boring and have to tackle large assignment that seem overwhelming. Many parents find the next phase, whether it is college, technical training, or a job, to be less stressful because your daughter will be maturing with better executive functioning skills coming online and able to pursue more avenues that interest her.

References

Americans with Disabilities Act of 1990, 42 U.S.C. § 12102 et seq. (1990). www.ada.gov/pubs/adastatue08.htm

Americans with Disabilities Act Amendments Act of 2008 €3(4) (E) (i), 42 U.S.C. €12102(4)(E) (2008).

Durheim, M., & Zeigler Dendy, C. A. (2006). Educational laws regarding students with AD/HD. In C. A. Ziegler Dendy (Ed.), *CHADD educator's manual on attention-deficit/hyperactivity disorder: An in-depth look from an educational perspective* (pp. 125–134), CHADD.

Forgan, J. W., & Richey, M. A. (2012). *Raising boys with ADHD: Secrets for parenting healthy, happy sons.* Prufrock Press.

Hinshaw, S. P. (2020). *Straight talk about ADHD in girls: How to help your daughter thrive.* Guilford Press.

Individuals with Disabilities Education Act, 20 U.S.C. § 1401 *et seq.* (1990). https://sites.ed.gov/idea/statuteregulations

Individuals with Disabilities Education Improvement Act, Pub. Law 1-8-446 (December 3, 2004).

Lovett, B. J., & Nelson, J. M. (2020). Systematic review: Educational accommodations for children and adolescents with attention-deficit/hyperactivity disorder. *Journal of the American Academy of Child and Adolescent Psychiatry*, 60, 448–457.

Section 504 of the Rehabilitation Act, 29 U.S.C. Section 706 et. seq. (1973).

Points to Consider

1 If your daughter's ADHD is impairing her school functioning significantly, she could meet the criteria for a 504 plan or Individualized Education Program (IEP).

2 Even though the disability perspective is difficult to accept, isn't it better for people to have an understanding of the neurobiological nature of her ADHD than to think she is just being difficult or lazy?

3 You are your daughter's most important advocate and always will be.

4 What specific struggles does your daughter have in her current classroom?

5 If your current school isn't working, are you aware of alternatives in your community?

7 Review your self-assessment responses to decide if there are any areas where you still need to learn more.

Action Steps to Take Now

1 Continue to educate yourself about your child's legal rights within the school system.

2 Think about your daughter's learning style, strengths, and weaknesses. What does she need in the classroom in order to do her best?

3 If she is struggling behaviorally or academically in the classroom with no support, contact the school about the necessity of a 504 plan or IDEA eligibility. Make sure you educate yourself so you can be a good advocate for her.

4 Develop a good working relationship with her teacher(s) and with other staff members who could assist her and stay in frequent contact with them.

5 Complete Step 5 in the **Dynamic Action Treatment Plan** with your daughter.

Chapter 9

Making the Most of Your Daughter's Future

The Dynamic Action Treatment Plan

Throughout this book I've given you action steps at the end of each chapter. Whether or not you've had the opportunity to fill anything in, please don't overlook the need to have a comprehensive long-term plan focusing on shoring up your daughter's deficits and fostering her strengths and passions. **The Dynamic Action Treatment Plan** you are creating is a reflective tool to help you prioritize your steps. As a parent myself, I've found that having a plan in writing helps me get closer to making it happen.

At times, you may be overwhelmed by your daughter's needs. You worry about what lies ahead. Despite her challenges, she is a unique person with a special purpose in life. You know there is hope for her future. You can use the **Dynamic Action Treatment Plan** to help your daughter discover her purpose and grow in her journey. Over time, you can see her growth.

Begin by identifying your daughter's strengths and needs to use as a reference point to guide your thinking. Consider all aspects of her life – school, family, friends, leisure time and extracurricular activities, health and fitness, religion, etc. – as you complete the plan.

DOI: 10.4324/9781003365402-10

The Dynamic Action Treatment Plan

<u>Step 1 Strengths and Needs</u>

I/we believe my/our daughter's strengths include:

_____

_____

_____

_____

I/we believe the following need to be addressed for my/our daughter to maximize her strengths:

_____

_____

_____

<u>Step 2 Vision</u>

The key here is to begin by reflecting upon where you see your daughter in a year, 3 years and 5 years from now, and if she's mature enough, to ask her to consider those timelines as well. Together, consider her age, physical appearance, personality, behavior, and self-esteem. Think about her ethics and character, decision-making skills, schooling, interests and hobbies, friends, and components of her treatment program.

I find that thinking about and predicting what your daughter will be doing in the future is an interesting exercise. For you, it will stir various emotions, and you'll realize just how fast those years will pass.

• In 1 year, I/we see my/our daughter doing/being …

_____

_____

_____

_____

• In 3 years, I/we see my/our daughter doing/being …

_____

_____

_____

_____

• In 5 years, I/we see my/our daughter doing/being …

_____
_____
_____
_____

If you and your daughter did not complete this section together, communicate the vision to her and motivate her to become an active participant in making it happen.

<u>Step 3 Action</u>
In order for my/our daughter to achieve the vision I/we have for her at the 5-year mark, I/we need to do the following:

• Today – Make a to do list:

_____
_____
_____
_____

• Tomorrow – Prioritize and begin following through:

_____
_____
_____
_____

• Within one month:

_____
_____
_____
_____

• Within 6 months:

_____
_____
_____
_____

Your daughter's involvement and participation is crucial to the plan's success.

In order for my/our daughter to achieve the vision I/we have for her at the 5-year mark, she needs to do the following:

• Tomorrow:

_____

_____

_____

_____

• Within one month:

_____

_____

_____

_____

• Within 6 months:

_____

_____

_____

_____

• Within one year:

_____

_____

_____

_____

Step 4 Support
In order for my/our daughter to achieve the vision I/we have for her at the 5-year mark, I/we need to obtain the support of the following individuals or professionals:

1 _____

2 _____

3 _____

4 _____

Step 5 Roadblocks

When I/we become discouraged or frustrated with her behavior or performance, I/we need to remember these things:

1 _____

2 _____

3 _____

When I/we become discouraged or frustrated with her behavior or performance, I/we can count on these people for support:

1 _____

2 _____

3 _____

4 _____

When my/our daughter becomes discouraged or frustrated with us or with her ADHD, she needs to remind herself of these things:

1 _____

2 _____

3 _____

When my/our daughter becomes discouraged or frustrated with me/us or with her ADHD, she can turn to the following people for support (other than myself):

1 _____

2 _____

3 _____

4 _____

Now that you've completed your daughter's **Dynamic Action Treatment Plan**, remember to review and refine it as necessary.

I'd like to close by thanking you for your effort on behalf of your daughter. In my experience as a parent, you won't often hear many people say "Thank you" for how you are raising your daughter with ADHD, but I know you deserve thanks. Each day you work hard at raising your daughter, and one day she'll realize this. Helping your daughter make the most of her capabilities will be an accomplishment you can cherish all your life. I can assure you that it will be worth every ounce of effort you put into it. My compassion and encouragement go out to you.

About the Author

Mary Anne Richey, M.Ed., a Licensed School Psychologist, worked for the school district of Palm Beach County for many years, and now maintains a private practice in Florida. She also has experience as a middle school teacher, administrator, high school guidance counselor, and adjunct college instructor. Mary Anne has assisted many students with ADHD and their families over the years. In 2012, she was honored as School Psychologist of the Year by the Florida Association of School Psychologists and was a nominee for the 2013 National School Psychologist of the Year to be chosen by the National Association of School Psychologists. Throughout this book, Mary Anne helps parents manage the issues they face and incorporate strategies to help their daughters succeed in school and life. She has presented at national conventions and has held many workshops for parents and professionals on strategies for helping children with ADHD maximize their potential. She is also the author of *Raising Boys With ADHD: Secrets for Parenting Healthy, Happy Sons*, 2nd edition. She co-authored *The Impulsive, Disorganized Child – Solutions for*

Parenting Kids with Executive Functioning Difficulties; Stressed Out! Solutions to Help your Child Manage and Overcome Stress; and The ADHD Empowerment Guide. She has a passion for helping parents and children understand and manage ADHD based on the latest research and her experience supporting girls and their parents on their journey.

Printed in the United States
by Baker & Taylor Publisher Services